WORLD IN DANGER

WORLD IN DANGER

Germany and Europe
in an
Uncertain Time

WOLFGANG ISCHINGER

BROOKINGS INSTITUTION PRESS
Washington, D.C.

The Brookings Institution is a private nonprofit organization devoted to research, education, and publication on important issues of domestic and foreign policy. Its principal purpose is to bring the highest quality independent research and analysis to bear on current and emerging policy problems. Interpretations or conclusions in Brookings publications should be understood to be solely those of the authors.

Library of Congress Control Number: 2020943109

ISBN 9780815738435 (hc)
ISBN 9780815738442 (ebook)

9 8 7 6 5 4 3 2 1

Typeset in Minion Pro

Composition by Elliott Beard

CONTENTS

Preface   *vii*

ONE   WORLD OUT OF JOINT   1

TWO   THE ART OF DIPLOMACY   31

THREE   AMERICA FIRST   51
Superpower, but the World's Policeman No More

FOUR   RUSSIA   77
From a Common European Home to a New Cold War?

FIVE   WAR IN SYRIA   115
Intervene or Look Away?

SIX   MAKING PEACE WITHOUT WEAPONS?   137
Foreign Policy and Military Power

SEVEN   THE UNITED NATIONS   167
Who Provides for Global Order?

EIGHT **EUROPE** 195
Only Strong Together

NINE **FOREIGN POLICY IN** 227
THE TWENTY-FIRST CENTURY
Challenges and Opportunities

Notes 243

Name Index 249

Subject Index 253

PREFACE

As I am finishing up the final editing of this book in spring 2020, the world is confronted with the greatest threat to international security since World War II. The coronavirus pandemic threatens the lives and livelihood of millions—if not billions—of people across the globe. It builds on top of—and often exacerbates—the multiple security crises that endangered the international community well before the virus broke out. And it occurs before the background of a world that was already out of joint and characterized by growing uncertainty.

In fact, events are happening in the world that seemed impossible just a short time ago: The president of the United States, once the uncontested leader of the "free world," is not only largely absent from the global response to the coronavirus crisis. He is also snubbing his closest allies, first by withdrawing from the Paris climate accord and the Iran deal signed after years of arduous diplomatic negotiations with the Americans, Europeans, Russians, and

Chinese; and then, just a short time later, by honoring the North Korean dictator with a summit meeting at which the U.S. president made far-reaching concessions. And while he appears to get along wonderfully with Kim Jong-un, Donald Trump has recently been at odds with the United States's closest partners and allies on trade issues. Thoughts in Washington have turned to more punitive tariffs. These could affect, for instance, German automobile manufacturers who export to the United States. Will our country become a target for Trump? What does this mean for the future of the transatlantic partnership and for the future of the West?

In Europe there are worries about the stability of the eurozone and the general development of the European Union—worries that are further amplified by the impact of the coronavirus pandemic. Many European countries have seen successful campaigns by parties that are critical of European integration. At home and abroad, populist voices are calling for more nation-state and less Europe. In some member states, fundamental European values and principles are being called into question. How is Europe supposed to function in the long term and become capable of formulating global policy?

In Moscow, Vladimir Putin continues his fourth term as Russian president. Under his leadership, the prospect of détente with the West seems dubious at best. Just recently he introduced new strategic nuclear weapons that the Russian military intends to deploy. At the same time, there is so far no progress on arms control—indeed, a new arms race is well under way. Since the Russian intervention in Georgia, the annexation of Crimea, and Russian interference in Eastern Ukraine, Germany's allies in Central and Eastern Europe have become even more worried. Several hundred German soldiers have been stationed in Lithuania in order to emphasize our solidarity. But for some, this is not enough. The Polish ministry of defense, for one, announced that it would prefer to have an entire American division on its own territory. What do such developments mean for European security? Can we guarantee our own security without entering into a new, spiraling arms race, which could bring insecurity for all?

Indeed, we are once again facing fundamental foreign policy questions: How do we deal with Russia, a neighboring power that continues to violate the fundamental principles of the European security architecture and attempts to weaken liberal democracies? What does it mean for European security when Donald Trump openly questions core principles of U.S. foreign policy since 1945? And what conclusions can we draw from this? What are the prospects for the future of the European Union in the age of Brexit and populist movements in Europe? What do we mean when we say that Germany must take on more responsibility?

In Germany, debate on these fundamental foreign policy questions of our time is avoided rather than sought: Sure, addressing these issues can be awkward and exhausting. But considering the deteriorating state of global security, I do not believe that we can afford to remain passive. On the contrary, in the years to come, our country will be facing even greater foreign policy challenges, and we are not yet adequately prepared. And because there are no simple answers, it is all the more important that we discuss these challenges and how we can deal with them.

The German government has realized this, too, by the way, declaring in the coalition agreement of 2018 that, "in view of the international challenges," Germany must "strengthen its capacities for strategic analysis and intensify its strategic communication." The coalition agreement thus emphasizes the necessity of increasing investment "in expanding expertise on security policy and development policy" in Germany, expressly mentioning the role of organizations like the Munich Security Conference.

The Munich Security Conference, of which I have been chairman since 2008, has also made intensive efforts in recent years to open up to the general public. As at the time of its founding in the 1960s, the purpose of each annual conference is to bring together the most important decisionmakers and visionaries in order to discuss, and often argue about, contemporary security policy challenges. This is becoming ever more important, as evident in the vastly increased interest in our main event in Munich. However, by no means do these challenges concern only the political elite. This is why today, in contrast to the founding years, the Munich debates are televised so that they can be followed by livestream all over the world.

This book is a further contribution to an essential public debate that is more necessary than ever in these turbulent times. The book's express purpose is not to address the experts among us. This is a book for anyone who wants to better understand what is going wrong in the world right now, what that means for us, and what we can and must do about it. If it also manages to offer insights into the world of diplomacy and some understanding of the complexity of foreign policy today, then it has achieved its goal.

All uncertainties and superficialities are my doing. I was not able to deal with all current security policy issues equally intensively. Some important topics, such as cybersecurity and the rapid rise of China in the international arena, could only be touched on briefly, in order to leave enough scope to deal with fundamental questions of war and peace, national responsibility, and discussion of our relations to Russia and the United States, which are currently subjects of intense debate in Germany. And while I wrote the book before the coronavirus pandemic struck the world, none of the dangers discussed in the pages that follow—from the serious straining of the transatlantic relationship to growing challenges to European integration and stability—will disappear with the pandemic. If anything, the pandemic will exacerbate these threats.

For their many ideas and suggestions, I would like to thank my friends and colleagues at the Federal Foreign Office, where I worked for nearly forty years. I would also like to thank fellow members of the world of diplomacy and the extensive international community of think tanks, as well as colleagues and friends at the Hertie School of Governance, where I have been teaching as a senior professor.

I also owe a warm thanks to both Strobe Talbott, who connected me to the Brookings Institution Press and whose members have done a marvelous job of editing the book. Special thanks also goes to Susan Richter, who did the lion's share of translating the German version of this book into English.

Without the continual and critical support and backing of my team at the Munich Security Conference (MSC), I never could have completed the project alongside all of the conferences, lecture events, and publications on my agenda. I would like to thank Dr. Benedikt Franke, chief executive officer of the MSC, and the entire MSC staff in Munich and Berlin.

Special thanks are due to the Policy Team of the MSC in Berlin, for their intensive and critical advice, particularly Dr. Tobias Bunde (head of policy and analysis), Adrian Oroz (who has since left for a foreign office career), and Lisa Marie Ullrich (head of my office), as well as Jamel Flitti and Randolf Carr. Dr. Sophie Eisentraut played a particularly important role in editing, updating, and refining this current English language version.

Finally, my office staff bore a heavy workload, especially Pia Zimmermann and Amadée Mantz, who had their hands full even without the book.

And without Jutta Falke-Ischinger, who backed the project with a combination of marital forbearance and professional journalistic advice, none of it would matter anyway.

BERLIN, MAY 2020
Wolfgang Ischinger

WORLD IN DANGER

ONE

WORLD OUT OF JOINT

In January 2005, while I was serving as ambassador to the United States, Jutta and I were invited to an opulent ball in Palm Beach, Florida. The dress code for men was white tie and medals; for women, a long gown. The location of the Red Cross benefit ball was Mar-a-Lago, and the host was Donald Trump. Young men dressed as Roman gladiators carried torches as the guests, among them several of my fellow ambassadors and I, with our wives, traversed a long, red carpet to approach the host and his new wife, Melania. A real Hollywood experience! Later that evening I chatted with Donald Trump about his grandfather's German roots—never suspecting that, to the surprise of almost everybody, this man would be elected the forty-fifth president of the United States of America in November 2016.

Since the very beginning of my diplomatic career, in the early 1970s, I have had opportunities to meet a great number of international political leaders. This began with Jimmy Carter in the late

1970s, followed by Ronald Reagan. In the 1980s I experienced the redoubtable Soviet Foreign Minister Gromyko, as well as the terrible Romanian dictator Nicholae Ceaușescu, and then Mikhail Gorbachev, George H. W. Bush, Maggie Thatcher, François Mitterrand, and Jacques Chirac. In the 1990s I had to negotiate with the Serbian President Slobodan Milošević, who was later put on trial in The Hague. During that process I also met Igor Ivanov, who later became Russian foreign minister, and whom I still call a friend today. As a member of the German chancellor's delegation, I then met Vladimir Putin and, as ambassador to Washington, attempted to improve relations between George W. Bush and Germany, which had suffered greatly in the wake of the invasion of Iraq. As the chairman of the Munich Security Conference (MSC) for the last decade-plus, I have met a great many other state leaders, ministers, and international decisionmakers, from secretaries-general of the United Nations to presidents of the European Commission, from Ukrainian president Petro Poroshenko all the way to Iranian Foreign Minister Mohammad Javad Zarif and his Saudi counterpart Adel al-Jubeir.

Several of these leaders were responsible for decisions with crucial geopolitical or historical consequences. Take Ronald Reagan, and his successor George H. W. Bush, or think of Helmut Kohl and Gorbachev: peaceful German reunification, the breakup of the Soviet Union!

But none of these many decisionmakers shook up and unsettled the world like President Trump has since taking office in January 2017. The entire established liberal world order is threatening to give way, and nothing is the way it was before.

That the world is more dangerous had become clear to many of us, of course, ever since 9/11, the Iraq War, and the bloody wars in Syria and then also in Yemen. When Putin annexed Crimea in 2014 and instigated the bloody conflict in Eastern Ukraine, many saw him to be the great alienator. Nobody could have known that the new American president, of all people, would be the one to challenge the whole established order—free trade as well as the Western canon of values and the principle of collective security anchored in Article 5 of the NATO treaty.

But how dangerous is the situation in actuality? "Global security is more endangered today than at any time since the collapse of the Soviet Union" is a warning I have heard affirmed repeatedly, in many lectures.

German President Frank-Walter Steinmeier expressed it in similar terms back when he was foreign minister: "The world is out of joint." We are apparently experiencing an epochal watershed; an era is ending, and the contours of a new geopolitical age are only starting to come into focus. The Munich Security Report published by the MSC in February 2019 called this the "great reshuffling of the pieces of the international order." To date, it is hard to judge whether someone will be able to pick up the core elements of the global order and piece them back together—or whether the old order will be destroyed before the work on a new one has even begun.[1]

What is clear: No matter where one looks, there are countless conflicts in the world and multiple crises whose effects extend even to Europe. Many of them will be further exacerbated by the effects of the coronavirus pandemic. Today there are around 70 million people who have fled their homes due to conflict or persecution—a dismal record. And according to the Stockholm International Peace Research Institute (SIPRI), where I long served on the governing board, in 2019 global military spending rose to unprecedented levels, indicating a crisis of growing tensions and bloody conflicts.

In Syria, whose coast is just 125 kilometers from the European Union (EU) member Cyprus, hundreds of thousands of people have been killed in the last eight years. Millions have been displaced. The United Nations (UN) has stopped counting the casualties of this conflict, because the lack of access to the country makes it impossible to verify this information. In April 2016, Staffan de Mistura, the UN special envoy for Syria, estimated 400,000 dead by that time. The latest figures estimate around half a million fatalities. That is about the population of Dresden, Germany, or Oakland, California.

Since the beginning of the Syrian conflict, more than 6 million people have been displaced within the country and 5.6 million more have fled its borders. These two groups of refugees comprise more than half of Syria's population. And we are still receiving reports about atrocities like barrel bombs thrown over residential areas and the use of chemical weapons. Syria, once a destination for culture tourists from all over the world, has become a country in a permanent state of emergency; city names like Aleppo, Afrin, and Eastern Ghouta have now become synonymous with horror, suffering, and death.

Syria is only the most terrible example of the many internationalized civil wars—that is, wars in which a conflict starts as a confrontation between local actors but gradually involves ever more external powers. A terrible war of this kind is raging in Yemen, too, where regional powers are muscling in—Iran on one side and Saudi Arabia on the other.

The neighboring continent of Africa has several countries in a permanent state of violence: just think of Mali, Sudan, Congo, or Somalia. Another hotspot is located right at the gate of the European Union, no further from Berlin than Paris: A military conflict is raging in Ukraine, which shares a border with Poland, Hungary, Romania, and Slovakia. Over 2,500 civilians have been killed there since Russia began its military operation in Eastern Ukraine in 2014. Even after four years of international negotiations on pacifying the situation, shots are fired on a regular basis.

Mind you, those are only the wars and conflicts that manage to attract international attention. Under this visible peak of the iceberg of violence is extremely thick pack ice, made up of numerous violent conflicts all over the world that receive less attention. Among them are the civil war in South Sudan, attacks in the Sinai in Egypt, the collapse of the state in Libya, the drug war in the Philippines, the conflict with the Taliban in Northwest Pakistan, and the war against Islamists in Mali. The list could go on forever.

Beyond the "crises of the day" are the "eternal" hotspots, including the confrontations between Turkey and the Kurdish Workers' Party (PKK), which have been conducted militarily and practically without interruption since 1984; the Somalian civil war, which has been raging for thirty years; the conflict over Tibet that has been simmering since 1950; the equally old conflict between China and Taiwan, and the territorial disputes in the South China Sea. Resolution seems just as far away in Nagorno-Karabakh, Transnistria, and South Ossetia and Abkhazia, breakaway regions of Azerbaijan, Moldova, and Georgia, respectively; Russia's conflict with Chechnya; the interethnic tensions in the West Balkans, including the still contentious status of Kosovo; the disputes about Iran's nuclear program; the turbulent relations between North and South Korea, which have been based on a truce but no peace treaty for 75 years; and, last but not least, the Israeli-Palestinian conflict.

And, finally, there are also those countries that have suffered through traumatizing civil wars which were ended only with great difficulty, and that are now struggling to rebuild a stable state—places where old conflicts could flare up again at any time: Rwanda, Côte d'Ivoire, Chad, Congo, and Sri Lanka, to name a few examples.

There is also great concern with those countries that may not be at war but can hardly be regarded as stable. Turkey was at the threshold of civil war during the attempted coup in summer 2015; since then it has persisted in a state of emergency that seems to be becoming increasingly authoritarian.

Joining the ranks of crises, military conflicts, and political instability are terror attacks all over the world. Their best-known perpetrators include the Islamic State, Boko Haram, al Qaida, and the Taliban. The large majority of these attacks in recent years were committed in Iraq, Afghanistan, Pakistan, Nigeria, and Syria.

Fortunately, as of this writing, Germany has not yet been a main terrorist target. Nevertheless, there have been attacks ranging from the insidious murders and robberies committed by the right-wing radical National Socialist Underground (NSU) to serious Islamist attacks with trucks or knives. Here at home the fear may be greater than the actual danger, but the Germans' increasingly anxious view of the chaotic global situation is certainly justified.

JUST MINUTES FROM A MAJOR WAR

The unusual abundance of dangerous and bloody crises and conflicts is "crowned" by a persistent nuclear threat, which has become so normal that it seldom attracts any political attention.

In Germany, the country where hundreds of thousands of people marched in the 1980s to protest against new intermediate-range nuclear missiles and for peace, one thing seems to have slipped everyone's mind: that the danger of a confrontation between the great powers, and of nuclear escalation, has by no means been averted. That the Nobel Peace Prize was awarded to opponents of nuclear armaments in 2017 is, thus, especially gratifying—although this will hardly prompt the nuclear powers to disarm.

While we here in Germany are in the midst of a heated discussion about whether the budget for the German Army should be increased at all, in many parts of the world an arms race is well underway. China's increasingly self-assertive behavior is being reflected ever more clearly in its demands for military respect. Beijing is upgrading its armaments. And in pursuing a more powerful role for China in Asia and the world, President Xi Jinping seems to not shun the risk of antagonizing others—most importantly the United States.[2] This raises the question, will the further rise of China take place peacefully or will it someday lead to violent conflict?

There are also new initiatives to upgrade defense efforts in Russia and the United States, especially in the area of nuclear weapons. Old nuclear bombs are being modernized, and completely new weapons systems are being developed as well. At the same time, there have been several near collisions between Russian military aircraft and NATO in recent years—occurrences that can easily get out of control in the tense situation the world is currently facing. How do we ensure that a misunderstanding does not spiral directly into escalation?

Last year, North Korea and the United States threatened each other with the deployment of nuclear weapons, and in the Middle East, rivaling powers that are armed to the teeth—for instance, Saudi Arabia and Iran—moved ever closer to the brink of conflict. What can be done to reduce the danger of an escalation that it might not be possible to harness?

A massive reduction in the number of nuclear weapons has occurred in the last decades, most recently initiated by the New Strategic Arms Reduction Treaty (START) negotiated by Putin and Barack Obama. But as we observed in the Munich Security Report 2019, these "arms control treaties, still following a bipolar logic, are unraveling, while there is not yet a new multilateral framework for arms control that would be fit for the emerging international system." The Intermediate-Range Nuclear Forces (INF) Treaty is dead, and with New START unlikely to be extended beyond 2024, "another element which limited dangerous competition between Russia and the United States is likewise imperiled."[3] Meanwhile, the United States and Russia still maintain a total of around 13,000 nuclear warheads so that they can react in the case of a hostile military offensive.[4]

Many believe that nuclear war is a mere specter of the past or a dramatically orchestrated backdrop from a James Bond movie. But the nuclear threat is real: Around the world there are about 1,800 nuclear warheads just a button away from deployment, standing ready day and night.[5]

We should keep in mind how often militarily relevant incidents have occurred in recent years. I am a member of the European Leadership Network (ELN), which has issued a series of publications that warn about such dangers and document how often there were near collisions or unnecessary provocations between Russian and Western airplanes or ships. According to ELN, sixty such near collisions occurred between March 2014 and March 2015 alone.

This includes cases like that of a Scandinavian Airlines plane that nearly collided with a Russian military plane near Copenhagen, Denmark. A catastrophe was barely averted. While most of the incidents designated as serious by the ELN were provoked by Russia, NATO must, in its own interest, do everything to ensure that the risk of confrontation is minimized.

RISKY BEHAVIOR ON THE BRINK

In any case, the danger of an international war between great and intermediate powers has clearly increased in recent years. Because of this concern, I chose to entitle the 2018 Munich Security Conference "To the Brink—and Back?"—meaning that what we observed in many places all over the world was, in fact, "brinkmanship": extremely risky behavior that placed countries on the brink of war.

The hope was that the conference would be able to send a signal of de-escalation and détente and present initiatives showing how the world could step back from the brink. Unfortunately, this was not the case. Instead, many speakers added further fuel to the fire. At the end of 2019, I am even more concerned than I was in 2018.

I do not mean to sound alarmist. A major war continues to be rather unlikely. But the risk is, unfortunately, clearly greater than it was just a few years ago. One reason is the growing perception of threat in the great powers' capitals, which bears the risk of becoming a self-fulfilling prophecy—after all, "If everyone prepares for a hostile world, its arrival is almost preordained."[6] The situation today is more strained and dangerous than we have seen since the end of the Cold War. So it is high time for political leaders all over the world to take this danger seriously and act accordingly.

GLOBAL TREND: MORE INEQUALITY, LESS FREEDOM

Obviously, not only war and violence are playing a greater role these days. A new systemic competition appears to be on the horizon. Liberal democracy and the principle of open markets—the only conceivable models of legitimate political and economic order back in the 1990s—are no longer the clear preference in today's world.

The 2018 Freedom Report issued by Freedom House states dryly, "Democracy faced its most serious crisis in decades in 2017 as its basic tenets—including guarantees of free and fair elections, the rights of minorities, freedom of the press, and the rule of law—came under attack around the world."

According to the Freedom House indicators, 2019 was the fourteenth year in a row in which there were more countries where political rights and civil liberties declined than countries that registered a positive trend. Similar conclusions were drawn by the latest Bertelsmann Stiftung's Transformation Index, which scores the development of democracy and the market economy in 129 developing and transitioning countries. The alarming trend identified by these researchers can be summarized as more inequality, less freedom.

In China the Communist Party developed a system of authoritarian state capitalism, which was thoroughly successful in opening the path from poverty to moderate prosperity for wide parts of the population. This made China into an attractive example for many authoritarian states to follow. This is despite the fact that the authors of the Transformation Index also emphasize that democracies are much more capable of combatting corruption, social exclusion, and barriers to fair economic competition. Autocratic states have a much poorer track record in this respect, not to mention human rights.

Nevertheless, primarily because of China's economic success, the Chinese government is completely confident that its system is a suitable export model for other states to imitate—even as President

Xi Jinping is having the constitution changed so that he can remain in office indefinitely. At the same time, Beijing matches growing assertiveness abroad with increasing repression and surveillance at home.[7]

Russia left the path toward a liberal, democratic state under the rule of law a long time ago. A true opposition, free media, and a vibrant civil society are not tolerated at all. And yet the idea of "strong leadership" is catching on more, not only with the Russians, but also in many other places in the world.

Even in the European Union, there are advocates of "illiberal democracy." They want to restrict freedom of the press and free speech, warn about the "Eurocracy" in Brussels, or fall for general xenophobia. They constitute an axis of fear that seeks salvation by retreating into the nationalism of years gone by.

And lastly, even in the United States, which used to be regarded as the land of freedom, defenders of democracy must now fight daily for compliance with those standards that were once considered unassailable.

Liberalism has come under pressure in another form as well. For decades the principle of an open global economy was considered a guarantee for gains in prosperity, but this is now being increasingly questioned. Negotiations about dismantling trade barriers in the framework of the World Trade Organization have been stagnant for years. Ratification of regional free trade agreements has become quite difficult, even between the European Union and Canada.

In the meantime, President Donald Trump has introduced new protective tariffs on steel and aluminum, and since June 2018 goods from the European Union are no longer exempted from these duties. There is a real danger that this is the prelude to introducing ever more measures, culminating in a trade war—which means nobody wins.

GLOBAL CRISIS MANAGERS UNDER PRESSURE

International organizations and agreements have also come under pressure. Successes like the Paris Agreement on climate change and the nuclear deal with Iran do show that it is still possible to find answers to questions of global concern. But precisely these examples also show that the compromises reached are built on shaky ground: Donald Trump announced the United States's withdrawal from the climate accord back in summer 2017. And after the withdrawal of the United States from the Iran framework in May 2018, its future has become highly dubious.

Important powers, first and foremost the United States under President Trump, are cutting back funding for peace missions or pulling out of specialized agencies of the United Nations. Just like during the Cold War, the United Nations is once again frequently paralyzed because the permanent members block each other in the Security Council. And because the council no longer reflects today's global distribution of power, frustrated states are switching to substitute formats; informal "clubs" like the G7 and G20 are gaining momentum. This is happening because these less regulated bodies allow for something resembling "effective multilateralism." But is that really true? Didn't the 2017 G7 summit, the results of which Trump later undermined by tweet, sow doubts about such alternative formats?

My friend Ian Bremmer calls this phenomenon the emergence of a "G-Zero world," a vacuum fed by the decline of Western influence and by many states focusing on their own domestic problems. The result, according to Bremmer, is a world in which no country alone, nor any group of states, is willing to develop a truly global agenda, let alone provide solutions for the world's problems.

In Europe the annexation of Crimea and Russia's continuing intervention in Eastern Ukraine demonstrate that our continent is no postmodern paradise in which the use of military force is impossible. The dream of 1990—that the end of German partition would allow for the emergence of a comprehensive Euro-Atlantic security architecture that integrates Russia—has gone up in smoke.

OVERALL, PESSIMISM PREVAILS

Only traces of the widespread optimism of the early 1990s remain. Scholars who believe in overall progress are striking a different note in their contributions to today's discourse. It is not all that long ago that they would have expressed the opposite opinion.

Just twenty years ago, we believed that the world would move more or less constantly in the right direction. Democracy, human rights, and the market economy were advancing everywhere. International organizations took on ever more tasks and appeared to epitomize the model of global governance—one that would be equal to taking on the challenges of environmental pollution, child labor, and infectious diseases. So much appeared to be on the right track.

The establishment of the World Trade Organization in 1995 was considered a milestone. An open global economy was considered good for everyone in the long run, and for this a shared regulatory framework was needed. That was a broad consensus in principle, even though unfair trade practices such as dumping and export subsidies did, of course, persist.

At that time, China was barely present on the geopolitical map. The Middle Kingdom was in the midst of an economic boom, but hardly anyone imagined that it might also become a political rival of the largest economic power yet, the United States. Many believed instead that China (as my old friend Robert Zoellick, the former World Bank president, put it) could become a "responsible stakeholder" if integrated into international organizations and, above all, the global economic architecture—and would thus assimilate into the existing liberal world order as a reliable partner.

The United Nations Conference on Environment and Development had been held in Rio de Janeiro in 1992. This is where Agenda 21, which defined common goals for sustainable development, was passed. The conference was the starting point for a whole series of important global initiatives on environmental and climate protection. In Rio the vision of functioning global governance to solve global problems suddenly seemed within reach.

People spoke of the "peace dividend" and hoped that money which had previously been poured into equipping armed forces in both the East and the West could now serve other purposes. Countries including Kazakhstan and Ukraine even voluntarily gave up the nuclear weapons stored on their territory. The Cold War was a thing of the past; the future promised disarmament and cooperation.

In the 1990s, Europeans saw Russia as a partner and as a country that was modernizing and would develop toward real democracy. The CSCE became the OSCE: Although only one letter changed, from that point on the *Conference on Security and Co-operation in Europe* became the *Organization for* this purpose. But behind this new name was a visionary idea, as Russian President Mikhail Gorbachev formulated it at the time, of a "Common European Home" where the West and the East would live together.

Overall, Europe was focused on cooperation. After decades during which a small but growing group of European countries were cooperating more closely on economics and policy, in 1992 the European Economic Community (EEC) became the European Union. Its membership has increased considerably since then, from 12 in 1992 to 28 today. Back then, nearly everyone believed that expansion and deepening of the EU were two sides of the same coin, and that we Europeans, as the founders had formulated, would inexorably proceed further along the path to an "ever closer union."

The United States supported the Europeans—not always unconditionally, but certainly in principle—in deepening their cooperation and endorsed the steps to enlarge the EU, accompanied by the integration of Central and Eastern European countries into NATO.

After the end of the Cold War, it seemed that these countries were finally taking their place in the West. In the United States, President George H. W. Bush expressed his wish for a "Europe whole, free, and at peace." While the country substantially reduced its military personnel stationed in Europe, no one seriously doubted that the United States would continue to be engaged in Europe and would thus remain a "European power."

For us Germans, these developments were a godsend. With the turning point in 1989–1991, from the fall of the Berlin Wall to the end of the Soviet Union, the core objectives of West German policy had been fulfilled. Germany was reunited and now "surrounded by friends." It was integrated into important international organizations, from the United Nations to the EU and NATO, and had once again become a respected member of the international community. No threat to its national security was in sight.

THE GOOD NEWS: IT IS NOT ALL BAD

Although some of these hopes for peace, democracy, human rights, and free trade have been shattered, from the historical perspective there are certainly grounds for optimism. Therefore, it would be wrong to paint only an apocalyptic picture. If we occasionally distance ourselves from the latest news of the day and try to look at the larger view, we can see a picture of humanity that is—in the historical perspective—not only more peaceful than ever, but also more healthy and prosperous. This picture, as Harvard professor Steven Pinker has emphasized over and over again in a number of publications, shows that we are moving in the right direction overall.

Some important current figures support Pinker's optimism. Despite how often wars and their victims are in the news, the fact is the number of victims has dropped significantly in the decades since World War II. And global poverty, as we are reminded time and time again, has also been reduced. Billions of people, many of them in in China, have risen out of extreme poverty to form a new global middle class. Between 2005 and 2010 alone, the number of people who had to live on less than US$1.25 a day was reduced by half a billion.

In 1950, only about every third person in the world could read and write (36 percent). In 2010 the literacy rate had risen to around four out of every five people in the world (83 percent).

Further, we have succeeded in conquering many serious diseases that regularly cost the lives of countless people just a few decades ago. The distribution of vaccines resulted in the number of measles victims dropping by 84 percent between 2000 and 2016. Polio cases have fallen by 99 percent since 1988. Child mortality has been reduced in most countries. According to the World Health Organization, 20,000 fewer children died each day in 2016 than in 1990.

Even death is less menacing. It still comes, but not quite so fast: The average global life expectancy climbed from about 46 years in 1950 to 72 in 2017.

All of this sounds quite gratifying—and it certainly is! All the same, wars, crises, and instability in the world regularly thwart this general upswing and sometimes even roll it back. One major war, and the number of victims climbs back up. A single deadly epidemic, and the life expectancy drops. This is why it would be a fatal mistake to sit back and let the world take its course, believing that everything always gets better.

Considering the many victims of war and violence, it would be more than cynical to tell them, "Too bad for you, but you are simply the exceptions on the path to peace and justice."

Every single victim who could have been saved is one too many.

REASONS FOR HOPE AND OPTIMISM

When I was born, after the end of the World War II, Germany was in ruins and the guilt-ridden nation seemed irrevocably brought to its knees—deindustrialized, occupied by the victorious powers, and shortly thereafter, sawed into two parts. Who would have wagered even a penny that by 2018 this country would be reunified, a politically stable democracy, and one of the leading economies in the world? I share this experience with many of my generation, and only those under age thirty can possibly believe that Germany had been on the sunny side of history "all along."

And in my professional life as a diplomat, first in Bonn and later in Berlin and various foreign postings, I was able to witness political events that nobody would have thought possible.

My colleagues and I held our breath when Foreign Minister Hans-Dietrich Genscher walked out on the balcony of the German embassy in Prague on the evening of September 30, 1989, and declared to hundreds of East German refugees that they would be allowed to emigrate by train to West Germany the very next day. I accompanied one of the later trains, representing the West German government. I will never forget the scent of cold sweat, of fear, in the crowded compartments of the night train, nor the rejoicing upon our arrival in the West the following morning. More on this in a later chapter.

I sat behind the German chancellor as a member of the German delegation in Paris, when the heads of state and government of thirty-two European countries as well as the United States and Canada declared the end of the division of Europe on November 21, 1990, and signed the final document of the CSCE summit, committing to democracy as the only form of government and promising their populations to guarantee human rights. The day on which the Charter of Paris for a New Europe was signed heralded the end of the Cold War, which had been a threat for the entire world until that day.

I was the chief German negotiator during the talks in Dayton, Ohio, in November 1995, when the bloody war that raged for years in Yugoslavia was ended after weeks of arduous negotiations. A peace treaty was later signed by Serbian President Slobodan Milošević, Croatian President Franjo Tuđman, and the chairman of the presidency of Bosnia and Herzegovina, Alija Izetbegović—three men who were such bitter enemies that they had refused even to sit at the same table before this event. What I learned from this was that, for the sake of peace, one has to negotiate even with war criminals, and that the goal of peace can sometimes be achieved only through the deployment of military force.

My first day in Washington, D.C., as the new German ambassador to Washington was September 11, 2001. Before I even figured out the telephone system, my staff and I had to provide assistance to the families of the German victims of the terrorist attacks, while at the same time organizing crisis communications between my own government and the White House. In so doing, however, I also experienced the extraordinary generosity of the German population in this time of need. Within just a few weeks, Germans donated many millions of dollars, which I was later able to present to the U.S. Department of Defense for the families of the victims of the attack on the Pentagon. The U.S. general who accepted the check was impressed, stating that he had never before received such a large donation from abroad.

As the ambassador in London, I was congratulated by complete strangers in 2006 for the World Cup's "fairy tale summer"—a soccer tournament that was so joyful and peaceful that the word "Germany" no longer made the British think of the trinity of Hitler, the war, and the kaiser.

And as chairman of the Munich Security Conference since 2008, I have encountered so many leaders from politics, business, and civil society searching for new solutions and ideas to make this world a better place.

The English language uses the expression "fog of war" to express the fact that even the best made plans are worthless in times of war, because the actual events remain obscured by surprises, imponderables, and uncertainty. Not even commanders can maintain a complete overview, yet they have to make weighty decisions even when they can no longer see beyond the hand in front of their face.

Yet over and again, I have experienced that conflicts can actually be resolved even from within the fog—that trust and optimism can replace hate and desperation, and that peace is possible.

The path to peace can be found. Sometimes we just have to look a very long time to find it. That is why good foreign policy also requires tenacity and endurance—we like to speak of "strategic patience" in such cases. And, sometimes the journey is the destination.

FIVE REASONS WHY PEACE AND STABILITY ARE SO DIFFICULT TO SECURE TODAY

So, what is it that makes peace and stability so difficult to achieve? Let us try to get to the bottom of this problem: It is not a monocausal explanation we are dealing with, of course, but a whole bundle of causes and developments. I would like to briefly present five of these:

The Epochal Break in Power Politics

The unipolar world of the U.S. hegemony that began in 1990 is coming to an end. The next epoch will be characterized, above all, by the rise of China—and thus by a relative power shift away from the United States (and Europe) toward countries outside the traditional West. But extensive power shifts also carry the risk of new crises and conflicts. After all, ascending powers have their own ideas about how the international order is to be shaped—and they may well contradict the ideas propagated by the previous great powers. What we are dealing with here is also known as Thucydides's trap.

The ancient Greek historian had observed in the tensions between Sparta and Athens that the rise of new powers rarely pro-
ceeds peacefully. This raises a question: Can the values of the West,
and the institutions that still protect and support the liberal world
order it founded, survive in the long term? Or is a new world order
emerging—an alternative to the Western order we have known?
The disconcertion is palpable, and it is growing. It is further magnified by the fact that the classic "policeman of the world," who
had provided for a semblance of order, has withdrawn: "America
First," the political slogan of the Trump administration, means that
Washington no longer feels responsible for global governance, international institutions, and global rules. But if the United States is
no longer willing to take on this role, who should or can? This question frequently surfaced during discussions at the 2019 Munich Security Conference and was a core concern raised in our Munich
Security Report 2019. In it, we drew the disconcerting conclusion
that "some of the candidates for an increased role as guardians of
the liberal order are willing but incapable, others are at least mod-
erately capable but unwilling or unable to bring their capabilities
to the fore."[8]

The Loss of Truth and Trust

One problem is that trust between governments—especially among
the most powerful of them—is virtually gone. And it is very, very
difficult to rebuild trust once it has been destroyed. In this sense,
relationships between states are not so different from a marriage.
What makes the situation all the more precarious is that we are
observing an alarming loss of trust on all sorts of levels in recent
years.

For starters, today we often cannot distinguish between fact
and fake. What is truth, and what is propaganda? This is not new in
the history of the world; as Aeschylus said, the first casualty of war
is truth. But it now seems to apply in times of peace as well. Citizens, like governments, are bombarded with information to such

a degree that it is often impossible, or at least difficult, to ascertain what is true.

In the battle of ideas, everyone is adamant about their own "facts." This is an essential element in our world of increasing uncertainty.

Trust is also being undermined by the fact that Russia and others are deploying the latest technologies in an effort to manipulate democratic means of shaping public opinion in Western societies. We can track this especially in the debate about the role of Russian hackers and social media campaigns in the lead-up to presidential elections in the United States. But in the past year, the Chinese also came under fire for very aggressive interference in politics, universities, and media in Western democracies. Interventions in the freedom of expression are especially problematic in this regard—for instance, when Chinese media in foreign countries are "brought into line" in the hopes of restricting critical debates on human rights violations in China or on the assertion of Chinese territorial claims. In Australia, massive Chinese donations were exposed, which had been funneled to political parties and individual politicians who subsequently expressed very favorable opinions about China.

Thus it may be difficult to consider Xi Jinping's China or Putin's Russia a reliable partner. But it does not mean that we should not work together with Beijing and Moscow where possible.

What makes the situation especially dangerous in the case of Russia is the combination of two factors: the current crises in which both Russia and the West are involved (first and foremost in Ukraine and in Syria, but also in Yemen and elsewhere) and the loss of political trust, which has resulted, for instance, in today's almost complete absence of contacts between the Russian General Staff and the Pentagon. These days it is a major geopolitical event when the Russian chief of the General Staff meets with his American counterpart. In the Clinton and Obama eras, there were multiple communication channels between various levels of Western and Russian military and civilian leadership and command head-quarters. Everyone knew their counterpart and who to call in order to clear up any misunderstandings. No one knows with any certainty who to call any more. The two sides barely know each other.

Yet this does not only concern the question of whether Putin trusts Chancellor Angela Merkel or whether Trump trusts Putin. It is also about whether citizens still trust their institutions. Surveys show that citizens' trust in their governments to make reasonable decisions has dropped dramatically in the twenty-eight EU member states. This loss in trust is not complete, but it is quite substantial. And this loss of confidence in politics extends all the way down to the local level.

The Loss in Predictive Power

Added to this is a new kind of loss in predictive power, or an inability to anticipate the trajectory or significance of world events. As chairman of the Munich Security Conference, which is attended each year by over 500 decisionmakers from all over the world, I think about which topics to put on the agenda months ahead of time. It is important for us to set the right priorities, but we also want to discuss what will be affecting people in the year to come. I try to accomplish this by spending time beforehand with friends, colleagues, and experts whom I believe to be the most intelligent and experienced people in foreign policy, whether they are from Brussels, Moscow, or Washington, from Berlin, London, or Paris.

In early 2014 the political and civil rights demonstrations on Independence Square in Kyiv were reaching their climax. Yet not one of my advisors and experts suggested addressing the Ukraine crisis as the start of a major European security emergency. Everyone considered these events to be a domestic topic for Ukraine.

Six weeks later, everything had changed: Russian soldiers and tanks invaded, Crimea was annexed, and the crisis was no longer an inner-Ukrainian matter, but a massive international security conflict with threatening effects even today.

Just as bad, at the same time not one of us had recognized the relevance of a second topic: key word "Islamic State" (IS). In retrospect, I know now that there were definitely experts at the German Intelligence Service (BND) and the U.S. Central Intelligence Agency (CIA), and certainly in the back offices of the German Foreign Office as well, who were already worried about the Islamic State. However, the topic had not yet been picked up by decisionmakers. Only a few months later, in June 2014, everyone who followed the news knew that the IS presented a major security policy risk on a global scale—one that would occupy us for many years and continues to do so to this day.

Alternatively, take the year 2016: Why was almost everyone caught off guard in the days before the Brexit decision? Why were the analysts not able to predict the result with any accuracy? And what about the U.S. election? Who saw that ending with a loss for Hillary Clinton?

In 2017 I had the opportunity to accompany the German Foreign Minister Sigmar Gabriel to a discussion with the Saudi Arabian foreign minister about the current situation in the Middle East. There were no signs beforehand that a crisis with Qatar would erupt overnight. Suddenly we were facing the threat of war. Who had seen that coming? No one! And this list of surprises will be continued in 2020 and beyond.

A lack of predictability can cause headaches for stockbrokers. But in foreign policy it presents a new—and significant—problem. It was never possible to plan foreign policy precisely, of course, but in the past it was possible to make a more reliable prognosis of strategic developments. Conflicts escalated more slowly, the actors involved were old acquaintances, and their arguments and interests, familiar. This is no longer the case. Conflict prevention, as good as it sounds, has thus become much more difficult.

We can no longer prepare for what is coming and always have to be prepared for surprises. Expect the unexpected!

The Loss of the Nation-State's Monopoly of Power

An entirely different phenomenon that complicates efforts toward peace is the loss of the nation-state's monopoly of power. When the German Empire was founded in 1871, Otto von Bismarck was able to assert that he, as chancellor of the new state, was capable of providing for its external and internal security and prosperity. Today's small European nation-state can no longer make such a promise. Angela Merkel is smart enough to not even insinuate to voters that, as chancellor, she could save us from polluted air, terrorism, or pandemics. Indeed, the solution to nearly all difficult questions we face today transcends the capacity of individual nation-states. Only global approaches to problem-solving have any prospect of success. The increasing popularity of authoritarian leaders and populists is based in part on the fact that they assert the opposite and deceive their supporters by telling them what they want to hear: that the nation-state that forged the country's national identity is alive and well, and potent.

The Fundamental Change in the Nature of Conflicts

A further problem is the changing nature of conflicts. When our grandfathers and fathers went to battle in World Wars I and II, those were conflicts between nation-states. The German kaiser, the Russian czar, Hitler, or the French or American president issued the marching orders. States fought against states.

In 2019, the long list of armed conflicts in the world does not include any classic wars between nation-states. Not a single one.

In Afghanistan the Taliban are fighting fellow Afghans; in Syria the combatants include the Shiites against the Sunnis. Nor are the conflicts in Yemen and Mali classic interstate wars, although they do involve some external powers. Of course, mercenaries and foreign influences are everywhere. But in essence, all of these conflicts are variants of civil wars, very different from the wars of the past. This intensifies the powerlessness of the international community, because the world order of the United Nations is based on states as the acting subjects and prescribes rules for their interactions. Now conflicts involve entities like the Islamic State, which calls itself a state but is not. How can the UN take action against them? We will not get far with classical international law.

Added to this are technological developments that further relativize the nation-state's monopoly on power. The conflicts of today, and those of tomorrow even more so, are conducted by drone or by cyberattack—"weapons" that can be procured by any group or even by individuals. How helpless are the military and the police if the electricity supply to a large city is cut off, or a drone loaded with explosives is flown into a sold-out stadium? Such events also blur the classic boundaries between the roles of the military and the police, between foreign and domestic policy, and between international and homeland security.

OVERTAXED PEACEMAKERS

The EU, the transatlantic partners, and Germany itself all ask themselves, are we sufficiently prepared for all of these epochal security challenges, some of which we have never seen before?

The European Union has certainly seen better days as a peacemaker. European integration is anything but a one-way street toward an ever-closer union. Brexit, the intra-European effects of the financial and economic crisis, and the disagreements among member states about how to deal with the refugee crisis have made this abundantly clear. By now it is no longer unthinkable that the process of European unification could actually be rolled back or will leave individual members, like Great Britain, behind.

Of course, there have always been severe crises in the EU. But they have never been waged as personally and as bitterly as is happening now on the issues of quotas for refugees or in the dispute about the basic principles of the rule of law. This even led to leaders of EU member states refusing to participate in the same panel discussion at the 2018 Munich Security Conference, which is an extremely alarming development, especially since the capacity for joint foreign policy action—an EU that speaks with one voice—is needed more than ever. How can we square that circle?

Sadly, we can no longer rely on our American partner, either. On the other side of the Atlantic, old certainties are being called into question. As stated so diplomatically in the coalition agreement of the new German government in 2018, "The U.S. is undergoing a profound transition, which presents us with great challenges."

In other words, since taking office, President Donald Trump has baffled America's friends by cossetting autocrats all over the world while never tiring of complaining about the United States's classical alliance partners, especially the Europeans. It took an effort to make Trump acknowledge Article 5 of the NATO Treaty, which commits the signatories to collective defense if any member is attacked. At the NATO Summit in July 2018, Trump even threatened that the Americans would "go it alone" unless his NATO partners raised their monetary contributions immediately. Understandably, all of this has triggered new thinking about the future of NATO and thus of the security of Europe. Or as others have put it, now it has become "painfully clear to America's allies that they will increasingly have to fend for themselves."[9] The United States's renunciation of the nuclear deal with Iran only heightened the shock in Europe about the unreliability of Trump's foreign policy.

Polling numbers published by the Pew Research Institute reveal the extent of this shock about Washington's retreat: According to results from September 2018, 37 percent of respondents from all over the world said that the United States is now doing less to help address major global problems compared to a few years ago. Only 14 percent said the United States was doing more. Among North Americans and Europeans, the number was even smaller.[10] Trump's predecessor, Barack Obama, had already signaled a sea change, speaking of the United States as a Pacific power that wanted to dedicate itself to addressing the dangers on the other side of the globe, thereby necessitating a "pivot to Asia." Although the events in Ukraine have since resulted in the United States increasing its military presence in Europe, one thing is clear in the long run: We Europeans will have to become much more self-reliant. What would happen if the United States actually renounced its treaty obligations someday?

Since the very founding of the Federal Republic of Germany, the United States—underpinned by the nuclear umbrella—has effectively provided our ultimate life insurance. Will it persist in this role forever? If not, what does that mean for us?

That is a quick overview of the general geopolitical situation in the summer of 2018. So there are plenty of reasons for concern. Our country will be facing a whole slew of new foreign policy tasks. The question is whether and how Germany wants to grapple with them—and whether it can.

THE CHALLENGE FOR GERMANY

How should Western foreign policy orient its compass, particularly to deal with the plethora of current violent conflicts in the world? At the moment the West's compass is spinning: Is the lesson to be drawn from Afghanistan and Iraq that we would be better off refraining completely from lengthy, laborious stabilization missions because they are generally fruitless? Did the international involvement there perhaps blaze important trails for development? Can the West stake any claim to moral leadership at all after Abu Ghraib and Guantanamo? If so, what should this leadership look like? Is the conclusion from the bloody, bumpy transition processes since the Arab Spring that we would be better off not undermining dictatorships? Or do we admit that the chaos in the Middle East today is in part also a result of Western realpolitik, which cemented apparent stability in the short term by supporting autocratic rulers? There are so many important questions we need to debate if we are to understand that we are not facing a cartoonish black-or-white decision between two archetypes: the fanatic democrat who would rather overthrow every dictatorship or the political realist who has no problem with the suppression of others' freedom as long as it keeps things calm in Western eyes.

No, foreign policy decisions are not carried out at these opposite poles; they take place in a spectrum of shades of gray.

The debate about such decisions in Germany, however, is often emotionally charged, as if there were only black and white. Some voices ask whether Germany, with its usual policy of staying on the sidelines, belongs to the West at all. Intellectuals are particularly bothered by Germany's behavior in the UN Security Council in 2011, when Germany, a nonpermanent member, abstained from voting on the no-fly zone over Libya. Others, such as Bernd Ulrich in the weekly *Die Zeit* in 2014, emphasize the burdens that have to be shouldered due to the Western policy of intervention: "In the last fifteen years it was stunning to see how Western heads of state bent, and sometimes broke, international law; what justifications they offered for the war and what alliances they switched how often. This mortgage must finally be expressed and accepted; the West will recover its capacity for action only by acknowledging this debt, not by refusing to mention it."

The best thing about the West is that it allows this dispute about the right foreign policy, as well as critical self-reflection. The kind of confrontation raging here would not be possible in newspapers in Russia or China. But the fact that we can conduct this discussion so openly—in contrast to many other countries—brings with it an enormous responsibility to draw clear conclusions from the debate. After all, what the West itself defines as its values and ambitions remains of paramount importance for people in many parts of the world.

Both within the Federal Republic and without, there is considerable skepticism about whether Germany can currently measure up to this responsibility. For example, the *Washington Post* on

April 27, 2018, called Germany's hesitation to accept international military obligations one of the greatest strains on Europe. "German passivity is deeply engrained," it explains. "Berlin's political class lacks strategic thinking, hates risk . . . and hides behind its ignominious past to justify pacifism when it comes to hard questions about defense and security issues."

This cautious German policy, as Michael Thumann commented in *Die Zeit* on March 9, 2018, simply does not do justice to the modern challenges and power politics upheavals of the twenty-first century: "In March 2014 Angela Merkel said that Vladimir Putin was living on a different planet. A distant star where might is right, where one conquers territory and no international law applies. Four years later, however, much has changed. Today it looks as if Putin fits in perfectly with this new, hard, real world. And as if Merkel is living on another planet."

In May 2018, Christoph von Marschall expressed a similarly harsh criticism in the Berlin daily *Tagesspiegel*:

> Wherever one looks, the surroundings are becoming more dangerous: wars in the Middle East, migration pressure and the threat of terrorism from Africa, an aggressive Russia. Relying on the U.S., the chancellor says, is no longer possible to the same extent. Europe must do more. [But] what is its contribution? . . . The political class and the majority of the media are content with the excuse that Germany's history makes it a special case. More than seventy years after the war, the Allies are no longer willing to make an exception. Germany's EU partners, especially France, are pushing for a common European defense.

Has Germany earned this harsh criticism? What is clear is that things are getting unpleasant. And Germany—and its partners in the EU—clearly need a wake-up call. But what role and what responsibility can and must Germany shoulder, along with its European partners? What does it actually mean to take on "more responsibility?" Is that meant politically, militarily, or perhaps "only" morally? To answer these questions, we have to widen our scope. Above all, we must explain in detail why good foreign policy and diplomacy are so very hard in the twenty-first century. There is no getting around discussing the fundamental issues of war, peace, and international law, without which it is not possible to understand the complex and dangerous global situation in which Germany and Europe are acting. It further requires an in-depth look at two states that have always been of tremendous importance to the security of Germany and Europe—namely, the United States and Russia. As I finalize this text, at the end of 2019, the debate in Berlin about whether and how to take on "international responsibility" is in full swing again. In my view, this is an important and urgent debate. All of this will be discussed in the following chapters. Let us start with the question of how diplomacy, the most important instrument of German foreign policy, really works.

TWO

THE ART OF DIPLOMACY

PROTOCOL: THE OFTEN-UNDERAPPRECIATED DETAILS OF DIPLOMACY

In summer 2017, Prince William and Kate, Duchess of Cambridge, traveled to Germany for an official visit. Over three days they traveled to Berlin, Hamburg, and Heidelberg. The British royals impress with the glamor and glory they emanate. But although most of the reporting on their visit was found in the tabloids, and focused primarily on clothing and hairstyle, handshakes and jewelry, in truth their visit was nothing less than foreign policy.

Accordingly, the British ambassador to Germany announced that the visit would "reflect the entire spectrum of the good relations between Great Britain and Germany and strengthen the connection between the young generation of our two countries."

The young heir to the throne and his wife are considered the miracle weapon of the now 94-year-old Queen Elizabeth II, and the purpose of their visit was to create "a good climate"—through state receptions, official visits, dinner speeches, handshakes, and even more handshakes. While the success of British foreign policy is hamstrung by the wake of the country's withdrawal from the EU, the royal family remains the emotional icebreaker for London's interests.

The Germans may not want a monarchy, but their adoration for the royals knows no bounds. The British queen enjoys much greater admiration than the German head of state, no matter whether he's called Gauck or Steinmeier. Federal presidents tend to be more respected than admired. The difference can certainly be credited in part to the queen's personality, but it is due primarily to tradition and protocol. Every royal appearance, every movement, every sentence is deliberated carefully and analyzed for its implications. After all, representing the state is a high art! And Great Britain is certainly the world champion of this art form. The Queen's receptions in the garden, the state dinners in Windsor Castle—this is not Hollywood, it is all real, as is the natural self-confidence with which this wealth of tradition and power is demonstrated. Nearly everyone who has experienced this presence is impressed.

In contrast to this, the German state protocol is rather modest. We Germans have an aversion to pomp on our own part, for historical reasons. After the destructive aspiration to put Germany "über alles" in the world, the general consensus is that a degree of humility is more becoming. The official residence of the federal president, Bellevue Palace, is Prussian in style: unpretentious and unadorned. Nevertheless, this former summer residence of Prince Ferdinand, Frederick the Great's brother, commands a certain admiration. By contrast, the prosaically modern office building in which Angela Merkel resides, the "Chancellery," has the charm of an underground parking garage, sending a clear signal: This place is for working, not for flaunting.

It is true: Ultimately what counts in foreign policy is not symbols and words, but decisions and deeds. The pomp and circumstance surrounding state visits and political summits often contrast with the seriousness of the foreign policy conflicts addressed there. In April 2018, Emmanuel Macron's elaborate state visit to Washington and Angela Merkel's brief working visit with Donald Trump right afterward offered a good object lesson: Does a grand state dinner really yield more than a serious work meeting during a brief visit?

Today as in previous centuries, communication between the powerful is more than the legal formulation of texts and treaties—it is always an interpersonal interaction as well. Otherwise there would be no need for summits and state visits. Instead, experts (or maybe even some kind of artificial intelligences) could draw up contractual texts, which would then be sent back and forth until an agreement was reached. But as anyone who has ever signed a contract knows, mutual trust that both partners will comply with the contract is more decisive for the signature than the small print. And this is what must be nurtured. The first thing anyone who works in diplomacy realizes is how complicated a meeting between two important political representatives can become. It starts with deciding on the location and agenda of the meeting, and continues with the body language and seating plan for all of the participants. This does not just apply to diplomatic meetings; the procedures for installing a new ambassador are also subject to strict rules. But these rules only become apparent when things get off to a bumpy start.

In early May 2018, a new U.S. ambassador took office in Berlin, after a protracted appointment process in Washington that had lasted an entire year. Finally installed, the new ambassador lost no time in tweeting, "German companies doing business in Iran should wind down operations immediately." Richard Grenell's tweet was directed at the nuclear agreement with Iran, which his president had just renounced, and reinforced Trump's threat to sanction foreign countries that made business deals with Iran.

In response, I offered Ambassador Grenell, with whom I had already been corresponding for some time—also by Twitter—the following well-intentioned suggestion: "Ric, my advice after a long ambassadorial career: Explain your own country's policies, and lobby the host country—but never tell the host country what to do, if you want to stay out of trouble. Germans are eager to listen, but they will resent instructions."

Within a few hours my tweet had generated nearly 3,000 "likes," over 700 retweets, and a broad debate in the media about the role and function of ambassadors, and about the rules and limits of diplomacy. Because an ambassador acts with the express permission of the host country, a good diplomat is one who explains his or her country and its politics in public everywhere but, if the need arises, only criticizes the host country in a "diplomatic" form—that is, not through public channels, but in direct conversation with the host government. This is just one of the ways diplomacy follows rules that have evolved and proven effective over centuries.

But let us start from the beginning: All of the rules start with accreditation.

"LET'S TALK ABOUT HORSES"

Upon arrival, a new ambassador is accredited by presenting a letter from his or her own head of state to the head of state of the host country.

In Berlin this process is not terribly glamorous. The new ambassador drives up to Bellevue Palace and has a cup of coffee with the federal president. The ambassador may be accompanied by a staff member, and a representative of the foreign office and an advisor to the federal president attend as well. They conduct a friendly discussion, exchange a few ideas, and become acquainted. The whole thing is usually over in half an hour.

The procedure may be much more elaborate, however, as is the case in London. There the ambassador does more than merely present the queen with his credentials—quite a bit more. Days before my appointment with the queen in 2006, I received a visit from "Her Majesty's Marshal of the Diplomatic Corps in the Royal Household of the Sovereign of the United Kingdom," who fortunately also bore the somewhat simpler name Sir Anthony Figgis. Sir Anthony explained to me that it would be unseemly to start a conversation with the queen myself, let alone ask any questions, and that the conversation would follow the queen's wishes from start to finish. I was told how to enter the room—this is quite important, please!—and to never turn my back to the queen. The dress code was obvious: tails, medals, and top hat. My wife would face even greater challenges, as the "lady in waiting" assigned to her explained in a separate meeting. She was to wear a dress; under no circumstances could it be black, but neither should it be white or royal blue. Her shoulders had to be covered, and her heels should not be too high.

On the day of the official visit as new ambassador in London, a royal carriage and four stood in front of the German ambassador's residence on Belgrave Square. It used to be that only the ambassador was allowed to ride in the coach—his wife had to be driven behind in another vehicle—but the customs are no longer so strict. The bobbies stopped traffic to clear our route to Buckingham Palace, then the coach drove around the palace into the inner courtyard. My wife had to wait in a parlor. The queen, protocol stipulates, speaks first with the ambassador alone. Later, Jutta was asked to join us.

Of course, I had asked around beforehand for tips about what I was allowed to, could, or should say to the queen. British colleagues said I would have to wait until she asked me something. But one good friend, the permanent under-secretary of state in the Foreign and Commonwealth Office, shook his head: "That's all nonsense," he said. "The poor queen, she has to conduct conversations like that all the time. Everybody waits until she says something. She would be thrilled if you would tell her something clever. Think of something smart to say! She has been in office for fifty years, and has known them all—from Churchill, Adenauer, Eisenhower, Kennedy and Reagan up to today. You'll see, she's an interesting conversationalist!"

Fine. But what is *something clever?*

We discovered by chance that Zara Phillips, the queen's grand-daughter and a very successful equestrian, would be competing in an international tournament in Aachen, Germany, the following week. So I called Michael Mronz, the impresario of the Aachen tournament and husband of the late Guido Westerwelle, who had served as German foreign minister, and asked him what I needed to know about the tournament, the British team, and Zara Phillips. Soon I knew all about who the rivals were, what the name of Zara Phillips's horse was, how the obstacle course would go; I knew the prospects for success, the betting odds, and so on. I went into the meeting with the queen fully briefed by the expert.

As my foreign office friend had recommended, I did not wait long for a question from the queen, but simply started out by saying how regrettable it was that she would not be at the equestrian tournament in Aachen the following week, although her granddaughter was sure to win the gold medal there.

Wide-eyed with amazement, she looked at me and asked how I had ever got this impression.

I was interested in equestrian sports, I said (which was true), and everyone was saying that Zara was favored to win, which is why it was truly a shame that she, the queen, would not be there.

"Ambassador, I'm afraid you have no idea." The queen leaned forward, "But you may not tell anyone, you know. . . ."

And then she revealed to me that Zara's horse had a lame back left foot, and that just yesterday they had tried out a new salve to treat it. She told me the whole story, from the animal to the veterinarians, all the way to her granddaughter's worry that the wonderful horse might not be able to compete in the tournament.

The queen went into such detail that all I had to do was throw in an occasional "Oh really?" to keep the conversation going. At some stage the chief of British protocol gave the sign that time was up, but the Queen waved him off. She was so enthusiastic—apparently I had pushed the right button. Not only did she talk shop with me far beyond the scheduled time on this day, but on further encounters she resumed talk on the subject of horses right away. She usually merely shook hands with the others, but to me she said, "Let us talk about horses." I was no longer just any ambassador, but the horse lover. My colleagues were quite jealous.

By the way, Zara Phillips did win the individual gold medal at that tournament in Aachen in 2006, and the silver medal with her team. For this, British television viewers voted her "BBC Sports Personality of the Year." So my briefing from Michael Mronz had been "golden."

I recount this anecdote because it shows how even insignificant gestures can make a huge difference in how a single conversation can build trust or generate resentment—important in many spheres of life but especially in diplomacy. Nothing can be accomplished in that field without trust.

HIGHLY SENSITIVE POLITICAL GESTURES

As a young diplomat in the office of Foreign Minister Hans-Dietrich Genscher, I learned how highly political, and even dangerous, questions of protocol can be. It was November 1982. After a motion of no confidence, Chancellor Helmut Schmidt had stepped down and, on October 4, 1982, Helmut Kohl had been elected federal chancellor. In Germany everyone was talking about the Free Democratic Party's (FDP's) switch—or as some called it, betrayal—from a coalition with the Social Democratic Party (SPD) to one with the Christian Democratic Union/Christian Social Union (CDU/CSU). Foreign Minister Genscher—along with Otto Graf Lambsdorff—was considered one of the powerbrokers behind this momentous transition, and remained in office afterward. The same year, I was transferred to Genscher's ministerial office, where my first task was to accompany the foreign minister to Oslo and to plan this trip meticulously.

There were not many exciting bilateral issues between Germany and Norway at that time, making it an uneventful visit with a neighbor. King Olaf would receive Genscher, and there would be talks with the Norwegian foreign minister, interviews, and declarations. A wreath-laying ceremony was included in the schedule: Pretty much the standard itinerary.

A few days beforehand, Genscher asked for some details: Where am I laying a wreath? "Where everyone does," I responded, "At the tomb of the unknown soldier. Three Bundeswehr soldiers will carry the wreath. Everything has been arranged." That is what had been conveyed to me from Oslo, and I accepted it without verification.

Three days later in Oslo, we were driven to Akershus Fortress, above the city. A stone slab on the ground there reads, "To the victims of the National Socialist dictatorship." So much for the tomb of the unknown soldier! We got out of the car to cameras and many journalists. The wreath was ceremoniously laid down.

Then a German reporter approached Genscher, held a microphone in his face, and opened the interview with the sentence, "You just laid down a wreath at the monument against the Nazi occupation. No German has ever done this before. I would like to compare this moment with Brandt's genuflection in Warsaw."

Genscher, as always, came up with an answer immediately, said something about reconciliation policy, and got back in the car. There he upbraided me: "Was that the tomb of the unknown soldier? Really? Or the monument for Nazi victims? Before making such a political gesture I need to consult with Kohl first. Kohl and the CDU will accuse me of seeking the spotlight and making policy on my own!"

I was crestfallen. For me a wreath-laying ceremony was a wreath-laying ceremony. That such an event stood for policy was something that had not occurred to me before.

So, I learned my lesson. Protocol is important, and details are important—often cloaking sensitive political or historical relationships. Who remembers the case of Bitburg, where Helmut Kohl invited Ronald Reagan to lay a wreath at a cemetery where members of the Nazi elite "Waffen-SS" soldiers were buried? It caused an outcry in the media and preventable tension in German-American relations.

EVERY STEP YOU TAKE: THE WORLD IS WATCHING

A colleague of mine had a similar mishap with a wreath-laying ceremony, on the occasion of Genscher's visit to Tehran in July 1983. In contrast to the United States, Germany had never severed diplomatic relations with Iran after the Ayatollah Khomeini's revolution. Now Genscher was one of the first European ministers to travel to Tehran. That alone was regarded with some suspicion, especially by the United States.

The Iranian protocol had suggested a visit to a gigantic cemetery in southern Tehran, where the minister would lay down a wreath—an established procedure: In Washington, one goes to Arlington National Cemetery, and in Moscow, to Novodevichy Cemetery. So far, so good.

The German advance party had paid less attention to the host's proposal to also visit the "Pond of Blood," which features fountains spraying red-colored water. The pond itself was bizarre enough, but my colleagues had overlooked the fact that the path to the pond led over a mosaic of the American flag embedded in the ground. So, everyone who walks to the monument treads on the U.S. flag—a sign of total contempt. Genscher recognized the danger at the last second, took a path that went around the flag, and thus avoided becoming the subject of a compromising photograph. Afterward there was quite a commotion. What would have happened if he had not noticed in time? How would Washington have reacted? Even before the trip, the Americans had hardly been enthusiastic about the idea.

MINOR GESTURES, MAJOR EFFECTS

Small gestures can make a big difference—positively or negatively. West German Chancellor Willy Brandt falling to his knees at the wall of the Warsaw Ghetto in 1970, performed at the spur of the moment, was a gesture of tremendous symbolic importance and thus a historical event included in every German history book. It became the symbol of the new German *Ostpolitik* and, as such, a visual milestone along the path to the reunification of Germany years later.

Diplomatic rituals and gestures thus have great potential as a signal of harmony, but also as an occasion for conflicts and division.

But sometimes the center stage is less important symbolically than the seemingly profane tasks going on around it. A case in point: a train journey in 1989 turned out to be one of the most impressive moments in my life as a diplomat.

EVERYDAY DIPLOMACY CAN CHANGE LIVES

Late September 1989: Thousands of East Germans had already fled to the West via Hungary, across the Hungarian-Austrian border. When it was rumored that the East German head of state, Erich Honecker, would soon close the border between the German Democratic Republic (GDR) and Czechoslovakia, more and more desperate East Germans fled to the West German embassy in Prague, seeking asylum while they still could. The embassy was soon overcrowded. Thousands of people made the best of the tight space and few sanitary facilities. The Red Cross set up a soup kitchen to provide for their essential needs. The weather was quite cool for the season, and most people had to spend the night in tents outdoors. Rain had turned the garden into a sea of mud. Pregnant women and small children were housed in the boiler rooms of the embassy, where it was warmer. The conditions were unbearable. But the refugees persisted.

At the diplomatic level there were difficult negotiations about solutions for the refugees. Foreign Minister Genscher wanted to spare them a stopover in the GDR and let them go directly from Prague to the Federal Republic; Oskar Fischer, the East German foreign minister, demanded that the refugees be returned to the GDR transitionally. The United States, Great Britain, and France supported Genscher, and at some stage Soviet Foreign Minister Eduard Shevardnadze, too, accepted a compromise.

And so on the morning of September 30, it was settled: Chartered trains were to take the refugees across the territory of East Germany into the Federal Republic. Genscher traveled to Prague and spoke to the crowd that evening from the balcony of Lobkowicz Palace, uttering the most famous half sentence in all of German history: "We have come to you in order to inform you that today, your departure . . ." The rest was drowned out by cheers.

Next, East German trains were brought to Prague. The refugees boarded their assigned cars and headed back to the GDR, where they were stripped of East German citizenship before emigrating to the Federal Republic—all without ever leaving the train.

As a diplomatic escort, I boarded one of the trains in the second wave of transports. The train pulled out of the station in the evening and rolled slowly through the GDR. At some stage it occurred to the East German government that these trains gave the virtual appearance of a torchlight procession made up of enemies of the republic. Officials also wanted to prevent further refugees from jumping on the train along the route through Saxony. Accordingly, the train was diverted to branch lines so that it would not have to roll into the major terminus at Leipzig Hauptbahnhof.

We finally rode through Plauen, where officers of Stasi, the GDR's state security service, boarded and confiscated the official papers of the East German refugees. That was part of the agreement. It also meant that they lost their citizenship. Since I knew that the officers would make their way through the whole train, I had already gone through every compartment and requested that passengers write down all of the information from their passport or identity card on a piece of paper, so that the Federal German authorities would be able to use this information to issue a new West German identity card. "We will accept this piece of paper as a replacement document!" I promised.

This was the official, agree-upon plan. I repeated this sentence in each compartment over the hours we spent traveling from Prague toward the German border. The train was not heated, and there was nothing to eat or drink. Everyone was freezing.

Before we got to Plauen, I took a few random samples. I went into a compartment and requested of one of the passengers, "Show me your paper, please! Did you write down everything? Can I please see your identity card as well?" Then I compared the identity card with the piece of paper. First name Sven, last name Müller. Single. I stopped short. His identity card said he was married.

"Herr Müller, what is this about?" I exclaimed. "If you supply false information, you may be liable to prosecution! And if you marry again later, you'd be committing bigamy!" "Well," Herr Müller explained, "you see, I only married back then so that I could get an apartment. My wife is not even here with me. The woman sitting next to me is my girlfriend." I reminded him that he would have to comply with the law and write down his passport information correctly, and then I began checking other passengers' transcribed information more closely.

I discovered a number of such cases, most of them concerning changes to marital status. That made me aware how many of the refugees had lived their lives under major constraints regarding housing, family, and profession. They were now on their way to freedom, and to give themselves a new identity: "I am going West to start over!" It was truly touching.

But during the trip I had other worries on my mind. How would things go when the GDR officers entered the train? What if they were suddenly to pick someone off the train, for instance, someone who was accused of a crime? How could I prevent the situation from coming to a head? What would I do if there were a scuffle? None of this was clear. I was not really vested with authority of any kind. I had a diplomatic passport, so I certainly would not be arrested, but what about the refugees? I was basically powerless and, accordingly, nervous. To dispel the fears of the people in the train—fears that they had every reason to feel—I told them over and again that I was there to protect them. I promised that nothing could happen to them in my presence. That was not really true, but nevertheless, I repeated, "Don't worry. I am here. You are under diplomatic protection!"

Fortunately, nothing happened. But I could virtually smell the fear when the police came through the train. And it was not a pleasant smell: cold sweat. It spread through the entire train. Everyone knew how little it would take for the situation to escalate. And everyone knew how the story might end if one of the Stasi agents were to pick someone out. Everyone knew that the alternative to a life in the Federal Republic could mean a life in the Stasi prison of Bautzen. So little separated the dream from the nightmare.

No one was pulled off the train. The GDR police just stoically collected everyone's passports. We rode on further through the night, and dawn was breaking as we approached the inner-German border. At first light—the searchlights were still on—we arrived in Hof, Bavaria. The whole train erupted in a deafening roar, made up of a single word. And I roared along with them: Freedom! Freedom! Freedom! Uncontainable joy, mass hysteria.

I endured more worries and emotions in this one night than I ever had before, only to experience massive relief and exhilarating joy just a few hours later, as the refugees' wave of fear for their lives and their futures crashed into their boundless delight at having made it to freedom. It was an incredible experience for everyone who was there.

This profoundly impressed my own understanding of the events of this year and the years that followed. Constitutional and international agreements were not the point. What mattered were personal feelings and fears; it was about hopes and frustrations, and also the hardships people had to suffer, and about deliverance. These first refugees left their children, their partners, or their parents at home, left behind everything they could not fit into a travel bag, because they were so desperate. There was no way for them to know that people would be driving their Trabant cars, called Trabbis, into the West over an open border just five weeks later.

Nearly three decades later, in 2017, I received an email after a flight from Berlin to Munich. It came from the woman I had been sitting next to on the plane:

> Unfortunately, it was only after the flight that I realized you had already "accompanied" me on a journey once before! Almost exactly 28 years ago today. For me, a 20-year-old young woman at the time, it was the advent of a new life into new worlds that would never have been open to me before! I remember very well; it was you who calmed the fears of my fellow "adventists" and myself, who prepared us back then for how they were routing us through the territory of the GDR. I had started out all by myself back then, to Prague, hoping for a future, and I got that future. By now I am proudly flying as a pilot for Lufthansa (this time I was on a personal trip). I was only able to scale these "heavenly heights" thanks to the dedication and commitment of people like Herr Genscher, yourself and others.

This email showed me what diplomacy is also good for, and what tremendous effects small diplomatic gestures and seemingly profane tasks can have on an individual. I later met up with Lufthansa captain Ina Krause for a longer conversation, and she allowed me to quote from her email.

My statements during the trip from Prague promised a security that I could not promise at all. How could I possibly guarantee that nothing would happen? But it was precisely this uncertainty that was making everyone on that train sweat. Whether consciously or not, they understood that I wanted to give them courage, reassure them, because panic would have been of no use in this situation;

presumably, it would have made everything even worse. In any case, neither Ina nor anyone else ever accused me of lying to them.

All of us have experienced the positive and the negative power of "self-fulfilling prophecies." When coaches encourage their teams by saying, "Don't let that goal by the other team rattle you. You'll outscore them and end up winning the game!" they project confidence, send a signal of trust, and potentially strengthen the nerves of the athletes so much that they transform the deficit into a victory.

Just like the coach, the diplomat, too, attempts to find clever phrases and friendly gestures to pave the way to success. But instead of "winning," the goals of diplomacy are security, peace, and trust.

Sometimes this includes saying things that may not entirely correspond to the objective truth, but that could become truth if all participants are willing—and if everything falls into place. It is a balancing act between truth and lies, between compliment and honesty, that diplomacy has to strike time and again. It is also an attempt to prevent misunderstandings.

MISUNDERSTANDINGS WITH SERIOUS CONSEQUENCES

In some situations, skilled diplomacy can help find a way out of an impasse of reciprocal misunderstandings and mutual distrust. Diplomacy can also provide important services in interpreting or breaking the ice. But this requires a great deal of patience and sometime does not pay off until years or decades later.

One of my oldest American friends is Bob Kimmitt, U.S. ambassador in Bonn in the early 1990s and later deputy secretary of the U.S. Treasury. Without disclosing too much inside information, even today Chancellor Merkel invites Kimmitt for an occasional chat whenever he comes to Berlin, although he has not held a government office for years. Why? Because Kimmitt sought out personal contact with Angela Merkel when he was ambassador and was able to build up a relationship of trust long before anyone even thought about Merkel becoming chancellor. Personal trust matters.

But while trust can be built up only gradually and with effort over years, the opposite is not the case: It is easy to suddenly destroy trust overnight. In this sense, too, the same principles apply to diplomacy as to personal relationships.

I saw how trust could be gambled away from another experience. There was not even any malicious intent involved; neither party was trying to fool the other. There was merely an unfortunate sequence of several misunderstandings.

A few hours after the terror attacks of September 11, 2001, I sent a message to Berlin, feeling it necessary to fulfill my duties as ambassador by assessing the political mood in the United States. My telegram included the sentence, "Doubtlessly, the U.S. will expect complete political and practical solidarity from us and its other close allies."

Those were the words. Later, the telegram was published; anyone can look it up. It did not say, "We recommend that we show complete solidarity." It merely stated that the American government expected such complete solidarity. Two days later, Chancellor Gerhard Schröder stated in a government address: "Ladies and gentlemen, I have expressed the deepest sympathies of the entire German nation to the American president. I also assured him of Germany's unlimited—I emphasize, unlimited—solidarity. I am certain that all of our thoughts are with the victims and their families. Our sympathy goes to them, our heartfelt condolences."[1]

Even at the time, some of us had a queasy feeling that this wording might be going a bit too far. Solidarity without the word "unlimited" might have been enough. But after 9/11, Germany stood firmly alongside the United States. And George W. Bush took the sentence seriously; Washington was impressed.

That statement resulted in misunderstandings and even led to a serious crisis of confidence. The following is how it unfolded.

In the fall of 2001, there were rumors that the Bush administration was not only considering fighting the Taliban in Afghanistan, but also contemplating taking action against Saddam Hussein in Iraq.

In late January 2002, Chancellor Schröder attended the World Economic Forum, which was not held in Davos that year, but at the Waldorf-Astoria in New York, in order to express solidarity with the city devastated by the attacks on the World Trade Center.

The chancellor took this opportunity to make a short side trip to Washington. After a discussion about the situation in the Middle East during dinner with President Bush at the White House, Chancellor Schröder said, "If action has to be taken, then quickly and without hesitation!"

It was a casual comment and certainly not a commitment that Germany would go along with the United States in the case of military action in Iraq. But taken in the context of the "unlimited solidarity" promised in September 2001, and mingled with the Americans' own wishes and expectations, it could be interpreted as an indirect promise by Schröder to stand side by side with the United States in the case of Iraq.

That is how it was—incorrectly—interpreted by the United States. Bush later felt he had been deceived when Schröder withheld his support.

THE CRISIS OF CONFIDENCE BETWEEN GERMANY AND THE UNITED STATES

In May 2002 the American president paid a return visit to Berlin. I was present for a conversation in which the two leaders discussed all kinds of topics. Before they headed to the subsequent press conference, Schröder said, "We may get some questions about the issue of Iraq."

And Bush replied, "Then we will tell the press, truthfully, that we did not talk about that. There is nothing to talk about, anyway.

I have not decided anything, and when I do, I will let you know."

No sooner said than done, the press conference proceeded uneventfully. And Chancellor Schröder believed that he would be informed by the White House whenever a decision on Iraq was in the making. But the notification from Washington never came. We know today that Bush was already working on plans to invade Iraq in the summer of 2002. We were not informed at all.

First, in late summer of 2002, there was a rather aggressive speech by Vice President Dick Cheney against Iraq, which set off all the warning bells in Germany. Then there was a scandal concerning Federal Minister of Justice Herta Däubler-Gmelin, who had supposedly compared Bush with Hitler. As ambassador, I received a special summons to the White House: The president felt he had been personally attacked and would henceforth meticulously track everything coming out of Germany.

As for Schröder, during the German election campaign, he ran on an anti-Iraq-war platform that ultimately ensured his reelection. As a result of all this, the mood between Berlin and Washington continued to deteriorate. In order to rebuild the seriously damaged trust between the two countries, I arranged with National Security Advisor Condoleeza Rice—on the basis of Bush's promise back in May—that I would come by her office every six weeks or so to hear whether there was any news on the issue of Iraq. And I did exactly that from late summer until Christmas 2002. Every time I was told no, there's nothing new! This was the information I then passed on to Berlin.

In January 2003 there were UN Security Council sessions in which it became ever clearer that something was in the offing. But still, we received no official information from the United States; we could only speculate. The French, who were also quick to express their opposition to intervention in Iraq, were even more suspicious than we were. In March 2003, Iraq was invaded. The promise made in May 2002 to notify us beforehand had not been kept. Schröder regarded this, justifiably, as a breach of trust.

Much, much later, I asked my American partners why they had left us in the dark. After all, I reminded them, we were NATO allies, close partners, quite apart from the fact that Bush had promised Schröder to involve him before the decision was made.

The answer was sobering and spoke volumes about the state of relations between Germany and United States at the time: "We deliberately did not initiate you into our plans because we knew that there was close coordination between Berlin and Paris. We assumed that if we were to inform you, the French would find out the very same minute. And if the French found out, Saddam Hussein would know one minute later. That was to be avoided at all costs."

It was shocking to learn that the White House did not trust the German government to handle secret information properly. It was equally shocking that the Americans thought that their NATO partner France was capable of passing such information on to their adversary in Iraq. The United States's decision not to inform its allies Germany and France was a drastic proclamation of distrust.

It was understandable that Schröder had every reason to be angry. The trust between Germany and the United States was in tatters for a long time. Both sides did not trust each other, and each side believed the other capable of just about anything.

This example shows the vast potential for misunderstandings, despite interpreters, minutes of meetings, and expert advisors. Each side believes it understands what the other is saying but takes it the wrong way or places it in a context of which the other is not aware. And that is all it takes to cause a deep crisis of confidence. This is why classic diplomacy and professional diplomats are not superfluous even today. Good foreign policy is, unfortunately, very complicated. Experience and competence help. The essence of diplomacy, the responsibility for war or peace, has probably never been summarized more poetically than by W. H. Auden[2]:

> *As evening fell the day's oppression lifted:*
> *Far peaks came into focus; it had rained:*

Across wide lawns and cultured flowers drifted
The conversation of the highly trained.

Two gardeners watched them pass and priced their shoes:
A chauffeur waited, reading in the drive,
For them to finish their exchange of views;
It seemed a picture of the private life.

Far off, no matter what good they intended,
The armies waited for a verbal error
With all the instruments for causing pain:

And on the issue of their charm depended
A land laid waste, with all its young men slain,
Its women weeping, and its towns in terror.

THREE

AMERICA FIRST

*Superpower, but the World's
Policeman No More*

WHAT WE CAN RELY ON: THE SPEECH AT TRUDERING

"The times when we could completely rely on others are, to an extent, over, and therefore I can only say that we Europeans must really take our fate into our own hands."

This somewhat awkward sentence hit the Western world like a clap of thunder. Federal Chancellor Merkel seemed to have uttered it almost incidentally during a forty-minute speech on a hot Sunday afternoon in a beer tent in Trudering, on the outskirts of Munich in May 2017. But it was certainly no mistake.

Many people in Germany regarded the sentence primarily as a response to President Donald Trump and a reaction to his appearance at the NATO summit in Brussels a few days prior.

But how was this message from the chancellor understood beyond German borders? All of the world's prestigious newspapers, from the *Washington Post* to the *New York Times*, from *The Guardian* and *The Economist* in Great Britain, to *El País* in Spain,

Libération in France, and *La Repubblica* in Italy, appraised Merkel's speech as "historic." Its brutally honest sentences, they reported, stood for a turning point that would change the direction of the transatlantic partnership and open up a new chapter in American-European relations.

The European-American relationship had indeed changed. And this is precisely what Merkel expressed. While the presidency of Donald Trump had dramatically accelerated this process, it had been initiated well before he took office.

The American "older brother" that held his protective hand over little old Europe is a construct from the Cold War era, when the two nuclear powers, the United States and the Soviet Union, kept each other in check through a strategy of mutual deterrence, with the Americans functioning as the patron of the Europeans. This was the basic logic behind NATO as well: In the end, it was not only about the mutual commitment—and the strength that arose from this—that we would help each other if a member of the alliance were to be attacked. Another central aspect was that Europe, and above all Germany, instead of arming itself to the teeth, would now entrust part of its security to the United States in the form of extended nuclear deterrence. Nonetheless, the Europeans did provide for much of their own security and extended the American guarantees by making extensive contributions of their own; the German Bundeswehr, for example, had a reputation as a capable and well-respected army.

This balance changed with the end of the Cold War. Defense expenditures were slashed throughout all of Europe. This was the right thing to do, on the one hand, since the Soviet Union no longer presented a threat. But it also resulted in a situation today in which many European armed forces are less than fully operational.

Year after year, it became ever more difficult for U.S. politicians to justify why the United States continued to spend enormous sums for the defense of its European partners, while the partners were cutting back their own contributions ever further—although, as strong economic powers, they should have had enough financial resources to do more for their own security.

In June 2011, and thus long before Trump, U.S. Secretary of Defense Robert Gates, who was highly respected both at home and abroad, gave a speech in Brussels that attracted lots of attention. He formulated a major concern. Previously he had warned that NATO was threatening to break into two parts: one group of members that would take over the lower-risk peace and development missions, and another that would lead the high-risk combat operations. Moreover, he stated it was not acceptable that the U.S. share of NATO's defense expenditures had grown from 50 percent during the Cold War to 75 percent. Gates warned that if this trend persisted, if the Americans continued to be the only ones investing in a common defense, then U.S. decisionmakers in the future would ask whether America's investment in NATO was still worth the cost. "Ultimately," Gates remarked, "nations must be responsible for their fair share of the common defense."

This was not a threat, but a warning. But even Gates had no idea how soon the United States would elect a president—Donald Trump—who actually calls NATO "obsolete" and openly threatens to fulfill U.S. treaty obligations only if the NATO member countries, as pledged in 2014, pay more for defense in the future, aiming for 2 percent of their gross domestic product. Only a few countries have met this target so far. Germany, currently spending 1.2 percent, has promised to raise this rate to 1.5 percent by 2024. This should be welcomed, but it still falls far short of the 2 percent agreed to at the 2014 NATO summit in Wales. If Germany is not even capable of implementing the Wales resolutions, it is hardly surprising that its smaller NATO partners are in no rush to meet their own targets.

After all, the Bob Gates critique struck a nerve: For decades, the Europeans, including and above all, Germany, have made themselves comfortable under America's protective umbrella. Without the United States there would have been no German reunification, no European Union, and no peace in Europe, including in the Balkans.

The question now is, can and will America continue to act as the patron of the Europeans and the whole world?

U.S. FOREIGN POLICY BETWEEN ISOLATION AND INTERVENTION

The history of American foreign policy is a history of contradictions. On the one hand, U.S. foreign policy is anchored in a deep-seated national pathos that pervades the rhetoric of American politics: American policy has always been imbued by the certainty that the country is called upon to play a unique role in the world.

The idea of American exceptionalism, its destiny to provide for order, peace, and freedom all over the world, and the view that the country was borne out of a special idea, and thus has the mission to propagate this idea—all of this runs deep. For Americans, pride in their nation is linked with their own independence and freedom, with the guarantee of human rights and democracy, and with the spirit of individualism and enterprise. In 1780, Thomas Jefferson dubbed his young country the "Empire of Liberty."

George W. Bush sharpened these ideas in his foreign policy program: "The survival of liberty in our land increasingly depends on the success of liberty in other lands. The best hope for peace in our world is the expansion of freedom in all the world." On occasion, interventions in other countries are necessary to achieve this goal. The decision to send a hundred thousand U.S. soldiers to Iraq, 4,422 of whom never returned, was based on this logic.

At the same time, the history of the United States has repeatedly featured phases of isolationism that alternate with those of interventionism. George Washington, the very first U.S. president, warned against political alliances with other states, as these would bring more problems than anything else. Another example is the

Monroe Doctrine: In 1823, President James Monroe made the principle of nonintervention a central anchor of American foreign policy. The United States should not intervene in European conflicts; vice versa, the Americans would tolerate no interference by Europeans in America.

The key principle of the Monroe Doctrine determined the foreign policy discourse in America over the following decades. Concentrating on America meant that until World War I, practically the only relationships with "Old World" Europe, and also with East Asia and South America, were economic in nature.

In keeping with this principle, when war broke out in 1914, President Woodrow Wilson declared that the United States would remain neutral. When the United States was forced into the war in 1916, cautiously isolationist tendencies still prevailed. And when the League of Nations was founded after the end of the war in 1918, thirty-two of the victorious powers of World War I—all except for the United States—joined. Although the American president received the Nobel Peace Prize in 1919 for the idea of founding the League of Nations, the U.S. Senate rejected membership in the organization.

Isolationism remained the prevailing foreign policy maxim in the United States up until the late 1930s. Even in 1937 the Senate was still passing neutrality acts. These laws forbade the president and his government from providing military support for any forces at war, regardless of whether they were attacking or defending. Franklin D. Roosevelt was ultimately able to intervene in World War II with congressional approval, but only after the Japanese attack on Pearl Harbor in 1941—one of the most traumatic events in American history.

The interplay between the imperatives of reluctance and interference continued to determine policy in the United States.

In his "quarantine" speech of 1937, which caused an international sensation, President Roosevelt attempted to convince Congress to cast off its isolationist stance. World peace was endangered.

Some powers were acting aggressively, disregarding the sovereign territory of other nations, and were violating treaties. No one should imagine that the United States would be spared from these dangers. Therefore, he argued, the peace-loving nations must enter into opposition to these criminal states, isolate them (place them under quarantine), and band together to preserve laws and peace: "When an epidemic of physical disease starts to spread, the community approves and joins in a quarantine of the patients in order to protect the health of the community against the spread of the disease." Withdrawal or neutrality, by contrast, would only fuel international anarchy.

Roosevelt did not name any names, but everyone understood that the aggressor states he was talking about were Germany, Italy, and Japan, and that he wanted to unite his own country with Great Britain and France against these aggressors. It was not until four years later that the United States actually became involved in the war, but Roosevelt had already planted the idea of the interdependence of all states.

World War II was a turning point in the way Americans thought about the world. Nationalism was increasingly replaced by internationalism: the idea that a state is never alone in the complexity of world events and that shared interests can be advanced only in cooperation with others. After the victory over fascism and the end of World War II, the idea gained ground that the United States would have to rebuild and shore up the international order, for its own security. The assumption was that only with a stable world order and strong international institutions would the world avoid falling back into the abyss a third time, after 1914–1918 and 1939–1945.

The order that America built and fostered, and from which West Germany and Western Europe benefited tremendously, admittedly applied only to the Western part of the world at first. What followed was the Cold War—the East-West conflict and the rivalry between capitalism and communism that led to a competition between the United States and the Soviet Union. This war was slugged out globally and concerned all possible areas of life, from sports and culture to science and space travel, all the way to the military—and thus, unfortunately, to an arms race, which nearly led to the ultimate war on several occasions. The two superpowers came closest to war during the Cuban Missile Crisis in 1962, when, for nearly two whole weeks, military escalation seemed imminent.

The U.S. policy toward the Soviet Union was called containment and entailed limiting Soviet power and expansion. This included a systematic policy of alliances that the United States pursued in an attempt to forge coalitions against the Soviet Union. In the foreground was the U.S. alliance with the Europeans and, in Asia, with Japan and South Korea. However, in keeping with the proverb, "The enemy of my enemy is my friend," the Americans did not shy away from cooperation with authoritarian systems of all kinds. For instance, in the 1980s they supported the Islamist Mujahideen in Afghanistan against occupying Soviet troops, which is why the United States today stands accused of having trained and armed the later terror organizations of the Taliban and al Qaida.

After the Cuban Missile Crisis, the United States and the Soviet Union began negotiations on disarmament. As a result, the two great powers mutually agreed to dismantle nuclear missiles.

With the beginning of Ronald Reagan's presidency in 1981, the American tone toward the Soviet Union became noticeably more confrontational. Reagan spoke of the "evil empire" and started an arms race on an unprecedented scale. Yet at the same time, he began to cultivate a personal dialogue with the Soviet President Gorbachev. In his second term, Reagan actually pressed ahead with disarmament talks. By that time the arms race had already contributed to the weakening of the Soviet economy, which then led to the political collapse of the Soviet empire a short time later.

Thus at the beginning of the 1990s, the United States became the last remaining superpower—some even referred to American "hyperpower" and spoke of a "unipolar moment." Against this backdrop, President George H. W. Bush called for "a new world order"—a world in which all nations can stand together for peace and justice. A clear commitment to an outward-looking, interventionist U.S. foreign policy, which he lost no time in putting into practice: When Iraqi troops invaded Kuwait in 1990, the United States intervened. In the Bosnian War in 1995 and in Kosovo in 1999, too, the Clinton administration ultimately intervened to end the conflicts and hurried to the aid of the rather helpless Europeans.

The Europeans, although they no longer required American protection against a Soviet threat, continued to rely on the U.S. military. Europe was in no hurry to bid farewell to this "nursing care" they had carried over from the Cold War era. The Europeans were confident: From now on, the United States would function as the world's policeman in Europe's interest as well as its own. Yet this expectation of the Americans was accompanied by a certain aversion to military interventions in the world. The mixed message sent by this "Old World" to the United States read: Be our world police, but please refrain from using violence!

THE GLOBAL EVENT OF 9/11

"So, time for you to head to Washington and enjoy the next few years!" With these words, Chancellor Schröder had said goodbye in Berlin when I assumed my new posting as German ambassador to the United States in summer 2001. It sounded as if I were going on a vacation.

Jutta and I flew to Washington, D.C., on September 10, 2001. Expectant, I walked over to the embassy, just a few meters from the ambassador's residence, on the early morning of September 11 for my first day of work. My adrenaline levels were high; I was in a cheerful mood, looking forward to this special occasion. I planned to spend the day at my desk, meeting with staff, with a few appointments on my schedule. I was in my new office at 8:00 a.m., intending to learn how to work the telephone and so on, when my assistant charged into the room a short time later and cried, "Turn the TV on!" The second plane had just flown into the World Trade Center.

The very first thing I did was to call Foreign Minister Joschka Fischer in Berlin, but he was already sitting in front of the TV himself. Shortly thereafter we saw clouds of smoke rise over Washington. A plane had just crashed into the Pentagon. My driver took me to see what had happened, as close to the Pentagon as the police allowed.

Everywhere you could sense that the United States had taken a blow to the heart. Americans asked, how can this be happening? We are the good guys! America was petrified. It soon became quite clear that what our delegation was experiencing here was a global event: "After this assault into the very heart of America, the everyday life of Americans and their self-perception of their place in the world will never be the same." This was the core message we sent from the embassy to Berlin on that very day.

It was a dramatic day that left its mark on the nearly six years I subsequently spent in the United States. From this time on, the embassy was in permanent crisis mode.

The shock for Americans was as great as after the Japanese attack on Pearl Harbor in 1941. There had been terror attacks on American facilities on several occasions in the past, of course, such as the bombing of the U.S. embassy in Nairobi, Kenya, in August 1998 and the bomb attack on a U.S. warship in the port of Aden, Yemen, in October 2000. But this was the first major attack on American soil.

In a historic session, NATO declared that the attacks on the World Trade Center and the Pentagon would trigger its mutual defense clause. The ministers of defense of all NATO states had come to Brussels for the extraordinary meeting—all, that is, except for U.S. Secretary of Defense Donald Rumsfeld, who sent his deputy, Paul Wolfowitz. From this point on, it was clear how the Americans would proceed in the face of this existential challenge: "We have been attacked. We'll take care of it ourselves!"

Today the unprecedented solidarity between Germans and Americans in the early days following the attacks has been all but forgotten. As mentioned earlier, Germans donated over US$70 million for victims of the attacks. However, the pleasant relations soon came to an end. The rift in German-American relations started in summer 2002. In late August, U.S. Vice President Dick Cheney issued the bleak warning that Iraq possessed weapons of mass destruction. This was his justification for military intervention—which then came in 2003, causing the serious turmoil between Chancellor Schröder and President Bush discussed in the previous chapter.

DAMAGE CONTROL

Germany's refusal to participate in the Iraq War ushered in the most difficult phase of my diplomatic career. I focused on damage control, soliciting compassion and understanding. Even if Germany was not sending soldiers to Iraq, I insisted, we were still good friends. I did not hole up in my office, but wrote op-eds for U.S. newspapers, gave interviews, went on talk shows, and held lectures at universities.

At the height of the conflict between Bush and Schröder—when emotions were running high, and America's conservative elite was raging—I received an invitation to appear on Bill O'Reilly's talk show on Fox News. O'Reilly was one of the best paid and most notorious moderators in the country. He was an ultraconservative TV professional, loved to provoke his guests, and liked to get loud and angry. He was even known to have a guest's microphone switched off when he did not like what he or she was saying. O'Reilly had already achieved dubious fame as a radio moderator, but his talk show "The O'Reilly Factor" was the flagship of Fox News at the time and one of the highest rated shows on any U.S. cable news channel.

In short, an appearance on his show required a lot of courage—

and my staff advised strongly against it. But I wanted to proactively defend Germany's position against the Iraq War, so I entered into this debate on Fox News. O'Reilly jumped right in for the attack, saying something to the effect of "We saved your asses after World War II. We rebuilt your country. With my money, my father's money, my grandfather's money. In the Cold War we protected you from the Russians. And now, when we want to fight against somebody who is a danger for entire world, you stand there and say no. Just what kind of ingrates are you?"

I tried to keep my cool: "Bill, I am really glad that you are not the president, because what you are saying there is just plain irresponsible!" And then I continued by explaining that, from the German perspective, there was no political and legal basis for a war against Saddam Hussein.

I knew that O'Reilly was merely stating what many Americans were thinking anyway, so I had nothing to lose. Afterwards, I received a lot of praise for my appearance, but it could have gone horribly wrong.

Although today we are certainly used to seeing an ambassador on TV every now and then, a press appearance of this kind was an uncommon sight at the time. During this period, I encouraged the press department of the embassy to commit to marketing American-style. First we launched a professional website. More than one million visitors were registered in the first year. We distributed free copies of the *Atlantic Times* newspaper, which my friend Detlef Prinz had founded, to journalists, politicians, students, and interested citizens. We invited managers and prominent journalists to submit articles on bilateral relations to this publication. We handed out T-shirts, refrigerator magnets, and coffee mugs. Printed on the mugs was the slogan "Germany Info: Caution, very hot!"

What motivated us most in our marketing campaign was to ensure that, whatever our differences, people on both sides of the Atlantic continued to keep the lines of communication open, so that trust would not erode further.

We practiced "public diplomacy," seeking out the media whenever the political doors in Washington were closed to us. Public relations is one of the most important tasks of diplomacy in the modern world. This is the complete opposite of Bismarckian secret diplomacy. After all, there is little need today for secret dispatches. Whenever our leaders feel the need, they can speak with each other directly on the telephone or arrange a meeting—as indeed they do.

My role as ambassador was not so much to serve as Schröder's or Merkel's ear in Washington, but more to be a lobbyist for German interests—above all, for the German interest in a resilient transatlantic relationship. I was assisted in these lobbying efforts by many—of course, by the embassy, our consulates, and the Goethe Institutes, and also by college professors, teachers on exchange programs, and, last but by no means least, the many German companies that had created hundreds of thousands of jobs in the United States.

BUILDING RELATIONSHIPS WITH A
DOG BOWL AND A COCKTAIL BAR

Around this time, we opened the "Berlin Bar" in the basement of the German ambassador's residence in Washington. It was a huge success. The grand opening party in spring 2004 was attended by Harald Schmidt, Germany's famous late-night TV host (who comes from the same town on the Neckar River as I do, so we had our own "Nürtingen summit" in Washington). Thanks to Harald's impromptu raffle moderation, we were able to dispel once and for all any fears that our hundred or so party guests may have harbored about German humor.

Opening the bar was also an attempt to give the cool, imposing architecture of the ambassador's residence a cozier touch. The building, designed by the famous architect Oswald Mathias Ungers of Cologne, Germany, and completed in 1994, did not correspond at all to American notions about German *gemütlichkeit*—such as an old brick house with columns and old trees, appointed with mahogany furniture in the colonial style. My wife and I were quite happy with the sleek, modern decor of the residence, but I saw that I would have to do something to counter the stark character of the building.

The bluntest advice came from my friend Richard Holbrooke, the legendary U.S. crisis diplomat: "The first thing you have to do is tear the building down!" Another American friend had a better recommendation: "This cold, imposing house needs life. Your average American with a large living room and an open fireplace always has a dog or two. Go get a dog!"

That is how Rocky, an Australian shepherd, came to live in the German embassy. The dog really did make a huge difference: When Colin Powell or Henry Kissinger stood on the patio and the dog showed up, the mood changed immediately. Rocky was petted, had to shake hands, and got dog treats. He was a wonderful bridge to an atmosphere in which everyone could take off their jackets and ties.

A second question was, where do we go after an official dinner at the embassy? German hospitality would not be complete without offering guests a nightcap after dinner: a glass of wine, a beer, or a schnapps. Jutta discovered the unused room in the basement and transformed it—in allusion to the Paris Bar in Berlin—into the Berlin Bar. Since it picked up on Ungers's architectural language, it was not "gemütlich" in the traditional sense; rather, it was cool and functional, with rooms in dark red, armchairs in black and white, black-and-white photographs of postwar Berlin on the walls, sofas from New York, and tables from California. The bartender served traditional beer on tap but also a specially created house drink called the Berlin Bar Fizz: ice cold orange juice mixed with cranberry juice and a shot of sparkling wine. The Berlin Bar was a hit and is probably the snazziest bar on Washington's Embassy Row today.

Here, but also on my trips throughout the country, I learned that the core of the German-American relationship is built on three deep foundations: The first is that generations of Americans spent some period of their lives in Germany, many as soldiers and others as students or businesspeople. The second foundation is the shared memory of the Cold War, the community of destiny in the face of Soviet nuclear weapons, and the success of European unification and German reunification. The third foundation is the economic relations between the two countries. No matter how bleak our interactions have looked at times, German investment in the United States and American investment in Germany have steadily continued to grow, to the tune of billions of dollars. Political tensions have not slowed it, even though some Americans did call the embassy during the Iraq crisis to tell me personally that they were so enraged about Germany's "no" to the Iraq War that they had just canceled their order for a new BMW. But such cases were few and far between. Nothing contributes so much strength and stability to bilateral relations as economic ties. For that reason, too, the punitive tariffs imposed on European goods by President Trump in June 2018 are worrying.

THE WELCOME ADVERSARY: "THE AXIS OF EVIL"

Until 2001 the United States had been a world power that faced no immediate danger to its national security. That changed on 9/11. In order to avert danger, the White House now demanded the largest possible freedom of action, both domestically and externally. There may not have been any clear aggressor state responsible for the attacks, but in its stead, Bush blamed the "axis of evil," the so-called rogue states of Iran, Iraq, and North Korea. As "state sponsors of terrorism," according to Bush they bore at least part of the responsibility. The instruments of the Cold War, deterrence and containment, were now replaced by a "preemptive security policy," which included preventative military missions to defend against even *future* security threats. This policy led directly to the Iraq War.

Foreign policy under George W. Bush was marked by the "global war on terror," which served to legitimize a permanent state of emergency. In the memory of the global public, this state of emergency is intimately linked with the repulsive images of torture in an American military prison in the Iraqi city of Abu-Ghraib, such as the photograph of a female soldier holding a naked, crouching man on a dog leash and the picture of a prisoner hooked up to wires, standing on a crate with a bag over his head.

Suddenly the United States, a historical pioneer in the fight for human rights, had to defend its own interrogation techniques that applied electric shocks, waterboarding, and hanging upside down—and did so unabashedly. The reasoning went something like this: "We are living in new circumstances. September 11 changed the rules of the game, and that is why we have to reconsider the complete ban on torture."[1]

During this period, the United States forfeited a great deal of trust worldwide.

President George W. Bush left behind a triple crisis. First, there was now a crisis of trust in the adherence to values and the reliability of the world's leading power. Second, there was a security policy crisis, which included the ongoing military conflicts in Afghanistan and Iraq as well as the charged relationship between NATO and Russia, the effective standstill in arms control and the peace process in the Middle East, and the neglected issue of climate protection. And on top of all this, there was a breaking crisis in global financial markets, which started in the United States and then intensified into a sovereign debt crisis and the euro crisis in Europe. The impacts of all three of these crises are still felt today.

OBAMA: A NEW BEGINNING

In 2008 there was a hopeful new beginning with the election of Barack Obama. As he had promised during his campaign, on June 4, 2009, the recently inaugurated U.S. president addressed the Islamic world in a keynote speech entitled "A New Beginning," which was presented at Al-Azhar University in Cairo. The location was chosen deliberately: In the words of then White House spokesman Robert Gibbs, Egypt was a country "that in many ways represents the heart of the Arab world," and Al-Azhar University, as Obama put it, "stood as a beacon of Islamic learning." In the speech, Obama called for mutual respect and for peace between Palestinians and Israelis, for religious diversity, and for equal rights for men and women. He advocated for a two-state solution to resolve the conflict in the Middle East, promised to return complete sovereignty to Iraq, and reinforced his aspiration to eliminate nuclear weapons.

It was undoubtedly a historic speech that met with positive resonance globally, although some in the Islamic world did express their skepticism, wanting to see deeds before applauding his words. Obama had anticipated this mistrust in his speech:

> [N]o single speech can eradicate years of mistrust, nor can I answer in the time that I have this afternoon all the complex questions that brought us to this point. But I am convinced that in order to move forward, we must say openly to each other the things we hold in our hearts and that too often are said only behind closed doors. There must be a sustained effort to listen to each other; to learn from each other; to respect one another; and to seek common ground.[2]

He closed his speech with words that were both religious and conciliatory: "The people of the world can live together in peace. We know that is God's vision. Now, that must be our work here on Earth."

A few months later, Barack Obama received the Nobel Peace Prize. This speech—and thus America's new rhetoric—was certainly an essential factor, even though the Nobel Committee in Oslo took a lot of flak over it. After all, previous politicians who had received the Nobel Prize were awarded it not for words, but for deeds, such as Willy Brandt for his *Ostpolitik*, Mikhail Gorbachev for his contributions to the end of the Cold War, and Shimon Peres for his peace policies in the Middle East.

Of course one can honor someone for their life's work. That is great for the honoree but does not serve any further political purpose. Such a prize can also inspire, stimulate, support, and spur on a peace process. It can also make a contribution to moving things in the right direction. That is what was attempted by giving the prize to President Obama.

The plans that the new American president initiated at the beginning of his term were many: nuclear disarmament, peace in the Middle East, a new relationship with Russia, an attempt to open a new chapter in the especially fraught relations with Iran, a new way of dealing with the Muslim world—all of these were (and still are) important political initiatives, which were welcomed enthusiastically around the world.

What makes this so special? If an American president had proclaimed such policies twenty or thirty years ago, the rest of us would not have been able to do much more than watch or perhaps help out a little. But as the Norwegian Nobel Committee quoted Obama in the last sentence of its justification for awarding him the prize, the prize was supposed to inspire "all of us to take our share of responsibility" that the goals defined by Obama can be achieved. If this award ceremony was an appeal to others to make a contribution, then it also expressed the realization that the solitary reign of a single world power is over. The United States can no longer handle all of the world's problems, certainly not alone.

OBAMA'S HERITAGE

The obstacles Obama had to overcome in order to realize his initiatives did not only concern foreign policy; many of them had to do with domestic issues. Enormous challenges awaited him in the area of U.S. economic and financial policy, including many fundamental debates about the state's role in the economy—on issues of energy and climate policy, but also regarding the health care system in the United States. And Obama struggled with a tremendous and ever-expanding polarization of society and politics in the United States, peaking in the "birther movement" fueled by many of his opponents on the right, which claimed that Obama had not been born inside the United States and was therefore not eligible to be president.

More support from Europe would have bolstered him and his political project. It was no coincidence that Obama had solicited European support even during his campaign, by speaking at the Victory Column in Berlin. Throughout his entire presidency, time and again he cultivated contacts with European leaders, especially with the most powerful one from the American perspective: Angela Merkel.

Unfortunately, Europe's partnership skills left much to be desired. Until the Treaty of Lisbon took effect in 2009, instituting far-reaching reforms of the European Union, the EU was too busy with its own affairs. Right after that, the effects of the European financial crisis kept the EU on edge, not exactly strengthening the transatlantic relationship.

Obama could not become the bringer of global peace everyone was hoping for, because he first had to clean up at home and lead a war-weary nation out of a serious economic crisis. Nation building at home in the United States was his goal, Obama said, not nation building in faraway lands.

Seven years after the beginning of the war, Washington was glad to finally be leaving Iraq and reluctant to send soldiers into new conflicts. Nowhere can the consequences of this reluctance be seen more clearly than in the Syrian civil war and its effects: hundreds of thousands dead, millions displaced, and a chaos in the heart of the Middle East that is still emanating in all directions.

In 2013, Obama drew a line in the sand, threatening consequences if Syrian President Bashar Hafiz al-Assad deployed chemical weapons. But when this actually occurred, Obama shrunk back from the threat to punish Assad militarily. The failure to follow through seriously damaged the credibility of the United States: A red line should be proclaimed only when it is 100 percent clear that the threat will be carried out when the line is crossed.

The withdrawal of the United States from its global leadership role was also facilitated by the reduction of its economic dependency on the Arab countries. The new technology of fracking suddenly allowed the United States to press a previously unattainable quantity of oil reserves out of the earth. As a result, the U.S. government saw less of a need to give highest priority to stability and security in the Persian Gulf.

America's reduced willingness to perform the role of global leader was apparent not only in the way it dealt with various crises, but also with an important new issue, the "global commons"— the climate, the environment, water, energy resources, the internet, space, and so on. Increasingly, the question was, who would take care of the common goods? Who ensures that these resources will be used in a controlled, sustainable way? Although the United States admitted that the West had a particular responsibility to deal with such issues, Americans were ever less willing to bear it alone.

Yet Obama also bequeathed to us some important foreign policy successes—above all, the nuclear deal with Iran, which was negotiated by the United States, Russia, China, Great Britain, France, and Germany along with the EU, and which has been hanging in the balance since the United States unilaterally revoked it in May 2018. The treaty is certainly not perfect, and it excludes deplorable aspects of Iranian foreign policy. But it did fence in Iran's nuclear ambitions and thus, probably prevented a war. The bitter realization of all diplomatic efforts is that what is achieved is often not what was desired, but what is desired often cannot be achieved. Diplomacy is the art of the possible.

Nevertheless, America's indecision under Obama—above all with regard to Assad and permissiveness toward the reinvigorated regional power Iran—and Obama's abandoning of Hosni Mubarak, the Egyptian president, in the course of the Arab Spring were assessed in the Arab world as signs of the United States's increasing unreliability. Trump garners so much support and applause in large parts of the Arab world in part because he distanced himself from this policy of reluctance, at least rhetorically—for instance, during his jubilant visit to Saudi Arabia in 2017. Whether it will be possible to achieve enduring peace and stability in the face of such explicit partisanship against Iran remains to be seen, however. To me it seems that the American withdrawal from the Iran treaty increases the danger of war in the Middle East rather than contains it. More on this later.

Obama did not start any new wars in the Middle East, aside from the intervention in Libya, but he did allow others to start wars—and this had harmful consequences. What's more, the status and reputation of America as a guarantor for the stability of the region sustained serious damage.

The relative retreat of the United States, or even the mere perception of a retreat, caused great uncertainty in the Middle Eastern region. What Merkel expressed in her speech in Trudering—"The times when we could completely rely on others are, to an extent, over"—is a feeling that was already widespread in the Arab world under Obama.

For Europe, too, the feeling that Merkel expressed has been around longer than the Trump administration. Just look at the Ukraine conflict: The United States has not been entirely absent from the attempts to find a solution over the last five years. However, the central diplomatic format in which the Minsk Agreement was negotiated, and in which its implementation is now being discussed, is the "Normandy Four": France, Germany, Russia, and Ukraine. For the United States not to be included would have been impossible to even imagine for the diplomatic negotiations that ended the Balkans war in the 1990s: Back then, the United States called the shots.

What the United States is doing today is "leading from behind." That is what an Obama advisor once called it in the context of the intervention in Libya. What he meant was that America's involvement in European and Middle Eastern security issues would continue, but under Obama, the United States would no longer insist on leading by standing on the front lines. Now the debate about the role of the United States has taken on a whole new dimension, as Trump is hinting at even more radical withdrawal options or—as happened at the NATO summit in July 2018—even implicitly threatening to leave NATO in order to force his treaty partners to increase their defense spending.

TRUMP AS THE PRESIDENT OF UNCERTAINTY

So, even during Obama's administration, America no longer wished to bear the burden of geopolitical leadership alone. And then came Trump.

The United States is still a growing nation, with a current population of 328 million (the third largest country in the world at this time, after China and India) and the strongest military power by far. It will take a long time for this to fundamentally change.

In fact, the military dominance of the United States could even increase, as President Trump is continuing to raise the defense budget. The United States also benefits from the preeminent technological productivity of Silicon Valley. Wall Street is still the center of the international world of finance. Aside from tanks and soldiers, American companies, including those in Hollywood, provide for impressive global "soft power."

But if America intends to reduce its role as a global protector and anchor, a fundamental challenge emerges: Who will take on these responsibilities? Who will provide for order in the world if the United States does not want to anymore? And the key question for transatlantic relations becomes, how should Germany, how should Europe, deal with an America led by Trump?

It has recently become especially difficult even to find out the

U.S. position on important issues. Trump and his team often send conflicting signals.

For example, in his opening speech during his trip to Saudi Arabia, Trump struck a conciliatory tone and called Islam "one of the world's great faiths." Right beforehand he had proposed banning Muslims from entering the United States, claiming that "Islam hates us." So, which is it?

Before or after his election, Trump said nothing critical about Putin. In 2018 his administration drastically tightened sanctions against Russia, but in June 2018, Trump proposed inviting Putin back into the G8 and agreed to hold a first bilateral summit with him in mid-July 2018.

So, which Russia policy does the United States intend to pursue?

The new national security strategy of the United States, which was published in December 2017, regards China and Russia as autocratic adversaries of the United States and emphasizes the importance of values for U.S. foreign policy. Trump, conversely, has repeatedly shown sympathy for dictators and talked down human rights or ignored them completely. Yet he has been unsparing in his critique of U.S. allies. So, are values important or not?

One could argue that while some statements are completely contradictory, they are all just rhetoric. Unfortunately though, in foreign and security policy it is extremely important who formulates certain statements and how they are understood. Especially in crisis diplomacy—for instance, between the United States and North Korea—clear communication is crucial. Currently, it is never clear: Is a threat Trump tweets serious, or is he just letting off steam?

Trump's lack of appreciation for his allies and his diplomacy based on uncertainty make the world more dangerous because trust is lost and crises can escalate more quickly and intensively. In addition, by publicly attacking the European NATO members—first and foremost Germany—from the very first minute of the NATO summit in Brussels in July 2018, he damaged this important alliance. His actions challenged the elementary foundation of NATO: its internal cohesion. "America First" is his policy. In principle there is, of course, nothing wrong with that. But Trump implements this policy as if it were supposed to read not "America First" but "America Alone"—and as a consequence, Europe alone. Yet it is written in the stars whether Trump's commitment to NATO, which he ultimately did bring himself to acknowledge at a press conference on July 12, 2018, will last. We Europeans will have to get used to the idea, at least during the Trump era, that the White House may no longer be interested in true alliance partners, but simply divides the world into friend and foe.

Since 1945, U.S. presidents have had very different ideologies and emphasized various policies. But all were convinced that the liberal international system that emerged after World War II, and spread even further after the collapse of the Soviet Union, was good for the United States, good for its partners, and good for the world: a system of multilateralism and cooperation, open societies and open markets, and close ties among the Western democracies. Trump's vision is fundamentally different. No major initiatives to strengthen or stabilize the international system can be expected from him. On the contrary, his focus is on power politics and national interests. From his perspective, America should not bind itself to institutions or standards, and should pursue a protectionist economic policy.

Recently the United States resigned from the United Nations Educational, Scientific and Cultural Organization (UNESCO) and turned its back on the Paris climate agreement and the Trans-Pacific Partnership (TPP), a major trade deal between Asian and Pacific states. In May 2018, Trump then also revoked the Iran nuclear deal.

This triggered a further threefold crisis:

- a resurgent crisis surrounding Iran's nuclear potential and Iranian foreign policy

- intensification of conflict in the region—already a powder keg—among Syria, Israel, Saudi Arabia, Turkey, Russia, and other warring factions

■ a serious straining of transatlantic relations—raising the question, is there still a meaningful transatlantic partnership at all?

With the retreat of the United States, the survival of the nuclear deal is highly uncertain. The three European partners, Great Britain, France, and Germany, have affirmed their intension to adhere to the agreement and to engage in a dialogue with Iran, but their chances of success are rather slim. Trump's decision is not only disastrous for the stability of the Middle East, raising the danger of a regional arms race, but also a serious blow to the transatlantic relationship. Since then, the question of whether, and to what extent, this may put an end to the transatlantic partnership has been the subject of intense debate. This is sad enough in and of itself. Angela Merkel made it very clear: The revocation violates trust in the international order.

Richard Haass, who worked for many years in the upper echelons of the U.S. State Department, got to the heart of the current developments in American policy, calling it "the great abdication" of the United States, or the voluntary relinquishing of responsibility. Or as my friend Strobe Talbott, the former deputy secretary of state, tweeted, "Britain is only exiting Europe. America is exiting the world." How bitter that sounds. But the scandal Trump provoked at the G7 summit in 2018 by revoking his approval for the closing communique when still on his way home from the meeting appears to confirm Talbott's assessment. So does the lack of U.S. leadership in the global response to the coronavirus pandemic that the world witnessed in the spring of 2020.

AMERICA: THERE IS NO ALTERNATIVE

In Germany many feel that Europe has to recognize which way the wind is blowing and finally stop clinging to the apron strings of the United States, and that what we are experiencing with Trump makes clearer than ever the necessity for Europe to become more capable of acting for itself.

And I agree: In the long run it is not politically sustainable for 500 million prosperous Europeans to outsource a significant portion of their security to a partner on the other side of the Atlantic Ocean. For this reason, we must be more vigorous about taking matters of security into our own hands, just as Chancellor Merkel said in her speech in Trudering. Europe has to become more operational, speak with one voice, and continue developing into a defense union.

Now comes the big "but": Cutting the apron strings is different from strengthening the ability to act. Independence is not an option. Anyone who wants to simply write off the United States as a partner is mistaken in three ways.

First, the Europeans cannot do without the American nuclear security guarantee in the short and middle term. We have a key interest in convincing Washington of the importance of a unified and peaceful Europe—and of the United States's contribution to this. The uncertainty triggered by speculation about decoupling European security from that of the United States can be recognized in the budding yet still vague debate about a European—or even a German—nuclear weapon. We need America, as a partner and as a security guarantor.

Second, it is not as if there were partners all over the world standing in line to defend the liberal world order at Europe's side. The EU and China may agree that a new era of protectionism would be harmful and that climate protection is important, but what we have in common beyond that is fairly limited. The liberal world order will endure in the long run only if it is supported by both pillars of the transatlantic partnership.

Third, we should not ignore the many millions of Americans who did *not* elect Donald Trump. The activism in civil society in the United States and the reactions of the American judicial system show that the America we know and love is alive. Instead of turning away from the entire country, we should work with all of those who are interested in preserving the transatlantic community of values. Among these are many congressional representatives, as well as many governors, CEOs, and civil society actors. Governors of some large states, such as California, share Germany's climate and energy targets, and have clearly communicated this. And even ultraconservative representatives from the American South, where Volkswagen, BMW, and Mercedes operate factories, highly value German investment in their districts. We can and must lobby for German and European interests at all levels, including in the present conflict about steel and aluminum tariffs. "Washington against Berlin and Brussels" is too shortsighted a strategy.

Europe has to become more independent, but it cannot do so without its alliance with the United States. So, what do we do? Engage, engage, engage! There is no alternative to engaging the new American government as strongly as possible—although it must be done without glossing over the unsettling developments. Even if many Europeans do not like the idea, this is precisely the realpolitik we need now.[3]

By continuing to engage, we can do our best to shape the next months, possibly years, while simultaneously laying a foundation for the time thereafter—helping us find common ground, actively advocate for our interests, and deal with conflicts. For instance, we will not find much common ground in trade or refugee policy, so in these spheres we should tread carefully and deal with each other without any unrealistic expectations. But in other fields, such as diplomacy in Ukraine or with North Korea, we may find renewed vigor to develop new policy approaches together.

Let us also remember that America has always found its way back from every wrong turn it has taken so far. And it remains—with all of its mistakes and weaknesses—the only Western world power. This is why it is in our own deepest interest to reject the proponents of "cutting the apron strings." We must not allow the idea of the West to be thwarted, for we know that there is no feasible middle road between the West and the East. That is the lesson of the twentieth century, especially for us Germans.

FOUR

RUSSIA

*From a Common European
Home to a New Cold War?*

RUSSIA, THE PSEUDO-GIANT:
SUCCESSFUL BY ITS OWN STANDARDS

When the topic is world order and world powers—even nearly thirty years after the end of the Cold War—many people still think of not only the United States, but also Russia. Indeed, the Russian Federation is the largest country in the world by area, has a population of 140 million—or around a third the population of Europe—and is one of five officially recognized nuclear powers. But a modern great power needs not only territory and military might, but also economic and political innovativeness—so, not just "hard power," but also "soft power" and "smart power."

In this regard, Russia is more of a "pseudo-giant," with a gross national product smaller than that of Italy, a limping economy, and a problematic health care system. Aside from military might and energy reserves, Russia has relatively little to offer.

"Good foreign policy consists in building trust, winning new friends and alliances, and reducing old enmities and distrust," was my regular sermon at the foreign office. If foreign policy is defined this way, then a country needs to ask itself some important questions: How many new partners have we won? With how many enemies have we reconciled? How much trust have we been able to build? How do things look overall with our own "soft power"?

Russia cannot provide encouraging answers to these questions. And its prospects for doing so look even worse in the future. Moscow's relations with the former Soviet republics Belarus, Kazakhstan, Turkmenistan, Uzbekistan, Armenia, Azerbaijan, and Kyrgyzstan are based primarily on economic or military dependency. In the Baltic states, in Poland, and all over Eastern Europe, people are afraid of Russia, and some in Moscow even find this desirable. Russia's disputes with Georgia and Ukraine have developed into sustained armed conflicts with no reconciliation in sight. In short, Russia has hardly any new friends, and relationships of growing suspicion and even hostility with neighbors.

At the same time, we have to recognize that Russia's definition of successful foreign policy is different from that of Germany and the rest of Europe. For Moscow, friends and allies do not count for much. Instead, its foreign policy is about power, about resurrecting Russia's great history, and about defying the West. I am convinced that this will not prove successful in the long run. But apparently it is good enough for Russia's short-term ambitions. And at the moment, as measured by its opportunities, Russia is in a pretty good position: In Ukraine and in Syria, Russia has achieved its goals, at least in the short term. And Russian intelligence and cyber activities—influencing the election in the United States, a nerve gas attack in Great Britain, hacker attacks in Germany—are unsettling the United States and democracies in Europe.

Russia's relations with the West, the United States, and the European Union have deteriorated, especially through the annexation of Crimea and the war in Ukraine. Since 2014 the EU has imposed economic sanctions against the Russian Federation. Moscow, in turn, banned imports of Western agricultural products and foods. Since then, Moscow has been turning to China, which signed a supply contract for Russian natural gas—though more as a symbolic surrogate deal than an economically profitable business. In the long game Moscow will be, at best, a junior partner of Beijing—and will run the danger of having little to offer in resistance to long-term Chinese ambitions.

On top of this, serious tensions between NATO and Russia have settled into prolonged conflict rather than cooperation. Although Russia had been admitted to the G8 summit of the eight most powerful countries in May 1998, Russia was ejected from the club in March 2014 in response to its annexation of Crimea. In 2018 we are further than ever from readmitting Russia, even though Trump demanded precisely this at the G7 summit in La Malbaie, Quebec, and more recently, when discussing the 2020 G7 meeting in the United States.

THE "COMMON EUROPEAN HOME": NO ROOM FOR RUSSIA

Russia and Germany have had a special relationship for centuries, which peaked for the first time in the days of Catherine the Great, and were traditionally allies up until the end of the nineteenth century. After the hostilities of the twentieth century—two world wars, millions dead, the Cold War, and the tensions in divided Germany—reconciliation in the course of reunification now dominates the thinking of most Germans and of many Russians as well.

The strained relationship changed abruptly with the fall of the Berlin Wall. Back then the Germans sported T-shirts with a portrait of Mikhail "Gorbi" Gorbachev; his famous remark of 1989, "He who comes too late is punished by life" ("Wer zu spät kommt, den bestraft das Leben"), has entered the canon of German proverbs. And when Gorbachev declared, "Europe is our common home," we thought that was a great idea. Germany was grateful, and Russia would benefit from Germany's support. As a result there are extensive German investments in Russia today, and around 12,000 young Russians are now studying at German universities.

Nevertheless, there is also mutual skepticism. Many Germans distrust Russia and fear too much dependence on Putin's energy empire. And the Common European Home has remained largely fictional. The American historian Mary Elise Sarotte picked up on this metaphor years later, stating, "A large European home was built with countless rooms, but none of them had Russia's name on the door."

On November 9, 2019, thirty years after the Berlin Wall came down, I summarized what had happened as follows in Politico:

> When the dividing line that had separated Germany and Europe for several decades vanished, the process of reunification that ensued was astonishingly peaceful. For many, this amounted to a miracle. Yet, as soon as October 3, 1990, during the Berlin unification celebrations, German Federal President Richard von Weizsäcker drew attention to a large project that was still awaiting completion—the pan-European one. Weizsäcker warned of the risk that the dividing line Europe had just overcome would simply move east: "The Western border of the Soviet Union must not become the Eastern border of Europe."
>
> Thirty years later, we have to admit: We were not able to prevent a new division. On a European level, we were unable to mirror what came true in Germany—unity. The objective of "a Europe whole, free and at peace" as formulated by U.S. Presidents George H. W. Bush and Bill Clinton has still not come to fruition.
>
> Sure, a lot was achieved since 1989: The EU and NATO integrated many Eastern European states, thereby contributing to their efforts to consolidate peace and democracy, and promote prosperity. Germany, suddenly surrounded only by friends, benefited disproportionately. Yet this did not give rise to a pan-European security architecture, a durable order of peace in Europe. Russia and other Eastern European states have not found their place in this order.

Quite the contrary: With Moscow's annexation of Crimea and its intervention in Eastern Ukraine, the prospects dimmed even further. A relationship based on trust was replaced by Western sanctions and Russian military aggression.[1]

Where did it go wrong?

FROM THE COLLAPSE OF THE SOVIET UNION TO PUTIN'S MUNICH SPEECH

When Gorbachev stepped down as president of the Soviet Union on December 25, 1991, and Boris Yeltsin, on the very same day, hoisted the white-blue-red flag of the Russian Federation over the Kremlin, it was a day of relief for the Western world. For the Russians, though, especially in retrospect, it was to become a day of defeat. The Soviet Union, the last empire of the twentieth century, had collapsed, and along with it, a huge piece of Russia's national pride. It was a consolation that the Russian Federation was the legal successor of the Soviet Union (and thus, of its seat on the UN Security Council), but reality soon showed that a rocky and winding path lay ahead. With the dissolution of the Soviet Union, the relationship to the now independent successor republics had to be restructured; at the same time, strategically important facilities had disappeared from its national territory, including the naval base of the legendary Black Sea Fleet in Crimea. The successor organization, the Commonwealth of Independent States (CIS), was initially joined by twelve of the fifteen former Soviet republics but soon became increasingly irrelevant.

By the time Vladimir Putin became Russian prime minister in 1999, frustration about Russia's loss of its previous importance in the world was prevalent throughout the population. Putin called the collapse of the Soviet Union the "greatest geopolitical catastrophe of the twentieth century." His nation suffered from this trauma. In Russia, Gorbachev, a revered figure in the West, is considered the involuntary initiator of this downfall.

And after years of growth, the Russian economy is now stagnating, and due to Western sanctions and a lack of innovation, this will not change in the foreseeable future. That former "brother countries" like Poland, the Czech Republic, Slovakia, the Baltics, and other Eastern European states are now EU members does not make things better from the Russian perspective. On the contrary, this—and even more so, the expansion of NATO to members of the former Warsaw Pact—is understood by Moscow as an intrusion into its sphere of interest and thus, as an aggressive act. Ironically, hardly anyone in the West was interested in the eastward expansion of NATO at first—the impulse came from the states in Central and Eastern Europe.

In the West and in these states, the expansion of NATO and the EU to the East was regarded as a manifestation of European states' flight to freedom, following the precedent set by the citizens of the GDR who "voted with their feet" back in 1989. After 45 years under Soviet occupation, these countries strove for security and prosperity in Western institutions—voluntarily and in sovereign self-determination.

This is indeed what had been agreed upon in the Charter of Paris when, on November 21, 1990, the closing document of the special CSCE summit was signed by thirty-two European countries including Russia/the Soviet Union, as well as the United States and Canada. This was a day that symbolized the end of Cold War confrontation and the division of Europe: "The courage of men and women, the strength of the will of the peoples and the power of the ideas of the Helsinki Final Act [of 1975, discussed in chapter 4] have opened a new era of democracy, peace and unity in Europe."

This is where Russia itself, still the Soviet Union at the time, committed to the idea that all states are equally free and can choose their alliances themselves—which is exactly what these states have been doing ever since.

I myself experienced a Putin who, in the years after 1999, strove to link Russia more closely to Europe. In 2001, Putin gave a speech before the German parliament, in which he recalled the fall of the Berlin Wall as a time in which "the ideas of freedom" replaced "Stalinist totalitarian ideology." This Putin—what I call Putin no. 1—spoke first in Russian and then ended his speech in German, appealing to Europe for cooperation and partnership with Russia: "Russia is a friendly European country." It was a pleasure to work with this Putin.

At the time I was a member of the German-Russian Strategic Working Group, the German side of which was headed up by Klaus Mangold, the chairman of the German Committee on Eastern European Economic Relations at that time. At the end of working group meetings, there were also sessions with Putin and Schröder. These meetings took place in a constructive spirit and yielded good results, in part due to Putin's personal commitment to move things forward.

And then came the break. Beginning in 2007 we were dealing with a completely different Putin, a Putin no. 2 if you will, who seemed to think, "I have had enough! You promised me a fair deal, but it has been reneged upon. Since Russia's interests are being violated, I have to advance my interests with other means." At the Munich Security Conference, Putin gave the participants a piece of his mind: He accused the United States of striving for "unipolar world supremacy," claiming that it had "overstepped its national borders in every way." He warned NATO of "an almost uncontained hyper use of military force." The North Atlantic alliance and the European Union were imposing their will on other countries and relying on force, according to Putin. Russia's president criticized the eastern expansion of NATO harshly, because it was putting its military infrastructure "on our borders."[2]

The shock waves traveled far, for it was clear that this speech was directed not only at the audience in Munich, but at the whole world.

NATO ENLARGEMENT TO THE EAST AND
THE NATO-RUSSIA COUNCIL

The sovereignty of states and their freedom to make alliances was, as mentioned above, enshrined in the Charter of Paris in 1990. It took a few years before the first states of the former Warsaw Pact were offered accession talks.

It must be emphasized that the accession of Central and Eastern European states to NATO was not an end in itself. The enlargement of NATO made all of Europe safer. Many smaller states now enjoy the protection of the alliance and do not have to arm themselves in order to feel secure. Just imagine Europe today without NATO: From Tallinn to Bucharest, from Paris to Berlin, there would be much more military spending, because everyone would have to take care of their own country's security and could not count on allies. Without NATO the number of nuclear states in Europe might be significantly higher. Would a Germany facing the Cold War without NATO have voluntarily and definitively renounced the nuclear option? Would Turkey have done so? Therefore, NATO was a very effective "proliferation inhibitor." This has not been recognized enough in Moscow and elsewhere, not then—and not even today.

Thus it was right in principle and good for Europe that NATO was enlarged. From the Western perspective, Russia benefited as well: The most secure external borders Russia has are in the West, toward NATO. This is the way we Europeans see it. Unfortunately, in Moscow they have an entirely different view: Even in the early 1990s, Russia expressed reservations against the plans to enlarge NATO to the East.

Back then Chancellor Kohl said he wanted to talk with his "friend Boris" first. Kohl talked with Yeltsin and brought back the message that Russia did not believe NATO enlargement was a good idea unless it was linked with an organic change in the relationship between NATO and Russia. What emerged from this was a "two pillar strategy": NATO enlargement on the one hand, a deepening of the relationship between NATO and Russia on the other. And from that point on we informally discussed the steps toward NATO expansion with the Russians. There was no veto for the Russians, but intensive consultations.

In order to dispel Russia's misgivings once and for all, both parties assured each other in the NATO-Russia Founding Act of 1997 that they were committed to developing a strong, stable, enduring, and equal partnership. This document was based on the two pillar strategy. So, it seemed clear that NATO no longer thought of itself as an alliance against Russia. With its signature, Russia, too, declared that it accepted the alliance's eastward expansion. Indeed, this was precisely the point: The framework conditions for enlargement are defined in detail in this document. Later Russian complaints that Moscow had been promised NATO would not expand eastward are unfounded and incorrect. That is why the Russian indignation in Munich 2007 was somewhat surprising.

As the chief German representative in the negotiations about the founding act of 1997, I can say the Russian side at no point stated that the West had agreed or promised not to enlarge NATO. If the Russian side was convinced that there had actually been such a promise, they should not have participated at all in these negotiations regarding steps toward NATO enlargement. Unfortunately, the Russian propaganda was quite successful: Today there are many, even in the West, who believe that we went back on our word. This is not the truth.

At the NATO summit in Madrid in 1997, Poland, the Czech Republic, and Hungary were offered accession to NATO, and they joined in 1999. This same summit yielded a partnership between NATO and Ukraine. There were also agreements reached on disarmament and arms control issues, on the transfer of weapons and technology, and on military training. Ever since, NATO has had an office in Kyiv, and Ukraine, a liaison in Brussels. At the time, this was no problem.

After Poland, the Czech Republic, and Hungary joined in 1999, the pressure on other Eastern European states grew even stronger: They all wanted to join NATO and sought its protection. In 2002, NATO decided to invite Bulgaria, Romania, Slovakia, Slovenia, and the three Baltic states—Estonia, Latvia, and Lithuania—to accession talks. In 2004 all seven states became members of NATO. Up to that point Moscow accepted this, in the spirit of the founding act.

At a summit in Rome, the NATO-Russia Council had been established to create better opportunities for dialogue between NATO and Russia, and to strengthen cooperation on issues of defense and security policy.

But the question of future NATO membership for Georgia and Ukraine sparked a conflict at the NATO Summit in Bucharest, Romania, in April 2008. One year after Putin's Munich speech, the crisis between NATO and Russia reached a new climax: Putin regarded NATO's expansion plans as a provocation, because Georgia and Ukraine would be the first parts of the former Soviet Union to join NATO.

To understand this better, we need to look back at the first NATO enlargement summit. It was held in Madrid in 1997, with heads of state and government meeting in a restricted session. I sat right behind Kohl as trouble brewed: The French wanted to admit five countries, but the Americans wanted a maximum of three new members. In the end, we proposed a compromise of dividing the enlargement into separate steps: three countries in the first round, the other Eastern and Southeastern European candidates and the Baltics in the second round. This allowed the first expansion to be reduced to three states in order to accommodate Washington, while Chirac was able to send a signal to Bucharest that it would be Romania's turn in the second round at the latest. I wrote this proposal by hand on a slip of paper and Chancellor Kohl read it out in German. After applause from Clinton, consent from Chirac, and a sigh of relief all around, the result was not exactly welcomed in Moscow, but it was tolerated.

At the NATO summit in Bucharest in 2008, eleven years later, the exact opposite happened: An American plan for Georgia and Ukraine, known as the Membership Action Plan, or MAP, was on the table. A MAP is not a NATO membership card, but it clearly lays out the path to accession. At the time, the German government and the French believed it went much too far. Contrary to NATO practice, member states went into the summit discussions with this issue unresolved, because no agreement had been reached beforehand. At the summit there was a no from Merkel and from Sarkozy, and a yes from Bush. In the following negotiations Bush declared that since he had already promised MAP to the Ukrainians and the Georgians, he could not back down now. At the last minute a compromise was reached, producing a statement without a date: "NATO welcomes Ukraine's and Georgia's Euro-Atlantic aspirations for membership in NATO. We agreed today that these countries will become members of NATO." Period. It seemed like a clever idea. Without a date, we thought, it was a nonbinding announcement, something like the agreed-upon goal of EU membership that had been the subject of negotiations with Turkey for decades.

But it was an announcement, nonetheless—and in Putin's ears, a very menacing one: "Sooner or later we will expand the alliance to include Georgia and Ukraine."

From the Russian perspective, what we thought of as a compromise formula was in fact an escalation. Three months later, in summer 2008, the Russian government started its little war with Georgia. From this point on, we were gradually heading into an ever-sharper confrontation, until Secretary General Anders Fogh Rasmussen stated at the start of a NATO summit in Newport, Wales, in September 2014, "Russia's aggression against Ukraine has been a wake-up call. It has reminded us, reminded all of us, that our freedom, security and prosperity cannot be taken for granted."

Suddenly there was war in Europe once more.

WAR IN EUROPE: UKRAINE UNDER FIRE!

What was the cause of the conflict in Ukraine and in Crimea? The port of Sevastopol on the southwestern tip of Crimea had been the main naval base of the Russian Black Sea Fleet since the eighteenth century. After the end of the Soviet Union, Ukraine became independent and the base of the Black Sea Fleet was no longer located in Russian territory. In the Ukrainian independence referendum of 1991, 54 percent of the Crimean population voted to detach from Russia—a majority, but a significantly narrower one than in other parts of Ukraine. In Donbass, over 80 percent voted for independence; in Kyiv and Western Ukraine, over 90 percent.

In 1997, then Russian President Boris Yeltsin and then Ukrainian President Leonid Kuchma signed an agreement about the fleet in Sevastopol: Russia was to lease the base for the next twenty years and would share its facilities with the Ukrainian Navy. The Black Sea Fleet Accords took effect in July 1999 and were supposed to last until 2017.

In April 2010 the two new presidents of Russia and Ukraine, Dmitry Medvedev and Viktor Yanukovych, met and agreed to renew the agreement for another 25 years; now the Russian fleet would be allowed to remain in Crimea until 2042. In return, Ukraine was granted a 30 percent discount on Russian natural gas. Not everyone in the Ukrainian parliament was thrilled about this contract; there were representatives who did not want to be bound to the Russian Federation for so long, especially since it might eventually be possible to obtain natural gas more cheaply from other regions. During this session of parliament, there was a great uproar; someone even threw smoke bombs. Nevertheless, a narrow majority approved the contract renewal. Opposition leader Yulia Tymoshenko announced legal steps against the contract and requested support from the West. Even then it was clear that the issue was about far more than lease income for the port and a fixed gas price.

The tensions between the Russian faction and the pro-Western forces in Kyiv escalated in late 2013. In November 2013, instead of signing a planned Association Agreement with the EU that was meant to strengthen Ukraine-EU political and economic cooperation, Yanukovych met with Putin in Sochi, Russia, raising suspicions he would sign an agreement on Ukraine's accession to a Russian-led Customs Union, which—apart from Russia itself— already included Belarus and Kazakhstan. The opposition assembled for a "Euromaidan," a massive protest movement on Kyiv's central square, Maidan Nezalezhnosti—"Independence Square." They demanded the resignation of the president, new elections, and the signing of the EU Association Agreement. In early December, hundreds of thousands demonstrated on the streets and were hailed as a transformative movement in the West.

In February 2014 the situation escalated further: Security forces opened fire on the demonstrators. In the end the city had over eighty casualties to mourn. And when Yanukovych then fled the country overnight, the result was indeed a change of power in Kyiv. From the Russian perspective, this was a coup against a legitimate government. Moscow spoke of a real danger to the Russian population in Ukraine and considered "antifascist" measures necessary for their protection. Shortly thereafter, armed "self-defense" forces from the Russian-speaking population of Crimea occupied the parliament building in the southernmost region of Ukraine, in February 2015.

CONTROVERSIAL REFERENDUM IN CRIMEA

Two thousand Russian soldiers had landed in Crimea—and from the perspective of the West and the Ukrainian government, it was an armed invasion and occupation by the Russian Army in violation of international law. By the Russian account, it was just a normal event covered by the Black Sea Fleet Accords. At the request of Ukraine, the OSCE dispatched unarmed military observers to Crimea, but they were refused admittance by pro-Russian units.

In April, Putin conceded that Russian forces had actively supported local "self-defense" forces in Crimea. In May he disputed that Russian troops had intervened in the events there. In June he admitted it once again.

The international confusion was reinforced by massive intervention in the media landscape. Instead of Ukrainian TV programs, now only Russian TV was shown in Crimea. Journalists were threatened and intimidated. The organization Reporters Without Borders spoke of a climate of censorship. Russian stations propagated false reports about gunfights in Kyiv and attacks on pro-Russian civilians. The Western world reacted with outrage but could do nothing. The whole propaganda spectacle served as a campaign for a dubious referendum on the status of Crimea, called at very short notice, which asked Crimeans to choose between remaining part of Ukraine or joining Russia.

The seven remaining G8 states, the president of the European Council, and the president of the EU Commission all declared that they would not recognize the planned referendum.

On March 16, 2014, the referendum took place nonetheless and resulted in—what a surprise—a vote of 96.77 percent in favor of accession to Russia. The rest went swiftly: On the next day, March 17, Putin gave a speech on Crimea's accession into the Russian Federation, and a treaty was signed the very same day. The Crimean government announced that the clocks would be reset to Moscow time, the ruble would be valid as a second currency, and the oil and gas sectors would be nationalized.

The latter was particularly provocative, as there were considerable oil and gas fields located just off the Crimean coast that had not yet been exploited. None other than the Russian company Lukoil, the world's sixth largest listed oil corporation, had lost the bid to do so in 2012. From 2017 on, these fields would have yielded so much gas that around 20 percent of Ukraine's gas imports could have been replaced, and thus reducing the country's import dependency on Russia. Instead, on March 18 the Russian state gas company Gazprom applied for the extraction rights for these oil and gas reserves, which no longer belonged to Ukraine.

PEACE IN GENEVA, WAR IN DONBASS

Within a few weeks the situation in Ukraine had been turned upside down. In Kyiv there was now a Europe-friendly government in power, but Crimea had been annexed by Russia, an obvious violation of international law and a breach of the Charter of Paris, which laid down strict rules for changing national borders in Europe. In the eyes of the West, the Crimea referendum had been mere theater: The United Nations and the OSCE had not been involved at all, and observers were not admitted—a serious breach of international law. In Moscow, by contrast, the accession treaty was understood as the natural return of Crimea to Russia—but how could such a decision be made without Kyiv?

The Russian annexation of Crimea thus could not and would not be accepted; everyone in the West agreed on this. Even before the pseudo-referendum, the EU, the United States, Switzerland, Canada, and Japan had imposed various kinds of sanctions in order to punish Russia for its course of action. Negotiations about facilitating visas were suspended, assets were frozen, and travel bans, issued. By the end of 2014 the list of EU sanctions was extended multiple times, and it remains in effect today.

Russia appeared quite unimpressed and reacted with countersanctions. They issued travel bans against U.S. Americans and Canadians, and then against eighty-nine European politicians.

And as if that were not enough, in spring 2014 an additional hot spot erupted in Eastern Ukraine, namely in the mining region of Donbass. The region, so valuable for heavy industry, is still occupied today by armed separatist "people's militias." Here, too, Russian soldiers were involved on the side of the separatists—but according to Russian claims, they were not there on an official mandate from Moscow, but just happened to be "on vacation" in Eastern Ukraine. These guerillas operated Russian military equipment and ultimately proclaimed the independence of the "people's republics" of Donetsk and Luhansk. So, the Russian annexation of Crimea was now followed by a covert invasion of Donbass. The West did not want to sit idly by, but what could it do?

The first peace efforts and attempts to reach an agreement led to "Geneva talks" in April 2014 between the foreign ministers of the United States and Russia, John Kerry and Sergey Lavrov, the EU's foreign policy head Catherine Ashton, and the interim foreign minister of Ukraine, Andrey Deschitsa. There all parties agreed that they would reduce tensions and restore security for all citizens. Yet the so-called separatists in Donbass were not willing to lay down their weapons.

THE OSCE INVITATION TO A ROUNDTABLE

In early May 2014, Russia demanded the recognition of the Donbass separatists and proposed holding a second Geneva conference to which the separatists would be invited—a proposal rejected by the Ukrainian government. However, Russia was at least willing to allow the OSCE to mediate.

As a result, a couple of days later my telephone rang in Washington D.C., where I had just started a sabbatical at the Wilson Center. The German government asked me to make myself available to organize roundtable talks on resolving the crisis in Ukraine. The OSCE chairman at the time, Didier Burkhalter, foreign minister of Switzerland, had welcomed this German proposal, and the Ukrainian government had already accepted the idea in principle. There was to be a dialogue among all political groups in Ukraine, accompanied by the OSCE, and based on the model of the roundtable talks in East Germany before reunification.

I accepted, hoping that roundtables could at least ensure a calm atmosphere for the Ukrainian presidential elections scheduled for May 25. The hope was that a newly elected Ukrainian president could then introduce a process that would lead to a peaceful solution, perhaps via direct or indirect channels to Moscow.

So, I flew to Ukraine as a personal representative of the OSCE chairman. The first session of my roundtable process took place in Kyiv on May 14, the second in Kharkiv on May 17, and the third in Mykolaiv on May 21—all of them under crisis conditions. But one aspect of all these talks was especially gratifying: Ukraine has a young, lively, and activist civil society, which was well represented in these sessions. Clearly, this was and is a great asset for the country's future.

Ultimately, the Ukrainian election was held on May 25, 2014—except in Donbass—and was as free and fair as one could possibly hope under the extremely difficult circumstances. The new president-elect was Petro Poroshenko, a critic of the Russia-friendly Yanukovych and a supporter of the Euromaidan movement.

The election was an important milestone, but the long path to stabilizing and reforming Ukraine was just beginning. In lectures and articles at the time, I warned that Europe would have to continue providing strong support for Ukraine and find new approaches for dealing with Russia. But what could such approaches look like?

In mid-July of 2014, Putin met with Angela Merkel in Rio de Janeiro, where they were both attending the final match of the World Cup soccer tournament. The two agreed that the Ukrainian government and the separatists should engage in direct discussions with each other as soon as possible. Merkel and Putin had been talking on the telephone regularly since the crisis erupted. I found the chancellor's extreme patience during these countless conversations, which often must have been quite frustrating, quite admirable. Good foreign policy often requires a great deal of patience, and sometimes impressive staying power.

In early September the first meeting of a trilateral OSCE contact group comprising representatives of Ukraine, Russia, and the OSCE took place in Minsk, Belarus. The group also included representatives of the self-proclaimed people's republics of Donetsk and Luhansk. The result, dubbed Minsk I, was an agreement by all parties in the conflict to a ceasefire, to be monitored by the OSCE, and an exchange of prisoners. But as it turned out, the agreement was not worth the paper it was written on: The ceasefire was not respected.

RUSSIA'S REVISIONIST FOREIGN POLICY

What began as a national political crisis in Ukraine had rapidly become a conflict that threatened the security of all of Europe. Something virtually inconceivable had become reality: a war in Europe, with constantly climbing numbers of casualties and no negotiated settlement in sight. On top of this, on its way from Amsterdam to Kuala Lumpur, Malaysia Airlines flight MH17 was shot down by a Russian anti-aircraft missile in Eastern Ukraine in summer 2014. All 298 passengers lost their lives, including 80 children and 15 crew members. Due to a Russian veto in the UN Security Council, it was not possible to set up a special tribunal to investigate the incident. Investigations conducted by the Netherlands have since concluded that it was ostensibly Russian separatists who shot down the plane. Because most of the victims were from the Netherlands, the perpetrators were to be tried in that country for their crime. However, as no one expects that Russia will extradite its own citizens, the suspects may never land in court.

Russia's actions in Ukraine paint the alarming picture of a country that no longer feels bound to the principles of security in Europe enshrined in the Charter of Paris and the earlier Helsinki Final Act, and is pursuing a "revisionist" foreign policy instead. Thus, Ukraine is becoming the staging ground for a confrontation between Russia and the West about the principles for organizing the world of the twenty-first century.

In this context it is worth taking the time to list all of the fundamental rules and agreements the West regards as violated by Russia's annexation of Crimea and invasion of Eastern Ukraine:

- the principles of the CSCE Final Act of 1975 mentioned above, in which European states (including Russia) committed themselves to the inviolability of borders and to the peaceful settlement of disputes

- the Budapest Memorandum of 1994, in which Ukraine was assured security guarantees for respecting its existing frontiers in exchange for Kyiv relinquishing the Soviet nuclear weapons stationed in Ukraine

- the 1990 Charter of Paris

- the NATO-Russia Founding Act of 1997

- the Friendship Treaty and the Black Sea Fleet Accords signed by Russia and Ukraine in 1997

- the Charter of the United Nations

All of these breaches of law were and continue to be disputed on the part of Russia, of course. The European security architecture has thus, de facto, collapsed—a fatal development in historical terms, after achieving so much reconciliation and trust, and after so much arms control and intensive cooperation.

The annexation of Crimea and the start of the war in Eastern Ukraine apparently heralded the development of an unofficial "Putin Doctrine," which goes something like this: Moscow has the right to intervene in order to protect Russian-language populations abroad—based solely on Moscow's assessment of whether, when and how this protection is necessary.

The assumption that the territorial integrity of European states is no longer threatened today has thus proven erroneous. With the annexation of Crimea, the continuing covert intervention in Eastern Ukraine, and the announcement of this Putin Doctrine, Russia has rolled back the history of European security to an earlier chapter, with alarming consequences.

At the 2017 Munich Security Conference, Chancellor Merkel got to the heart of why this Russian policy simply cannot be tolerated: "The principle of territorial integrity . . . is something on which the European peaceful order has been based since the Second World War. That is why we need to be so strict on this issue. If this principle no longer exists, the entire European order will be destabilized." If we allow states to simply assimilate parts of their neighbors, the world order of the twenty-first century will be a cruel one indeed, taking us from international law back to a world where only the powerful survive.

Russia is not the only threat to the principles of territorial integrity and basic respect for international law that Merkel mentioned. China's behavior is also causing concern for Europeans and Americans, but first and foremost for the states of East and Southeast Asia. In the South China Sea, Beijing is waging territorial conflicts with, among others, the Philippines, Malaysia, and Vietnam, as well as enforcing its territorial claims more and more vehemently by means of new military bases and artificially reclaimed islands. A decision by the Permanent Court of Arbitration in The Hague on the territorial conflict between China and the Philippines, in which the judges ruled in favor of Manila, was simply ignored by Beijing. For that reason it is hardly surprising to hear from China's neighbors that the South China Sea is for them what Crimea is for Eastern Europe.

But back to Russia and Ukraine: Back in November 2014, Angela Merkel had given a speech in Brisbane during the G20 Conference, in which she warned against the resurrection of the Cold War and a division of the world into spheres of influence. At the Munich Security Conference in February 2015, she posited that the Ukraine conflict could not be won militarily: "The problem is that I cannot imagine a situation in which upgrading the military equipment of the Ukrainian Army would so impress President Putin that he would believe he might lose on the battlefield."

So it was time for crisis diplomacy. Together with French President François Hollande, Merkel first traveled to Kyiv in early February 2015 to meet with Ukrainian President Petro Poroshenko and then to Moscow for a meeting with Putin. The U.S. Secretary of State John Kerry got involved as well. In mid-February, Minsk II was announced: According to this agreement, Minsk I was now to be implemented fully so that a ceasefire would take effect at long last.

Nevertheless, Eastern Ukraine remains in the hands of separatists today, and Crimea remains annexed by Russia. The war has not escalated further, but otherwise we have made little progress. And it remains fully unclear whether Russia is interested in peace at all.

EUROPE'S SECURITY: AGAINST, FROM, OR WITH RUSSIA?

Over the course of the last five years, the situation in Ukraine has hardly changed—neither for the better nor for the worse. There is a real risk of creating a protracted, "frozen" conflict, with Ukrainian territory permanently divided. And the danger of continued economic malaise has not been averted, either. These problems cannot be resolved without Russia. The hard truth is, neither the integrity and security of Ukraine nor its economic rehabilitation can be realized in the face of continuous conflict with the big Russian neighbor next door.

A sustainable security architecture for all of Europe can be shaped only together *with* Russia. But it is no less true that European countries today also need security *from* Russia.

A dual strategy is needed, offering and conducting a dialogue with Putin on the one hand—as difficult as that may be under the current circumstances—while, on the other hand, denying Russia opportunities to threaten European countries and preventing Russia from exploiting Western European weaknesses: as much defense as necessary, and as much cooperation as possible!

A clear military message and enhanced defense capabilities are still imperative. NATO was right to react as it did to the Russian annexation of Crimea and Russia's continued support for the separatists in Eastern Ukraine, putting forward a program of political and military reassurance. Just as the alliance demonstrated solidarity with West Germany during the Cold War, it is now doing the same for its allies in Eastern Europe.

So today the German people are called upon to provide our Eastern NATO partners with the very same solidarity we ourselves received not so long ago. Anyone who can remember how important it was for us that Americans, British, Frenchmen, Canadians, and others were stationed in West Germany, so that they would be involved directly in case of conflict—and thus eliminate any doubt about whether the mutual defense clause would apply—will understand why our alliance partners on the Eastern flank desire their partners' presence just as strongly. Therefore, it is right and proper that the German Army has taken command of one of the four multinational battalions that NATO sent to Poland, Estonia, Latvia, and Lithuania. Incidentally, this is the first time the Bundeswehr is actually providing military protection for a NATO ally.

Aside from NATO, it is a different matter for those countries with the bad luck to not belong to any alliance. Ukraine is one of them. What is the NATO partners' and Europe's responsibility for this country? Ukraine must have the right and the possibility to defend itself. For this reason, too, it is understandable that NATO partners decided to supply Kyiv with defensive weapons like anti-tank missiles, radar systems, and improved communications systems. For a long time, all of the weapons coming into Ukraine were from Russia, so the separatists had equipment at their disposal that the Ukrainian Army could do little to oppose.

Yet, what is even more important is financial and economic support for Kyiv, coupled with assistance in fighting corruption. This is existential for Ukraine. Equally important is the promotion of Ukrainian civil society. The young generation that demonstrated on the Maidan—not against Russia, but against a corrupt Ukrainian elite that robbed Ukrainian youth of their chances for a European future—is hoping for a better Ukraine, a European Ukraine. Europe can contribute a great deal to strengthening this young generation, for instance through visa waivers, scholarships for Ukrainian students, and support for nongovernmental organizations on the ground.

In addition to various funding instruments, the sanctions imposed against Russia since 2014 are an important instrument of solidarity with Ukraine.

THE PURPOSE OF SANCTIONS

Sanctions are never a panacea. Sometimes they have no recognizable effect at all. They often hurt the wrong people. On occasion, sanctions are imposed for the simple reason that we find nothing better in the diplomatic toolbox. There are risks and side effects, and therefore this tool should be used sparingly, and its effectiveness should be examined critically on a regular basis. In the late 1990s, Henry Kissinger pointed out that the United States had imposed sanctions against nearly half of humanity at the time, asking whether this was a promising route that we should continue to take. He was warning against the G8 considering sanctions against India and Pakistan because of their nuclear tests at a time when sanctions were already in effect against Russia, Cuba, Libya, Iran, China, and others.

Therefore, it is never wrong to be skeptical about sanctions. But the sanctions imposed on Moscow because of Russian policies in Ukraine should remain in effect as long as Moscow and the separatists fail to comprehensively implement the terms of the Minsk II agreement. Anyone who thinks the supposedly ineffective sanctions should simply be lifted is failing to recognize the signal this would send: Putin would get away with his aggression in the end, just by waiting long enough.

Of course, Kyiv must also fully engage in the implementation of the Minsk agreement; otherwise the sanctions will not make any political sense. From time to time, the Ukrainians need some straight talk about implementing Minsk as well. Nevertheless, the fact remains that Kyiv is the victim of this war.

De facto, the question of NATO membership for Ukraine has long been decided in the negative by the alliance. It is certainly understandable that the government in Kyiv does not want to give up hope, but discussions about NATO membership will not help us to resolve the current crisis. What is important here is to develop political alternatives to NATO membership, such as Ukraine following the examples of Finland, Sweden, or Austria, and defining itself as a bridge between East and West. What is at stake here is credibility. We cannot and must not simply leave Ukraine, Georgia, Moldova, and other states "between East and West" out in the cold.

Unfortunately, there is no easy answer.

In the end, all signatory states of the OSCE, and thus also Russia, must work together to seek ways to strengthen the European security architecture. Conventional and nuclear arms control must be put back on the agenda as mutual projects to prevent crises and build trust. In view of the persistent nuclear threats, there must be no room in Europe for flexing military muscles. Visions of strategic economic cooperation with Russia also deserve more attention. As recently as 2010, Putin himself was dreaming of a free trade zone in Europe "from Lisbon to Vladivostok." But one thing is clear: Many constructive proposals are destined for the wastebasket as long as Russia is unwilling to return to cooperative politics. *It takes two to tango.*

So, what is to be done? I will come back to our options for action later on.

"IT'S GREAT IF THEY'RE AFRAID OF US!"

When I took up my job as director of the policy planning staff of the German Foreign Office in 1993, a self-critical look at my own experience told me that I understood quite a bit about the United

States, NATO, and the EU, but very little about Eastern Europe. This is why I took a trip to Warsaw, Kyiv, and Moscow—for four days, all told. When I arrived in Moscow on the third day, I was greeted by Vice Minister of Foreign Affairs Georgiy Mamedov. Over dinner, I reported what I had learned in the past two days:

"I've just come from Warsaw and Kyiv. In both countries, I encountered a great amount of anxiety about Russia."

My dinner partner nodded, so I continued: "We Germans know what it means to have neighbors who are afraid of us. That is why we undertook all possible measures to put our neighbors at ease— the French, Danes, Dutch, Czechs, and Poles—and allay their fears of Germany. More and more, our neighbors perceive us as their friends."

Mamedov nodded once more, so I asked the question at the top of my mind: "What is Russia doing to alleviate anxiety about Russia in Poland, Ukraine, and the other Eastern European states?"

Mamedov looked at me and replied, "My dear friend, what is wrong with our neighbors being a little afraid of Russia? If they fear us, that's fine!"

Unfortunately, this is still the thinking of many in Moscow: It is a good thing if they fear us! This is also one of the reasons why the desire to join NATO was and remains so great in Warsaw, Kyiv, and elsewhere—they are afraid of Moscow. As small states without major military power, in times of crisis they feel they are at the mercy of the strong bear in the East.

INCOMPATIBLE NARRATIVES

The contrasts between Russian and Western perspectives became especially clear in a body that was convened by the OSCE in 2015, the "Panel of Eminent Persons on European Security as a Common Project." I was entrusted with its chairmanship.

The OSCE itself has a total of fifty-seven member states from North America, Europe, and Asia. This makes it the largest regional security organization, with the stated objective of striving to ensure "that more than a billion people can live in peace, democracy and stability."

As mentioned in the opening chapter, the OSCE was originally called the Conference on Security and Co-operation in Europe (CSCE). The proposal for the organization initially came from the Warsaw Pact, in the midst of the Cold War. Yet the conference did not actually open until after the success of Willy Brandt's *Ostpolitik*, when the West German chancellor endeavored to thaw the frosty atmosphere between the two blocs in the early 1970s. Arduous negotiations took place between 1973 and 1975, finally yielding the Helsinki Final Act (mentioned earlier) on August 1, 1975. It was supposed to put an end to the confrontations of the Cold War. The negotiations involved seven states of the Warsaw Pact, thirteen neutral countries, and the fifteen NATO states; today the meeting would presumably be dubbed the "G35."

Moscow hoped for recognition of the European borders that were still disputed at the time. The West hoped for the enforcement of human rights on the other side of the Iron Curtain. And the bartering succeeded: In the Helsinki Final Act, the participating states committed to the inviolability of boundaries and the peaceful settlement of disputes, as well as to nonintervention in the internal affairs of other states and the protection of human rights and basic freedoms.

Because the conference was such a success, it was followed by subsequent meetings in Bucharest, Madrid, Vienna, and once again, Helsinki. In 1995 the conference members decided to create the Organization for Security and Co-operation in Europe (OSCE) and to rotate its chair among the members. Unfortunately, the OSCE led a fairly low profile political existence in the period that followed, in great part due to the complicated procedure for making decisions. Resolutions could pass only by unanimous vote, and there was almost always at least one member state ready to use its veto power. That is why it was downright sensational when the

Swiss OSCE Chairman Didier Burkhalter succeeded in taking on a mediating function in the Ukraine crisis in 2014, not only sending OSCE observers to the region, but also initiating a political dialogue.

The "Panel of Eminent Persons," of which I became chairman in 2015, was supposed to develop proposals for the future OSCE role in conflict prevention and management, and on the fundamental questions of security architecture in the Euro-Atlantic and Eurasian regions—in the spirit of the Helsinki Final Act and the Charter of Paris, of course—with a particular view to the unresolved conflict in Ukraine. The panel comprised a dozen high-ranking individuals with long years of practical experience in various areas of European security. They came from a wide spectrum of OSCE countries: Greece, Turkey, the United States, Ukraine, Latvia, France, Switzerland, Georgia, Russia, the United Kingdom, Poland, Finland, Kazakhstan, Serbia, and Germany.

As a group we soon discovered that, in terms of our perceptions of the current situation in Europe, there were such great differences between the West and Russia that it was simply impossible to agree on a joint text. The incompatible narratives were a real catastrophe, especially for me as chairman.

In the end the only solution we saw was to present both narratives—Western and Russian—as separate documents. For the sake of completeness, we added a third narrative as well—namely, the viewpoint of the countries "in between" and thus particularly of Ukraine, Georgia, and other states that did not belong to NATO or the EU but also did not consider themselves part of the Russian sphere of influence.

Unfortunately, this "narrative trench" between Russia and the West has not filled in at all since then—in fact, it seems to have become even deeper.

THE CRUX OF ASYMMETRICAL CONVERSATION

The Russian side of the argument on the current crises in Eastern Ukraine, in Crimea, and even in Georgia, goes something like this: The root of all problems is the intolerable behavior of the West, such as exploiting Russian weakness in the 1990s by making empty promises about restraint while pushing forward with NATO expansion to the East. This is generally followed by a long list of transgressions by the West, some of which go way back and do not always have something to do with the current conflict: interventions in Kosovo, Iraq, and Libya; the way the West supposedly tried to force Ukraine into the EU with an Association Agreement—a treaty paving the way for enhanced cooperation between the EU and Ukraine; the way the Central Intelligence Agency (CIA) supposedly launched the color revolutions in Poland and later in Ukraine; and so on. The West imposes its own ideas of order on the entire world and is then surprised when states that want a different order fight back. Now Russia concludes it is finally strong enough again to defend itself.

The argument in the West, in contrast, is the following: After the end of the Soviet Union, hundreds of millions of people in Central and Eastern Europe were finally free to decide their own fates. That many of these countries wanted to be in the EU and NATO, and strived for freedom and democracy, is not the fault of the West. Its goal was merely to create a Europe in peace and freedom. That Russia does not want to take this path is regrettable and worrying.

At the same time, the Western nations ask self-critically, how much of the current conflict situation is our doing? How much did the Iraq War damage the world order? Did we not take Russian interests into consideration enough when Ukraine's Association Agreement with the EU was on the table? Was it wrong for Western foreign ministers to go to the Maidan and shout out their support for the demonstrators?

And yes, the West accepts that it made some mistakes. Yet, does that justify the Russian annexation of Crimea? Does this justify

Moscow keeping the militant separatists in Donbass for a fifth year and supplying them with weapons? Does this justify the Russian intervention in Georgia in 2008?

Thus, the asymmetrical debate becomes an infinite loop—two narratives that are diametrically opposed to each other, with no shared foundation. And while Americans and Europeans grapple with self-critically analyzing where they may have gone wrong, Moscow continues to see errors only on the part of the West. Self-criticism is considered fouling one's own nest.

The result is speechlessness and tension in equal parts. And the only way to surmount that—like in a major marital crisis—is finding a form of conversation in which both sides are ready and willing to admit mistakes, to show respect and appreciation for the other, and seek a way forward together. That, however, requires a basic minimum of trust.

We in the West are distrustful because we feel the Russians tricked us, and because in recent years Russia has damaged—that must be stated clearly—the security order in Europe and has attempted to weaken European democracies politically. Many leading politicians in the West also feel personally disappointed because the Russian leadership lied to their faces time and again. At some point it becomes difficult to make any kind of reasonable agreement at all.

The Russians mistrust the West because they feel encircled by NATO—which we, for our part, find difficult to understand, because no one in Moscow can seriously claim that the NATO alliance policy, which is so clearly oriented toward defense, is any kind of attempt at encirclement. The West adheres expressly to the agreements in the NATO-Russia Founding Act, which amounts to only around 4,000 soldiers rotating through Eastern Europe. On this point, Russian fears are extremely far-fetched. It is no exaggeration to call the Russian border with NATO countries the most secure border segment of the Russian Federation. Unfortunately, they do not see it that way in Moscow.

What is easier for us to understand, however, is that the Poles are unsettled when Russian military exercises simulate a nuclear attack on Warsaw. It is also comprehensible when the Baltic states say that the thought of Russian "little green men" worries them—that is, the never actually admitted but proven presence of Russian soldiers in Crimea and Eastern Ukraine. The small Baltic states, which have sizeable Russian minorities, are concerned about what could happen if their territory was suddenly also visited by "little green men," about whom Moscow claims to know nothing. These are quite understandable concerns.

RESOLVING THE CRISIS WITH RUSSIA—BUT HOW?

An unacceptable idea is to simply make our peace with the unresolved situation in Crimea and in Eastern Ukraine, and to accept it as an indefinite provisional arrangement. Such a measure would certainly not bring true peace to Eastern Ukraine—nor, incidentally, win any trust in all the other Eastern European states. Accepting border transgressions in violation of international law would send the message that Russian interventions in the guise of "self-defense with the support of volunteers" were no longer taboo and would open the floodgates for further violations. Standing one's ground against such acts requires perseverance.

By the way, here we are dealing with a historical precedent: For many decades the United States and Great Britain were committed to the eventual independence of the Baltic states, which in the past century experienced occupation by the Nazis and integration into the Soviet Union. Support for the Baltics' independence proved helpful when the countries insisted on their independence after the collapse of the Soviet Union. The same thing may apply to Crimea as well someday.

The question today must first be about the options for action we currently have at our disposal. What can be done to solve the

Ukraine crisis? Over 10,000 people have lost their lives in the eastern part of the country by this time, and the number grows nearly every week.

The so-called Normandy negotiation format, in which Germany and France are negotiating with Russia and Ukraine, is reaching its limits. The Minsk agreements that were reached under this framework remain valid, but even the simplest implementation steps have been faltering. How can things continue? From my perspective, a partial withdrawal of weapons from the line of demarcation and the enforcement of a ceasefire must be the first steps, along with trust-building measures such as more prisoner exchanges. Since fall 2017, negotiations have been underway with Russia about a UN peacekeeping force to secure peace in Eastern Ukraine. It is a good idea that has, admittedly, foundered on the most fundamental of all issues: Where should and may the UN force be active? The Russians insist that the hot spot is not the Russian-Ukrainian border, but the inner-Ukrainian front. This would stand the very idea of a peacekeeping force on its head.

Former American President Dwight D. Eisenhower would have recommended his favorite recipe: "If you can't solve a problem, enlarge it!"

What would that mean in this case? Well, first we could try to enlarge the negotiation format—for instance, by inviting the EU to the negotiating table, along with the United States, which has participated only indirectly so far. The result would be a format like the one that achieved agreement on the nuclear deal with Iran in 2015. Especially considering the debate about a UN peacekeeping force in Donbass, it would certainly make sense to include the Security Council veto powers—especially the United States—as early as possible, rather than sticking with the as-yet unsuccessful Normandy format. And as far as the idea of UN peacekeeping force is concerned, this new beginning could take place without any of the parties losing face.

A further argument in favor of a larger negotiation format: If

Putin has any interest in ending the Ukraine conflict, it is improbable that he would sign a peace treaty for Eastern Ukraine negotiated only with the German chancellor and the French president. He will want to be sure that the result is also supported by the White House. After all, Putin has never made a secret of the fact that a central motivator in his Ukraine policy is NATO enlargement. And indeed, Russian policy in Ukraine, as well as in Georgia, precludes the envisioned NATO membership of these countries, because both of them now have disputed borders, disqualifying them for membership in NATO. However, the question of NATO enlargement—in the Russian view—will ultimately be decided not in Berlin or Paris, but in Washington. Thus, no matter how difficult it may be, the United States should be at the table.

Admittedly, the prospects for a constructive United States-Russia policy do not look bright. So far, Trump's hands have been tied by the U.S. Congress on this issue due to the persistent suspicion that Russia interfered with the 2016 American election in his favor.

THE RETURN OF THE NUCLEAR QUESTION

And yet, after years of silence between Moscow and Washington, the reemergence of American-Russian summit diplomacy would be more than desirable. Therefore, it is a very positive development that Trump and Putin met in July 2018—as long as the concern that Trump might make "deals" with Putin over the heads of American allies (and at their expense) does not prove justified.

After all, although Russia may be merely an intermediate power in economic terms, we must not underestimate Moscow's military power. Together, Russia and the United States possess over 90 percent of the global stockpile of nuclear weapons, and Russia has the most nuclear warheads in the world—6,850 compared to the United States's 6,450.[3] Russia's military spending doubled between 2004 and 2014.

Such numbers are never good news. One would much rather recall better times: In 1987 the Intermediate-Range Nuclear Forces (INF) Treaty—one of the most important arms control treaties— was signed. The treaty stipulated a "double zero" solution requiring, among others, the elimination of all 857 deployed intermediate-range missiles with 1,667 deployed nuclear warheads on the Soviet side, and of all 429 deployed missiles and warheads on the American side. This was the first treaty to completely prohibit a certain category of weapons—a great diplomatic success that signified the end of the rearmament debate and made an essential contribution to the end of the Cold War.

In 2019, the INF Treaty fell victim to the breakdown of communication and trust between the United States and Russia. The United States accused Russia of violating the treaty by developing a new intermediate-range missile that can be armed with nuclear warheads. Additionally, NATO has expressed its concern, urging Russia to dispel these accusations with concrete proof. Russia, for its part, regards the U.S. anti-missile shield for Eastern Europe as a breach of the treaty, because it sees the American system, with its installations in Poland and Romania, as directed against Russia— not against missiles from Iran or other states. In February 2019, both countries suspended the treaty indefinitely, and in August the United States completely withdrew from it.

All of this has unpredictable and negative consequences on the security situation in Europe. Since the INF Treaty was a contract between the Russian Federation and the United States, disputes could be resolved only between these two states. But such disputes concerned us Europeans quite directly, and we should have gotten involved much more forcefully. For us, the end of the INF Treaty is a catastrophe. And the failure of the INF Treaty also practically excludes the possibility of renewal for the New Strategic Arms Reduction Treaty (START)," which was signed back in the Obama and Medvedev era and led to a considerable reduction in American and Russian strategic nuclear weapons. Incidentally, the initiative for New START was born at the 2009 Munich Security Conference and the ratification papers were exchanged at the 2011 Munich Security Conference. This makes me quite proud! But there may no longer be a single nuclear arms control treaty between the United States and Russia by 2021. In the worst case, this could lead to a new wave of nuclear rearmament in Europe as well.

Yet what Europe needs is not nuclear armament, but the resumption of arms control. Disarmament talks are a necessity.

TALKS, TALKS, AND EVEN MORE TALKS

So, what we need are concrete and implementable proposals that reduce mutual distrust, build trust, and provide the foundation for a comprehensive Euro-Atlantic security community in the long term. Such proposals have been made and continue to be offered.

Back in 2013 an international expert panel, in which I participated, submitted a report entitled "Building Mutual Security in the Euro-Atlantic Region." It was the result of a series of meetings that had begun at the 2012 Munich Security Conference. Under joint American, Russian, and European chairmanship, around thirty political and military experts from the United States, Russia, Poland, France, Great Britain, and Germany pondered the security of Europe and the prospect of peace stretching from the Atlantic to the Urals.

The report recommended talks and negotiations in a multitude of areas: The first order of business, of course, was nuclear weapons. Missile defense, armed forces, and conventional weapons were the next topics, but the subjects of cybersecurity and activities in outer space also made the list—each from the short-term perspective over the next five years and from a longer-term perspective over the next fifteen.

Because this report was ready and the experts were ready but no implementation was in sight, the four chairmen of this expert panel made yet another push before the G20 summit in Hamburg, Germany, in summer 2017.

The four were Des Browne, former British minister of defense; Igor S. Ivanov, former foreign minister and ex-secretary of the Security Council of the Russian Federation; Sam Nunn, former U.S. senator and chairman of the Senate Committee on Armed Services; and myself. A joint initiative by the West and Russia.

The four of us and our fellow committee members are old foreign policy hands, with plenty of diplomatic experience, and have dealt with disarmament and peace policy in various roles. We have encountered each other in all kinds of places; for instance, Ivanov and I had already worked together at the peace negotiations in Dayton, Ohio, in 1995. All four of us experienced the Cold War, including the construction and fall of the Berlin Wall, and the hope for a united, peaceful Europe. All four of us know all too well how difficult it is to create peace and maintain it permanently.

Concerned about the current situation, we wrote an open letter to President Putin and President Trump:

> The chasm between Russia and the West appears to be wider now than at any point since the Cold War. In the absence of new initiatives, the knot of distrust is being tightened, choking off the ability of governments to discuss, let alone advance, steps essential for improving the security of all people living in the Euro-Atlantic region.

We pointed out to the two most powerful men in the world what a unique opportunity their first meeting, at the G20 summit in Hamburg, would offer for "urgently pursuing practical steps now that can stop the downward spiral in relations and reduce real dangers."

At least they did take this opportunity in Hamburg to really talk to each other, although a rapprochement between the two seemed nearly impossible due to the domestic policy discussions in the United States.

In the letter to Presidents Putin and Trump, we suggested the following items: a joint declaration that a nuclear war cannot be won and must never be fought; restarting bilateral military-to-military dialogue between the United States and Russia; a joint initiative to prevent terrorists from acquiring weapons of mass destruction; and informal understandings on how to deal with cyber threats.

Unfortunately, the 2017 Hamburg summit did not bring any real progress on any of these issues, which means they remain relevant today. That is why we repeated the appeal in 2018. Our concern that Russia and the West are drifting ever further apart has intensified. One of Putin's closest advisors, Vladislav Surkov, wrote in 2018 that Russia was now facing 100 years of geopolitical solitude. Russia's epic journey to become part of Western civilization was now at an end after 400 years. Hopefully, that will not be the last word from Moscow.

The events in Ukraine in 2014 were a wake-up call for European security. A sustainable Euro-Atlantic security architecture requires all participants to work together with respect. Russia must be neither excluded from the European house nor forced to sleep in the hall. It needs its own room, provided that it refrains from vandalism.

Skeptics say, you want us to build an addition to a house while it is on fire? Truly, this is quite a challenge. But we should nevertheless attempt to keep tinkering to improve the building.

This is the great antagonism in our relations with Russia. Today we are—unfortunately—rivals, even adversaries, on many issues. Russia is engaged in expansionist foreign policy and in weakening Western democracies. Nevertheless, we continue to make an effort with Russia and the Russian population. In my view it would be a strong positive signal if the EU were to lift the visa requirement for Russians, despite all of the political trouble with Putin. After all, Ukrainians already enjoy this privilege—so why shouldn't Russians as well?

This may sound like a contradiction, but it is actually a classic example of a foreign policy dilemma. Foreign policy conceived for the long run is always more convincing than breathless reactions to short-term provocations or crises. What we are left with today, unfortunately, is a severe crisis of confidence between the West and Russia, a great threat to international security and stability. The consequences are clearly visible, for example in the flash point that is Syria.

FIVE

WAR IN SYRIA

Intervene or Look Away?

FROM THE ARAB SPRING TO A
FOREIGN POLICY NIGHTMARE

Syria: What has dominated the news cycle for years as a draining, endless war of nearly unbearable misery started rather harmlessly—actually, with a certain euphoria. In spring 2011 the Syrian people took to the streets to demonstrate. Their protests were directed against their long-standing president, Bashar Hafiz al-Assad.

The demonstrations in Syria followed a multitude of events in the Middle East watched enthusiastically by the public in the West; "Arab Spring" was the optimistic catchphrase that made the rounds via television and newspapers. Bit by bit, the people in the Arab world seemed to be fighting back against their oppressors—and doing so peacefully.

And yet, the events had been kicked off by a horrible event, not in Syria, but a couple thousand kilometers further west along the Mediterranean coast, namely in Tunisia.

On December 17, 2010, a young Tunisian named Mohamed Bouazizi committed suicide. He had muddled along as a greengrocer in the small provincial town of Sidi Bouzid, but then local authorities confiscated his vending cart because he did not have a sales license. With a little cash for a bribe or with ties to the right people, the poor vendor would have been able to solve his problems. But he had neither. A scuffle broke out; a policewoman hit him in the face. He submitted a protest to her superiors, but it was rejected. Humiliation and powerlessness ultimately brought him to such desperation that the 26-year-old sat down in front of the local administration building, doused himself with gasoline, and set himself on fire with a cigarette lighter. His death changed the world.

At first everything looked like it was made for Hollywood. Protests started in Tunisia, then the spark jumped further, and the "Arabellion" began. Spontaneous demonstrations erupted almost everywhere in the region. People in Tunisia, Algeria, and Libya, in Jordan, Kuwait, and Oman, took to the streets chanting, demonstrating for freedom, and dancing on the squares of their cities.

From the perspective of many in Europe, this seemed like the beginning of a fairy tale summer. Just over twenty years had passed since the peaceful revolution in East Germany, when GDR citizens rattled the Iron Curtain with regular demonstrations every Monday and finally cast off forty years of Soviet repression without a single shot fired. The memory was still fresh.

The world was astonished. Were we experiencing a historical moment comparable to the fall of the Berlin Wall and the freedom of Eastern Europe? The miracle of the peaceful revolution of 1989 appeared to be repeating itself in 2011.

But the Arab Spring did not last long, and the story has yet to find a happy end. On the contrary, the one death was followed by thousands. Tunisia continues to fight for a democratic future today and has made considerable progress, but the spring was followed by winter in several other Arab states: terror, violence, and civil war. The socioeconomic situation in most of these countries deteriorated further, and many a dictator was able to restore his regime after a transitional period full of uncertainty. In some cases, one unjust regime was simply replaced by another.

One problem is that even dictators watch TV and read newspapers. They do not wait for history to repeat itself, and for peaceful protests to rob them of power and status. By observing what happens in other countries, they learn which behavior yielded their idea of success and which ended in what they regard as failure. They adjust their own behavior accordingly.

The despots in the Arab world noticed what happened, first in Tunisia and shortly thereafter in Egypt. And just as the citizens were inspired by the courageous demonstrators and went out on the streets in droves, so, too, did their rulers copy the defense strategies of their peers.

Germans were not the only ones to associate the events in 2011 with the German revolution of 1989: Intellectuals in Tunis and Cairo wrote articles and op-eds referring to the peaceful demonstrators from Dresden, Leipzig, and other East German cities. And the authoritarian rulers, for their part, sought role models who had succeeded in securing their power.

And these despots found what they were looking for: After all, in 1989 there was not just a peaceful revolution in Germany; a few months earlier—in early June—there was the brutal suppression of student protests on Tiananmen Square in Beijing. In the GDR, fortunately, the tanks stayed in the barracks yards. This difference and its consequences provided a valuable lesson for regimes whose sole interest was preserving their power.

"WE WILL SHOW NO MERCY."

Egypt: The protests in the country on the Nile began on January 25, 2011, a Tuesday. Exactly one week later, on February 1, President Hosni Mubarak declared that he would not run for reelection in September. But the people continued to protest, demanding his resignation. Tahrir Square in Cairo was the focus of international press coverage. The authoritarian state attempted to break up the demonstrations. There were mass casualties, many of them fatal. In just one week, more than 800 people were killed. On Thursday, February 10, Mubarak declared he would remain in office but turn his official duties over to his deputy. This was again not enough for the people, so the protests continued. On the afternoon of the following day, Mubarak announced his resignation and handed the affairs of the state over to the Supreme Military Council.

What happened in Egypt repeated itself bit by bit in other Arab countries in similar ways: At the start, everything went quickly. The despot tried to defy the protest movement as long as possible and gave up his power just one piece at a time. In the end, he was defeated by the pressure from the streets. From this point on, everything happened in slow motion. The process of building a new democratic state was tough—and succeeded almost nowhere. In many places there were more steps backward than forward.

The conflict about a new order in Egypt escalated, leading to violence and finally to military rule, with the end result of consolidating the authoritarian system that the protesters actually wanted to overthrow. And thus, many an external observer came to the conclusion that, "The Arabs just can't deal with democracy," which is completely wrong. I will come back to this later.

Libya: In various parts of the country, February 17, 2011, was proclaimed the "Day of Rage." The protest rallies made clear that the people would be neither fobbed off by minor reforms nor deterred by state repression; aggressively and violently, they expressed their dissatisfaction.

The country's ruler, Muammar Qaddafi, did not stand by and watch these goings-on for long. It had not escaped his notice, of course, that his Tunisian neighbor Ben Ali had beat a hasty retreat four weeks prior, and that his Egyptian colleague Mubarak had stepped down one week earlier. When Algerian President Bouteflika announced on February 22 that he might relinquish his office "for health reasons" and then bowed to the pressure on the streets on February 23 to lift the state of emergency that had been in effect for the past 19 years, it was foreseeable how the situation might develop in Libya as well. That is why Qaddafi chose a more drastic way to retain his power.

With massive repression and savage violence, he cracked down on the demonstrators. Dozens were killed. But instead of the stabilization Qaddafi had hoped for, the opposite ensued. The crisis led to the collapse of the state apparatus and military establishment. High-ranking officers and diplomats joined the insurgents in order to protect themselves and their family clans, and then began organizing the resistance. As a result, former high-level representatives of the regime allied themselves with veteran members of the opposition and formed a national transitional council in Benghazi. They appealed to the international community to intervene and support them in their struggle against the dictator's repression.

Qaddafi raged. When he announced publicly on March 17, "We are coming—tonight ... and we will show no mercy," it was as if the incipient catastrophe could be followed on live television: preannounced genocide.

The global public reacted surprisingly quickly and with an unexpectedly broad consensus. With the abstentions of Russia, China, India, Brazil, and Germany, the UN Security Council passed a resolution that allowed the establishment of a no-fly zone in Libya. Great Britain, France, and the United States sent combat aircraft.

And then, yet another player entered the stage of the Libya conflict—the Arab League, in a rare show of unity.

The states of the Arab League cover an area about three times the size of the European Union and are populated by 350 million people, which amounts to around two-thirds of the population of Europe. In contrast to the EU, the Arab League is not a close community, but a loose association of interests. Founded in Cairo in 1945, it was initially little more than a reminiscence of the old Ottoman Empire, which collapsed in World War I. It aims not for the long-term integration of states and societies, but, on the contrary, for the long-term preservation of national sovereignty—and to arbitrate inner-Arab disputes.

Considering the noninterference rule and the much-exalted sovereignty of the member states, it was all the more astonishing that the Arab League was able to make a decision so quickly after civil war in Libya erupted, proclaiming a no-fly zone and mandating that its member states take military action against Qaddafi. Libya's membership was suspended, and later Syria's as well, on the grounds—unique in the history of the league—of human rights violations.

This could be interpreted as progress toward the league's opening up to liberal values and human rights. It is more probable, however, that the quick consensus on intervention in Libya was reached because most of the states of the Arab League had a score to settle with the Libyan ruler. Qaddafi had never missed an opportunity to make himself unpopular, especially with Saudi Arabia. For instance, he was suspected to have been involved in a plot to assassinate the Saudi Arabian crown prince in 2003, and showered King Abdullah with such verbal abuse during a public session at the Arab League summit in Doha in 2009 that his microphone had to be turned off.

Instead of basking in a glorious Arab Spring, which the people had dreamed of as a peaceful victory of a democratic civil society, Libya found itself at war.

SYRIA: SPRING BECOMES WINTER

In Syria, too, protests gained momentum over the course of summer 2011, and it appeared that nearly fifty years of single-party rule were coming to an end. Since 1963, the country had been ruled by the Ba'ath Party, a secular socialist party. Since an inner-party revolt in 1970, the party and the country had been controlled by Hafiz al-Assad, father of today's President Bashar al-Assad. The father wielded an iron fist. His methods for dealing with the Muslim Brotherhood were particularly brutal. When Bashar al-Assad succeeded his late father in 2000, many hoped for an opening of the strict regime.

In fact, there was a spring back then, the "Damascus Spring," which brought open political debates on issues like the cancellation of the state of emergency and the abolition of martial law, women's status in society, and relationships to Palestine and Israel. Demands included the release of political prisoners, the right to found parties and nongovernmental organizations (NGOs), and at some stage, the abolition of Article 8 of the Syrian constitution, which stipulates that the Ba'ath Party leads the state—and thus a demand for nothing less than the right to free elections.

After just a few months, however, Assad junior shifted back to the course of his father, arresting members of the opposition, prohibiting political salons, and sentencing activists to prison. I met him personally during this phase, when I accompanied the German chancellor to Damascus. Assad, it was pretty clear, had been walled in politically by the old men of the Ba'ath Party, who did not leave him alone with the German delegation for a second. No hope for reforms!

Nevertheless, the Damascus Spring lived on in the minds of many Syrians. When the Arab Spring broke out in 2011, the government responded to the first signs of protest with massive repression. The wave of protests began in the periphery of the country, reaching the large cities of Hama and Homs in the summer, and finally Damascus as well.

President Assad initially tried a carrot and stick approach, announcing a reform process parallel to the repressions. But the reforms were slow to materialize, the demonstrations grew, and the suppression of the protests by the military cost more and more human lives. Month for month, the situation in the country grew worse. The repression mobilized the opposition.

The conflict soon escalated: In April the Syrian government sent tanks against the demonstrators. In May, Syrian troops advanced into residential areas in Homs and other cities. In June the Syrian regime expanded its military operations. Government troops stormed the border city of Homs and prevented refugees from leaving the country. In July, ten thousand people assembled in Hama for the largest demonstration since the protests had begun. Overall, hundreds of thousands of demonstrators took to the streets in many parts of Syria. The subsequent decision by the Syrian cabinet to allow political parties other than the ruling Ba'ath Party was too little too late. In August, troops marched into Hama; there were more than one hundred fatalities. Protests in the port city of Latakia prompted attacks by warships, tanks, and ground troops.

Meanwhile, international pressure was growing. While NATO members, with a mandate from the UN Security Council, were advancing against Qaddafi in Libya, the international community initially reacted cautiously to the events in Syria. In April, EU Foreign Policy Representative Catherine Ashton condemned the violence in Syria, and U.S. Secretary of State Hillary Clinton demanded an end to the violence. At the UN, General Secretary Ban Ki-Moon and High Commissioner for Human Rights Navanethem Pillay also condemned the violence against demonstrators, while Turkey increased diplomatic pressure on Syria.

In May the United States imposed sanctions against Syria. The UN Security Council was split: Russian President Dmitry Medvedev rejected a condemnation of Syria by the United Nations. The EU passed an arms embargo and joined the United States in imposing sanctions against President Assad and other members of the political leadership. The Arab League condemned the violent crackdown against demonstrators, while the U.S. government, in consultation with the EU, explicitly demanded for the first time that President Assad step down. In September it looked as if the Assad era was going to end.

In the meantime, Syria's neighbors were vacillating between

accidental entanglement and intentional interference in the Syrian conflict. Saudi Arabia supported the rebels—and made no great secret of the fact, because Assad was a thorn in the side of the Saudis—as did Turkey. Qatar, which played a leading role in the international military operations in Libya, recognized that Syria offered a further opportunity to raise its international profile and step out of the shadow of Saudi Arabia. Accordingly, Qatar also financed the political opposition. The idea was to have an established government in exile and ready as soon as Assad finally stepped aside.

REGIME CHANGE: KNOWING WHAT COMES NEXT

The Western public vehemently sympathized with the Syrian rebels and wanted to support the people in their struggle for freedom and democracy. It was pretty obvious that such support also meant supplying weapons and ammunition.

This was in spite of the fact that previous wars and conflicts had made it clear that supporting rebels can backfire in the long run. The United States can tell us a thing or two about that.

Who could guarantee that the very opposition groups to be supported in their struggle against the regime would not join forces with the same Islamist fighters that were battling American allies in other contexts?

Assad complained about the intervention by Syria's neighbors and demanded that they respect the country's sovereignty. This argument made an impact in Russia. The Kremlin chief was displeased by President Obama's words, "Assad must go!" After all, this put a name to that elephant in the conference room of the UN Security Council, about which the Russians had already expressed their reservations when the issue of Libya and Qaddafi was on the table in 2011: forcing "regime change" meant overthrowing the autocrat.

In European capitals, too, and with particular enthusiasm in Germany, this single goal was stated time and again: Assad must

go. From today's perspective that was irresponsible politics, because there was not any actual strategy behind it: If Assad were
gone, what precisely was likely to happen? Did politicians in Berlin
or Brussels have a plan B? Of course not.

A blogger, the Yemeni human rights activist Tawakkol Karman,
had warned the world about this. She is the one who wrote the
warning sentence that everyone who demands regime change
should take to heart: "We must know what to do when it is over."[1] In
the early phase of the Arab Spring, the 31-year-old mother of three
children and member of Yemen's moderate Islamist Islah Party had
rallied hundreds of women to her side, becoming a main voice of
the opposition in her country. In 2012, I invited her to the Munich
Security Conference. The inspiring activist appealed straight to the
conscience of her listeners and gave one of the best speeches I ever
had the joy of attending as chairman of the conference.

On the day after the Tunisian despot Ben Ali was overthrown
in January 2011, Tawakkol Karman called for rallies in the Yemeni
capital Sana'a. She was arrested, locked up, and later released. Her
arrest triggered mass demonstrations. In October 2011 she was
awarded the Nobel Peace Prize as a representative of all protest
movements in the Arab world.

The warning not to overthrow a regime without having a convincing strategy for what comes after is true not only for Yemen,
which, by the way, has sunk into chaos like Libya and Syria. Throughout history the idea of regime change has rarely led to success. Just
having one less dictator does not make for a democratic summer!

After revolutions, societies have often required years or decades to stabilize, and only few revolutions have spawned democratic structures. The French Revolution was followed first by times
of brutal terror and then by Napoleon, who brought war to all of
Europe. The Russian Revolution in 1917 brought no democracy,
and nor did the Cuban Revolution in 1959 or the Iranian in 1979.
Authoritarian regimes disappeared in all of these places, but neither freedom nor democracy took their place.

And Germany has a laboratory on its own territory: After forty years of Soviet rule, millions of citizens of the GDR switched to a democratic system more or less overnight. Nearly thirty years later, however, scholars are discovering that even over this long period, it has not been possible for everyone to fully celebrate a sense of community—a requirement of no small importance for a functioning democracy.[2]

If this change in mentality and perception is a problem even in Germany, a highly developed political system, how can this possibly work in countries where identity and loyalty are generally functions of whichever religious or ethnic group to which a given citizen belongs? Most Arab countries do not yet have a tradition of democratic structures in the Western sense. Europe also needed centuries to develop parliamentary democracy and to accept the division of powers and an independent judiciary. It was a laborious process, which was interrupted over and over again by turmoil and wars. Democracy will not develop overnight, nor can it be imposed from the outside.

THE 2003 IRAQ WAR:
"OR ARE YOU A RACIST, ISCHINGER?"

Nevertheless, it is a popular idea that democracy can be exported like a new car model and that "scrapping" an old model will lead to a new political system modeled on the West. The idea is still cultivated and nourished by many—above all by the neoconservative intellectuals known as neocons. I met a number of these neocons when I became ambassador in Washington in 2001. Among them were Richard Perle and Paul Wolfowitz.

In the neocon view, there was a unique time in the 1990s when the Soviet Union had just disappeared as a world power and the United States experienced a special "unipolar moment." It looked as if the United States, because it no longer had any rivals in terms of military power, would be able to shape the world according to its preferences: eradicate conflicts, create peace, and spread capitalism and freedom. In short, a certain arrogance had inserted itself into American thinking.

It was from this arrogance that the idea to get rid of Saddam Hussein emerged. As described briefly in chapter 3, this plan was effectively implemented in 2003: On the grounds that chemical weapons had supposedly been detected, the United States attacked Iraq. The American war plan divided the EU into supporters (Great Britain, Poland) and critics (Germany, France). The transatlantic alliance was under severe strain.

The U.S. military was able to declare a quick success: Saddam was defeated in the air and on the ground in just a few weeks, especially due to the fact that his rule had already been weakened by UN sanctions and regional isolation.

But the dream of regime change soon vanished into thin air: The United States did not manage to secure Iraq and promote a sustainable process for rebuilding the country. Today, Iraq is still suffering under a strained security situation, in which terrorist militias wreak havoc, the Shiite majority demands the highest government offices, and tensions between the Kurdish regional government in the North and the central government in Baghdad are not fully under control.

In the midst of the transatlantic argument about intervention in Iraq, I had a discussion with U.S. national security advisor Condoleezza Rice. I told her it would be an illusion to believe that democracy would grow and flourish in Iraq as soon as Saddam was out of the way.

Rice responded indignantly, "But we taught you Germans, and the Japanese, how to build a democracy. Why wouldn't that work in Iraq?! Or are you a racist, Ischinger?"

In any case, the U.S. invasion of Iraq in 2003 did not have the effect envisioned by the neoconservative intellectuals in Washington. As it turned out, the Iraq plan was a veritable caricature of the United States overestimating its possibilities. Instead of moving toward democracy, Iraq descended into a civil war. This war claimed countless lives, tilled the soil from which the so-called Islamic State was able to emerge, and will continue to have lasting negative effects on U.S. foreign policy—perhaps similarly to the Vietnam War.

In retrospect, what happened is hardly surprising, because where do people find a sense of belonging? With whom do Iraqi Kurds or Shiites identify? With a state that oppressed them for decades? Saddam Hussein, a member of the Sunni minority, had ruled the land with an iron fist. Obviously, an incredible amount of rage had built up by 2003. And it is understandable that the various groups were not anxious to reconcile their differences. Similarly, it was to be expected that the Sunnis who had dominated the country were not about to simply relinquish their privileges. In short, it was foreseeable that trying to introduce a new and peaceful system in Iraq would be quite a challenge.

And incidentally, yes, introducing democracy in Germany after World War II did work. But in this case the United States and its Allies were willing to remain present for decades and assist in a very expensive, laborious process of rebuilding. And the historical preconditions were completely different. It makes a big difference whether the country in question has a long tradition of elections, self-government, and an independent judiciary, and thus a tried and true division of powers—as opposed to a country that is lacking all of this. So the idea that what had been achieved in Germany post-World War II in a relatively short period, namely reintroducing the rule of law and democracy, could also be achieved in Iraq was too simplistic.

The no from Berlin and Paris to the Iraq intervention in 2003 was thus justified, not only by the lack of legitimacy under international law but also because "no" turned out to be politically and historically correct. Nevertheless, it would be wrong to derive from this that a no to military interventions is *always* the right answer.

NO TO EVERY KIND OF VIOLENCE?

Various arguments are evoked over and over again whenever German participation in military interventions comes up. The first argument is pacifist and rejects every kind of force as wrong. Yet this often leads to a moral dilemma. After all, it is also possible to be guilty of inaction.

In the discussion about the Libya intervention, the French philosopher and writer André Glucksmann dismissed the question of just war outright: "No one . . . has the right to claim he is conducting a war that is right, or even just. There are only wars that are necessary, and wars that are not. In order to prevent the worst, one accepts the lesser evil."[3]

Even before he became Germany's president, in 2012 Joachim Gauck attempted to clarify that foreign policy is often a choice among several evils. "What measures would committed democrats then have to take so that everything would be 'all right' in Afghanistan?" he asked, then described the dilemma faced by politicians and diplomats alike: "Only in paradise is everything all right. But here where we live we have to deal with limited, faulty, even terrorist people and despotic systems. What is shaped where we live is nothing ultimate, not a paradise, but rather what is feasible and less bad."[4]

Military interventions are thus never simply just or good—but neither is avoiding them. Decisions for or against, like foreign policy decisions as a whole, are often a choice among several bad options. When politicians and diplomats manage to choose the least bad of these options—and implement it successfully—much has been accomplished. This may sound sobering, but it is the way things work.

POLITICAL REALITY IS NOT BLACK AND WHITE

Indeed, decisions are seldom simply either-or. As mentioned above, there are many intermediate levels between those who, when in doubt, would bring about democracy by force and those favoring realpolitik, who accept repression as the price of stability. The foreign policy reality is not black and white, but countless shades of gray.

The skepticism that a regime change forced by the West does not automatically produce democracy is justified, as is the critique that interventions are not morally justifiable when bombs are dropped without a plan and a commitment to rebuilding, financing, and providing for long-term political stability.

The debate must be fought in the gray areas, rather than confronting the dynamic upheavals surrounding us with artificial black and white—noble ideas versus egoistic interests. How much intervention makes sense, how much "sitting on the fence" is smart, and when does inaction also have political and moral consequences—these are the most difficult questions in foreign policy. They can be solved only by accepting that we often have to choose among several unsatisfactory options.

QADDAFI'S REPUTATION AND THE
LIFE OF THE WALLERT FAMILY

On the subject of the unsatisfactory, the Federal Republic of Germany was helped in a situation of extreme distress by Qaddafi, of all people. Here's what happened: On Easter Sunday, 2000, adherents of the Islamist terror organization Abu Sayyaf kidnapped twenty-two tourists and hotel staff on the Malaysian island of Sipadan off the eastern coast of Borneo, taking them to a camp in middle of the jungle on the Philippine island of Jolo. Among those kidnapped was the Wallert family from Göttingen, Germany—Renate, Werner, and their son, Marc. A rescue attempt by the Philippine

Army failed. At some stage, around three dozen journalists had taken up quarters in the hotels on the island and were reporting more or less live. This drama, with constant threats of violence and even death, lasted for weeks and then months. The images of the terrified mother were run by all TV stations. She was released after twelve weeks, but her husband and son remained in captivity.

The German government had grappled with the kidnappers for months. There had been demands for ransom, of course, but paying ransom was strictly forbidden, to prevent kidnapping from becoming a business model and endangering more tourists. We seemed to be at an impasse.

The consequences of failure in any way would have been terrible. Each passing day was a matter of life or death for the Wallert family. Any mistake could have cost them their lives.

Then the German government heard that the second son of the Libyan leader Qaddafi was well connected with the Philippine Muslims. He was also chairman of the Qaddafi International Foundation of Charitable Associations (GIFCA). It turned out that the foundation was willing to help and to take on the financial demands, so that Germany would not have to pay any ransom. In return, the Qaddafi regime had an interesting request: Libya's involvement in the Lockerbie bombing, an attack on a Pan American airplane that had taken place in 1988, meant that the country was isolated internationally. Tripoli hoped that a visit to Libya by the German chancellor might help to reestablish the international standing of the Libyan government. So we agreed to the visit. This is the way diplomacy works sometimes. The Wallerts were freed and the case was solved, without any ransom payment from Germany.

When the Libyans requested the promised visit by the chancellor a bit later, the German government pleaded scheduling difficulties and offered a visit by Foreign Minister Joschka Fischer instead. He did a stopover in Libya, but did not actually meet with Qaddafi personally. But we did try to fulfil our promise. Checkmark, task accomplished.

Was it wrong to accept this help? Was it wrong to, in a sense, shake Qaddafi's hand, as the price for liberating the Wallert family?

Let me point out one thing: If we categorically refuse to work with dictators and violators of human rights, then we will have to suspend relations with more than half of the world. This cannot really be really the answer, can it? This is why it would also be wrong to denounce Donald Trump's meetings with North Korea's Kim Jong-un. Diplomacy includes negotiating with aggressors if necessary, and accepting the political and moral risks that come with it.

GERMANY'S HISTORICAL GUILT AND THE PRINCIPLE OF NONINTERVENTION

The second German argument against intervention—the reference to Germany's historical guilt—was addressed by President Gauck in his 2014 speech in Munich. From German guilt, he criticized, we must not derive the "right to look the other way." Otherwise, he argued:

> Restraint can be taken too far if [we] start making special rules for [ourselves]. Furthermore, it should today be natural for Germany and its allies to not simply refuse to help others when human rights violations multiply and result in genocide, war crimes, ethnic cleansing or crimes against humanity. Not only do all Western democracies consider respect for human rights to be one of their defining features, it is also a cornerstone of any guarantee of security, of a peaceful and cooperative world order.[5]

In short, not everything can be excused by pointing to a difficult childhood. At some stage it is time to grow up and accept responsibility, even—and especially—for the more unpleasant tasks in life.

The third argument from intervention critics is presented over and over again by Putin, for instance: We are not allowed to interfere in the sovereignty of other states. We should respect all governments regardless.

Gauck offered a convincing response to this, too, back in 2011:

> I would take such reproaches very seriously if they came from the oppressed, from human rights activists in authoritarian states. But not when the ones who criticize our Western culture grant their own citizens only a fraction of the freedoms which are a matter of course in Western democracies. All the despots and dictators of this world are protecting is themselves and injustice, the Dark Ages against progress.[6]

The reference to state sovereignty and the principle of nonintervention is attractive for the Russians, of course—and for the Chinese, who are also fond of pleading this argument—because they do not want to be told how to treat their own citizens, be they dissidents or members of the opposition, Chechens or Uyghurs.

Above all, however, insisting on state sovereignty means reverting back to a worldview from earlier centuries. The Treaty of Westphalia in 1648 laid down the maxims of nonintervention into the sovereignty of states and the unrestricted right of every nation to control its internal affairs itself, and these have been nurtured ever since. This makes sense insofar as states are the central subjects of international law and their relations to each other must be regulated. But does that mean a state can really do anything within its borders—including slaughtering minorities? That can hardly be the answer in the twenty-first century!

This international debate was refueled around the turn of the millennium. Too many genocides, crimes against humanity, and war crimes had been committed, too many people murdered as, for instance, in Rwanda and in Bosnia. After long discussions, in 2005 the General Assembly of the United Nations, with an overwhelming majority, accepted that national sovereignty reaches its limits when rulers start massacring their people rather than protecting them. The "Responsibility to Protect," abbreviated R2P, was born.

THE RESPONSIBILITY TO PROTECT OTHERS

The idea behind R2P was this: Genocide, war crimes, crimes against humanity and ethnic cleansing are such serious violations of human rights that they require the international community to fulfil its Responsibility to Protect, especially when the states in question are not themselves willing or capable of saving their citizens from these crimes.

The international community attempted to apply this principle in Libya. UN Security Council resolution number 1973, which ultimately passed because Russia and China abstained from the vote, referred to this global Responsibility to Protect. The resolution, within a certain framework, allowed an armed intervention in Libya. Its purpose, as André Glucksmann summarized it in spring 2011, was "only to protect, by no means to invade the country, set up a democracy, or build a nation."[7]

Anne-Marie Slaughter, a professor at Princeton and one of the best-known experts on international law, who headed up the planning staff at the U.S. Department of State under Hillary Clinton, gave a speech advocating for intervention in Libya in April 2011. She emphasized precisely this request for protection and the criteria according to which it should be realized from the perspective of the United States:

> The U.S. was only ready to vote for resolution 1973 when certain criteria had been met: An appeal for help from the Libyan opposition, and an endorsement of a no-fly zone by the Arab League. Every step toward consensus is an indirect indication of the scale of the atrocities. Only when the brutal actions of a government stir the conscience of the region is the regional organization willing to take action. If it demands that the UN take measures against one of its members, the United Nations will probably consent. Yet if the regional organization behaves passively, the nations outside of the region will act against the regional consensus only if the actual or threatened crimes permanently shake the conscience of the world.[8]

Germany also abstained on resolution 1973 at the time. I disagreed with this decision then and still do now. In contrast to the Iraq War in 2003, the point here was to effect an intervention on the basis of international law, not a "coalition of the willing." The German abstention sent the wrong foreign policy signal. As a country with a history of genocide, Germany could have—indeed, should have—shown what it means to take on responsibility, especially since the action was backed by a multilateral mandate.

It would have been more elegant to approve the resolution and then submit what is called an "explanation of vote" to clarify that approval did not mean Germany was considering participating with its own military—and that it urged it was imperative to plan for the period after a possible end of the Qaddafi regime. Such an explanation would surely have been acceptable to everyone.

In hindsight, we know the project of applying R2P in Libya failed because the Western powers were not content to prevent a genocide, but instead insisted on bringing about regime change without having any corresponding plans for afterward. The question of "What happens after the end of the dictatorship?" was relegated to the bottom of the agenda.

Since 2011, Libya has been embroiled in a state of virtual civil war. No end is in sight, not even in the seventh year after Qaddafi's fall. Was the intervention worth the price, the bulk of which is being paid by the Libyan population? The dictator is gone, but now there is chaos. Terrible. But it does not justify, as many believe, Germany's abstention at the time.

THE LESSON FROM LIBYA: THREE
CRITERIA FOR INTERVENTION

We can learn from Libya to identify three criteria that should guide us in making reasonable decisions for or against military interventions:

1. Every deployment of military power, every intervention, should be backed by legal and political legitimation, a mandate. Generally, authorization should come from the UN Security Council. However, exceptions are conceivable, namely cases in which veto powers such as China or Russia prevent a mandate for intervention, even though it appears unavoidable for political and moral reasons. The Kosovo intervention in 1999 is one dramatic example of such a case; others are the airstrikes against Syria, because of its use of chemical weapons, by the Americans in 2017 and by the Americans, British, and French in spring 2018.

2. The countries of the region concerned should actively support such an intervention or, ideally, ask for it directly. That is the way it was in the Libyan case. For the first time in its history, the Arab League concerned itself with abuses by one of its own members. Without a certain degree of support from the region, successful intervention is virtually impossible, as experience has shown.

3. Perhaps the most important criterion is, we must define a clear objective to be achieved with the intervention, and it must be clear whether this objective can be achieved with the means at our disposal. The goals-means relation must be positive. An intervention based on the responsibility to protect may arise from the noblest of motives, but if we lack a clear objective, the means necessary to achieve it, and the willingness to support, potentially, a highly complex rebuilding process after intervention, then intervention is hardly justifiable. A military mission that ends in chaos is a disservice to the population, the people who were actually to be protected. Simply put, action should be taken only when it is clear that the objective can realistically be achieved. In the case of Libya this would have meant that the West, parallel to deploying military power, would have committed to helping Libya build a sustainable political future.

We must be humble and only tackle what we are ready, if needed, to make a sacrifice for. And we must not overestimate our chances. Otherwise responsibility can turn into negligence all too easily.

But how can wars be ended? What can we do within the scope of our limited capacity? These questions are particularly glaring in the case of Syria.

SIX

MAKING PEACE
WITHOUT WEAPONS?

Foreign Policy and Military Power

EVERY WAR HAS COME TO AN END SO FAR

The war in Syria involves numerous countries and interests, entan-
gled in a Gordian knot. This is not a completely novel phenomenon.
Yet all wars have come to an end at some stage, even the Thirty
Years' War. Its conclusion, settled by the Westphalian peace treaty
of 1648, is considered by some to be the first precursor of the European Union. This is why experts are fond of looking back at the
five-year peace negotiations in seventeenth-century Münster and
Osnabrück to find inspiration for solving today's geopolitical crises
and religious conflicts.

Yet we do not have to look so far back in history, just twenty
years, to recall the last brutal war on European soil, albeit beyond
the borders of the EU: The Balkan wars of the 1990s seemed almost
as tricky as the Syrian War does today. It is worth taking a closer
look at these crises, as they offer important lessons for foreign
policy decisions of today and tomorrow.

How relevant is the use of military force in conflicts like the one in the Balkans? Are military means perhaps even a necessary element of effective peace policy? One thing is undisputed: Even if things in the Balkans are still far from perfect today, and we continue to be very concerned about the region, the application of military force did put an end to years of raging, horrifying Yugoslav Wars.

Let us take things one step at a time: What happened?

At the beginning of the 1990s, a country with a population of 23 million fell apart within a very short time.

From its creation at the end of World War I, Yugoslavia was a multiethnic state in which members of various ethnicities and religions lived: More than a third of the population were Serbs, a fifth were Croats, and the rest were Bosniaks, Slovenes, Macedonians, Albanians and Turks, along with a small minority of Montenegrins and Hungarian-speaking Magyars. A third of Yugoslavia was Catholic (predominantly the Slovenes and Croats), a second third was Christian Orthodox (mostly Serbs and Montenegrins). And around 11 percent of the population were Muslims (mostly Bosniaks, but also Albanians and Turks), as well as a small group of German and Hungarian Protestants and a minority of Jews.

Josip Broz Tito, who ruled Yugoslavia from 1945 until his death in 1980, succeeded in reconciling the various demands of these many subgroups through a federal system. The idea was that over time a Yugoslav national identity would emerge, which was encouraged by targeted educational measures but also through massive repression. For instance, Croats, Serbs, Bosniaks, and Slovenes were explicitly forbidden from referring to their ethnic identity.

That worked for decades, but after Tito's death in 1980, the individual regions' ambitions for autonomy became stronger—in part, due to the pressures of an economic recession. They based their appeals on the "right to national self-determination."

The president of the Serbian republic within Yugoslavia, Slobodan Milošević, contributed in no small part to these sentiments by striving for the restoration of "Greater Serbia" (on the territory of then-Yugoslavia), but the different ethnic groups were not willing to be integrated again. Yugoslavia disintegrated, and ethnic and religious differences increasingly broke through.

BALKAN WARS: THE MASSACRE OF SREBRENICA

In 1991, the regional independence movements within Yugoslavia led to military conflicts that lasted nearly an entire decade and brought with them considerable brutality. One war followed another: It began with the ten-day war in Slovenia (1991), followed by the Croatian War of Independence (1991–1995), the Bosnian War (1992–1995), the Kosovo War (1999), and finally the Albanian insurgency in Macedonia (2001).

The Bosnian War was the most barbaric. Even today we do not know the definite number of victims, because each of the three warring parties cites different statistics, and even today, mass graves are still being opened to identify bodies. Nevertheless, we can say with some degree of certainty that overall, more than 130,000 died in the Balkan wars—around 100,000 of them in the Bosnian War. Around 14,000 persons are still listed as missing. Added to these casualties are 2 million refugees and displaced persons. Much of what happened back then resembled the more recent images from Aleppo, Eastern Ghouta, Homs, or Palmyra in Syria. Just a few short years ago, Syria was one of the most beautiful and popular travel destinations in the Middle East. But in many places, marvels of Syrian culture have been transformed into a desert of rubble. Similarly, during the period of wars in the Balkans, whole regions were depopulated and contaminated with land mines, cities and villages ravaged, and mosques, churches, libraries, and other cultural monuments irreparably destroyed.

The Balkan crisis began with the two northernmost provinces, Slovenia and Croatia, declaring their independence from

Yugoslavia after corresponding referenda won in each republic. Bosnia-Herzegovina followed their example and held its own independence referendum in March 1992, in which 99 percent voted for sovereignty; however, only around two-thirds of the population had participated. Immediately, ethnic tensions rose. A majority of the Serbs living in the region were in favor of remaining in Yugoslavia, while Bosniaks (Bosnian Muslims) and Croats from the Western region of Herzegovina preferred a state of their own.

The "losers" and boycotters of the referendum were recruited by the army of Bosnian Serbs to take action against the "rebels" in order to preserve what they viewed to be the legitimate confederation. They were supported by the Yugoslav (predominantly Serbian) Army.

The separatists themselves consisted of two distinct groups: On the one hand there were the Bosnian Croats, who received support from neighboring Croatia. On the other, there were the Bosniaks, who were the least prepared for a war and had the least materiel at their disposal, and who initially received support only from Muslim countries and later from the United States as well.

In the rest of Europe, at first many did not realize (or did not want to realize?) what was going on at their doorstep. It was not until large numbers of refugees—yet another parallel to our present—began streaming into the EU countries that attention turned to the region.

Today everyone shivers when they hear the name Srebrenica. This town was the site of the most serious war crime in Europe since the end of World War II: In 1995 more than 8,000 Bosniaks, boys and men between 13 and 76 years of age, were murdered by Serbs and buried in mass graves. It took years until the International Criminal Tribunal for the former Yugoslavia in The Hague had enough evidence to prosecute the perpetrators for genocide.

Before the war, Srebrenica had a population of 36,000. But at the time of the massacre, it harbored an additional 40,000 Muslims who had fled there from various towns in eastern Bosnia. They

were surrounded by Bosnian Serb troops and bombarded with gre-
nades. With the siege holding for ten months, people were already
dying of starvation by the time UN aid convoys finally began to
arrive in March 1993.

The reports from the city were so horrible that in April 1993
the UN, for the first time in its history, set up a protected zone: 750
UN "Blue Helmet" peacekeepers (first Canadian and later Dutch
soldiers) had the mission to disarm the Muslims who were defending the city and to deter the Serbian attackers. They failed on both
counts. Believing that the peacekeepers would protect them, the
Muslims handed over their heavy weaponry. And on July 6, 1995,
the Serbs began an attack on the enclave, taking Srebrenica within
five days—without any intervention by the UN. Panic broke out
in the city. Before the eyes of the poorly armed Dutch peacekeeping soldiers, who abandoned their observation posts and barracks
to the Serbs, any Bosnian men who seemed fit for military service
were singled out. Women and children were loaded into buses and
shipped out to nowhere, left to make their way on foot into safe territory controlled by the Bosnian government. They would never see
their fathers, husbands, brothers, and sons again—for, when peace
was proclaimed in November 1995, four months after the massacre,
not a single Muslim was left alive in Srebrenica.

"ETHNIC CLEANSING": UGLIEST WORD OF THE YEAR

The reports from the war zone finally roused the world community. Something had to be done. Subsequently, various measures
followed—most of them ineffective, and some that experts deemed
more likely to stoke the conflict, such as the UN arms embargo,
which various parties circumvented by smuggling weapons. In
Germany the original hope was that diplomatic recognition of Slovenia, Croatia, and Bosnia would serve to end the conflict, but this
gesture was shrugged off by the Serbs. Russia supported the Serb

government, similar to the way it supports Assad today, by arguing that external interference in a sovereign state was prohibited.

Thus the hate raged on while the global public watched more or less helplessly. There were ceasefire efforts; however, the Serbian side immediately used these opportunities to continue its crimes against the Bosnian population. The term *ethnic cleansing* caught on to describe the dirty work of murder and expulsion. In Germany, a panel of linguists proclaimed the term (*ethnische Säuberungen*) the "ugliest word of the year 1992."

Back in early January 1993, the "Vance-Owen plan" had been proposed. It was a peace plan named after its authors, the two chairmen of the International Conference on the Former Yugoslavia in Geneva: former U.S. Secretary of State Cyrus Vance and former British Foreign Minister David Owen. Their idea was to preserve Bosnia-Herzegovina as an independent state but create within it autonomous provinces, which would consist, to the greatest possible extent, of regions divided by ethnicities. However, it was not possible to convince the parties to the conflict to accept this solution; the Serbs, in particular, preferred to keep shooting. The situation appeared hopeless.

In July 1995, with the massacre of Srebrenica, it gradually became clear: The idea that the costs of inaction were lower than the potential costs of intervention was a miscalculation.

In that summer of 1995, the European public finally understood that it had just experienced one of the greatest defeats of the postwar period—namely, that tens of thousands of people in Bosnia had lost their lives and the EU had not been able to prevent it. A dramatic defeat, a devastating realization.

All of a sudden, things started moving quickly: Washington became more actively involved. There was talk of military operations. A few weeks after the massacre, NATO actually initiated an intervention led by the United States, which forced the Serbians to the negotiating table.

The goal of these negotiations was to get the parties involved in the conflict to commit to the formula proposed in the Vance-Owen plan: 51 percent of the territory for the Bosniak-Croatian federation, and 49 percent for the Bosnian Serbs. However, in spring 1995 the Serbs controlled some 55 percent of the country. Therefore, they saw no incentive to enter into negotiations, as it was clear that they would have to give ground.

What I learned back then was that sometimes there are only bad options in foreign policy: bad, really bad, and dreadfully bad. It means choosing between a rock and a hard place, especially when the stakes are the most terrible events of global politics: war and genocide. What happens when good words are not enough? What if every kind of diplomacy reaches its limits? What is to be done then—and with what means?

Fortunately, many crises can be solved without military action. But in some crises, unfortunately, military means have to be deployed in order to reach a solution. Yet military means are not necessarily combat operations or warfare. Talking about military means does entail deploying troops, but it does not necessarily require that shots are fired. Sometimes it is enough to threaten military means in order to defuse a conflict. And often, the mere fact that a state has military force at its disposal is a reason for avoiding a conflict with this state or its allies.

"Make peace without weapons" is a not a bad motto. Yet the "culture of restraint," which Germany cultivated for decades, must not lead to the demonization of military means in general. Sometimes the threat of these means is needed to generate the willingness of warring parties to communicate. This is neither cynicism nor militarism, nor "old power politics," but rather a lever that is sometimes, unfortunately, necessary in an otherwise nonnegotiable conflict. As bitter as this realization may be, soldiers, airplanes and warships are sometimes essential elements of international peace efforts.

"The instruments of war do have a role to play in preserving the peace. And yet this truth must coexist with another—that no matter how justified, war promises human tragedy," as Barack Obama phrased it in his Nobel Prize speech in December 2009. He continued: "War itself is never glorious, and we must never trumpet it as such. So, part of our challenge is reconciling these two seemingly irreconcilable truths—that war is sometimes necessary, and war at some level is an expression of human folly."

In the Balkan wars, ultimately it was only military means that helped find the way to peace: In early summer 1995 the Croatian armed forces, supported by the U.S.-executed "Operation Storm," soon won so many enlistees that they were able to take back enough territory to reestablish the 51:49 ratio within just a few weeks, according to American radar satellite images.

Then, from late August until mid-September, NATO executed the "Deliberate Force" mission on behalf of the UN: airstrikes on Bosnian Serb targets. The mission sent a clear message to the Bosnian Serbs and their President Milošević: We will not permit you to continue this way. And the message was received.

Along with Operation Storm, this mission created the prerequisites for the archenemies to meet at the negotiating table. Now the Serbs were willing to talk, because they had to fear that continuing hostilities might lose them even more territory. Otherwise the civil war would presumably have continued for years and cost many more lives.

This was a formative experience for me and one of the reasons why I believe it is unreasonable to exclude military options from the outset. A real chance for peace negotiations often only exists when all participants are convinced that they cannot successfully continue to pursue their goals on the battlefield. If even one party believes they can improve their negotiating position through military means, they will not negotiate seriously. Precisely this is the case in Syria today: Assad will keep his army fighting as long as a military victory is within reach. But more on that later.

THE CONFERENCE IN DAYTON:
AT THE TABLE WITH YOUR ENEMY

The peace negotiations took place in November 1995 in strict seclusion, far away from the Bosnian battlefields, at Wright-Patterson Air Force Base in Dayton, Ohio. The idea was simply to force all participants together until they made peace. The head of the U.S. delegation was Richard Holbrooke, who had previously been ambassador to Germany. I headed up the German delegation myself.

The delegates stayed in modest officers' quarters on the air base. In the evenings, we met for drinks at the bar. The American hosts launched the conference with a dinner at the National Museum of the U.S. Air Force. Between fighter aircraft and a mock-up of the Nagasaki atomic bomb, Serbia's President Milošević listened as U.S. generals offered a comprehensive description of one of the bombers that was on exhibit. Not a word was spoken about the fact that such American airplanes had been used against the Serbian Army just a few weeks before.

The negotiations began officially on the morning of November 1, 1995. It was the first time in years that Serbian President Slobodan Milošević, Croatian President Franjo Tuđman and Bosnian Präsident Alija Izetbegović had been in the same room.

The atmosphere was tense. That changed when the chairman, U.S. Secretary of State Warren Christopher, asked the three men to shake hands with each other. It was apparent that this cost quite an effort, especially for the Bosnian leader, while outwardly at least, the Serb played it cool. The wounds were deep.

Then Christopher opened the meeting: "Today we have an urgent and important task. We are here to give Bosnia and Herzegovina a chance to be a country in peace, and not a battlefield, a place where people can sleep in their homes, go to work, and worship in their churches, mosques and synagogues, without any fear of violence or death."[1]

There is a photo of this opening ceremony.[2] It was ten people sitting around one large round table. To the right of Secretary Christopher was Richard Holbrooke, and continuing counterclockwise were Carl Bildt of Sweden as representative of the EU, Pauline Neville-Jones from Great Britain, and Jacques Blot from France; the three main protagonists, Milošević, Tuđman, and Izetbegović; and then myself representing Germany and to my right, the Vice Foreign Minister of Russia, Igor Ivanov. Behind us sat our staff, a total of around forty people.

The negotiation process was unusual in the history of modern diplomacy, indeed, even unique. The pressure to succeed was tremendous, the consequences of the four-year war were terrible, and the risk of failure was clearly greater than the chance of success. There were simply far too many unknown variables at play.

Outside the gates of the conference site, a few dozen people displayed banners with messages that some of us mediators could certainly relate to: "Milošević belongs in The Hague, not in Dayton!" meaning in The Hague, facing the UN War Crimes Tribunal.

On top of all this, there was a policy dispute in the United States: Congress and the White House were at odds about Bill Clinton's plan to secure a peace settlement by sending 20,000 American soldiers. During the preparations for the conference, Secretary of State Christopher had made no secret of what he considered a precondition for deploying American troops to rebuild Bosnia, stating in an interview, "You can't seriously expect NATO forces to be deployed as long as those individuals are still in power."[3]

One of "those individuals" was actually sitting with us at the negotiating table. Milošević also represented the Bosnian Serbs because their leaders, Radovan Karadžić and Ratko Mladić, were already indicted by the international tribunal for war crimes.

Milošević was focused, above all, on damage control and on getting sanctions against Serbia lifted as soon as possible. Everything else was subordinated to this goal. He could talk himself into a rage on the topic of sanctions.

He was an important negotiating partner in Dayton. As my del-

Dayton Accords, opening ceremony, November 1, 1995

egation wrote in one of its diplomatic missives to Bonn at the time, "He enjoys his new role: Within just a few hours yesterday, the Americans Lake, Perry, Joulwan and Christopher came to speak with him." The visitors mentioned were U.S. National Security Advisor Tony Lake, U.S. Secretary of Defense William Perry, NATO's supreme allied commander in Europe, General George Joulwan, and U.S. Secretary of State Christopher.

For Milošević, the United States was the most important power at the table, of course, but he courted and flattered us Germans, too: For him, he claimed, Germany was the most important country—besides the United States—in the contact group; in times of peace, relations with Germany would be among the most important. "Mr. Ischinger," he said to me right at the start, "you are the second most important man in Dayton." Presumably he said the same to the leaders of the other delegations as well. But when I brought up the topic of Kosovo, he exploded, insisting that was an internal affair of his country.

NEGOTIATION MARATHON— A TWENTY-ONE-DAY WAR OF NERVES

"Let's sit down and get to work. And let's not forget our promise to succeed here," Warren Christopher urged the three presidents.[4] Dayton was to go down in history as a synonym for peace.

What ensued was a diplomatic tour de force. We had hoped to reach an agreement quickly. It was to take twenty-one days.

The contact group, which had taken over crisis management in the Balkans a year and a half before and was now leading the negotiations, comprised five states: the United States, France, Great Britain, Russia, and Germany. The EU was also included. The fact that the Federal Republic was allowed to play a part on this stage had prompted critique from countries like Italy and Spain, especially since Germany had not provided any peacekeeping troops for the mission in the former Yugoslavia. However, Germany had held the presidency of the EU Council in the second half of 1994, and during this time the German government had also occupied the EU seat in the contact group. At the end of the EU presidential term, we remained in the contact group at the request of the other four members.

Over a period of months, the contact group had prepared drafts for an agreement. Now we used diplomatic tricks to help get these implemented. Among the strategies were "proximity talks," a model in which the embittered enemies who were not willing to negotiate with each other directly held sessions in different chambers rather than meet in the same room. The members of the contact group then resorted to "shuttle diplomacy," carrying the information and arguments from one group to the other, back and forth.

I was assisted by a small, outstanding team. My deputy at the time, Michael Steiner, was subsequently appointed the EU's deputy high representative in Sarajevo and thus became one of those responsible for the implementation of the Dayton Accords.

Yet the decisive power in Dayton was, of course, the United States. In the critical final week, with failure looming, the U.S. secretary of state—seventy years old at the time—took control of the negotiations. He proved to be a subtle, tireless, and insightful mediator, who, even after several sleepless nights, always appeared in a flawlessly ironed suit and remained exquisitely polite.

How difficult the process was, and how close we were to failure, can be traced in detail by studying the fifty-three telegrams that my delegation sent from Dayton to Bonn during the peace negotiations. In a departure from the rule that files and dispatches from the German diplomatic service may not be published until thirty years later, the foreign office made these telegrams public as early as August 1998.[5] We wanted to add a German perspective to the all too American-centric narrative provided by Richard Holbrooke.

The warring parties had been divided up between different buildings around a parking lot. We negotiators walked back and forth as Bosnians, Serbians, and Croats pored over the map of the future Bosnian state. They fought tooth and nail over every square kilometer.

On November 7 we still believed that the talks would last for no more than ten days, but anxiety was mounting.

On November 10 we were able to report an encouraging success. Hans Koschnick, the man commissioned by the EU to coordinate the rebuilding, administration, and infrastructure of the Bosnian city of Mostar, which had been destroyed in the war, had met with the two mayors of the divided city to negotiate steps necessary to secure peace. So on this day, in the presence of the U.S. secretary of state who flew in at short notice, an agreement on the "Interim Statute of the City of Mostar" was signed. Ten days after the Dayton conference had started, this seemingly small success was a glimmer of hope on the horizon and boosted our momentum for the difficult negotiations.

On November 13 we were already talking about the "endgame." Everything would be done in a few days, it seemed.

But instead we were stuck in a situation in which nobody wanted to stand up from the negotiating table, because everyone believed that if they stayed a little longer, they might be able to strike a slightly better deal.

When after a good two weeks the warring parties still did not look ready to sign an agreement, despite various ultimatums, the U.S. negotiators demonstratively set their suitcases out in front of their quarters, signaling that they were ready to break off the negotiations. Holbrooke was already editing an address in which he would announce their failure. We Europeans recommended continuing on; I had instructions from Bonn to leave Dayton only when none of the warring parties was willing to negotiate any longer.

The tension rose on November 19. Secretary of State Warren Christopher had returned in the meantime, and negotiated day and night with impressive physical stamina. His personal role in the success of the negotiations deserves the highest recognition. Everyone was physically and mentally on the edge of exhaustion, from nocturnal negotiations, growing frustration about the reluctant negotiation partners, the close physical proximity of all participants, the apparent impossibility of reconciliation, and the political pressure to succeed that each of us felt from his given capital. In the critical final phase on the weekend, the German chancellor and foreign minister became involved from afar, urging both the Croats and the Muslims to sign: "People, grasp the straw!"[6]

None of us—neither the members of the contact group, nor the Bosnians, Croats, or Serbs— could have lasted much longer. But it was precisely this physical exhaustion that contributed to the negotiations' success.

The negotiation drama on the air base had now endured for three weeks. But it was Alija Izetbegović, of all people, the 70-year-old president of Bosnia-Herzegovina, who could not bring himself to sign the agreement. I knew that he thought the world of Helmut Kohl, so together with the chancellor's team in Bonn, I thought about how we could induce the Bosnian's consent. Then we had an idea, and I ran with it.

It was around midnight when I attempted to persuade the Bosnian president in a private conversation. I said that Helmut Kohl had given me a Bismarck quote to recite to him: "History with its great events . . . does not roll on like a railway train at an even speed. No, it advances by fits and starts, but with irresistible force when it does."[7]

Chancellor Kohl, I explained, had steadied himself in the difficult hours of German reunification with this quote by Bismarck: "One must just be permanently on the look-out and, when one sees God striding through history, leap in and catch hold of his coattail and be dragged along as far as may be."[8]

When Izetbegović actually did relent the next morning, he thanked me and asked me to give his best to the chancellor: "His words helped me through the night."

I'm not sure whether his greetings ever reached Kohl. But the bottom line was that on November 21, 1995, the deal was done. The peace treaty was initialed in Dayton. On December 14, 1995, it was signed in Paris. That is what is written in the history books.

However, it was far from settled.

DAYTON ERRORS: A LEAP THAT FELL SHORT

Of course, everyone was relieved that the signatures were inked, and everyone was looking forward to a break. But in this, diplomacy is like soccer: After the game is before the game.

There was plenty to process, follow up, and prepare. The formal signing of the peace treaty in Paris was approaching, plus conferences in London, Moscow, and Bonn. In the very next month, December 1995, disarmament negotiations between Serbs and Croats in Bosnia were to begin in Bonn, with high-ranking experts of the international contact group and representatives of the OSCE. Now trust-building measures were the order of the day. But there was not really any chance of calm setting in.

On top of this came the fact that the Dayton Accords were not exactly a masterpiece of international diplomacy, but merely what had been negotiable under the most difficult conditions in this terrible situation. It was anything but a perfect document. Some of it had been thrown together hastily and would need to be corrected and expanded over the course of the coming weeks, months, and years.

In 2018, I was starkly reminded of this when facing the decision by U.S. President Trump to withdraw from the nuclear deal with Iran. The agreement had been negotiated over ten years, and of course some Western concerns were accommodated insufficiently or not at all. It was—as in Dayton—what was feasible, but at the same time not what was desirable. But in both cases, what was feasible was still much better than no agreement at all.

But back to Dayton. All across Europe, politicians rejoiced. The peace agreement not only meant the liberation of the oppressed population in Bosnia from war and violence, but also was of the greatest importance for enduring security and stability in all of Europe.

Leaders pointed to the Charter of Paris, which had been signed in November 1990, and in which the member states of the CSCE had agreed to an enduring and just peace framework with respect for human rights and democracy, economic freedom, social justice, and equal security for all states. With the Dayton Accords, they announced, Europe had come a great deal closer to this goal of an enduring and just framework for peace.

And this was true. Thousands of refugees began to return to their home countries. Public institutions began working again: schools, kindergartens, trash pickup—aspects of everyday life. But the task of reestablishing peace was not completed and, unfortunately, has not been completed to this day.

Among the unfinished business was the Kosovo conflict. In February 1998 this led to the renewed eruption of war in the region, which, again, cost the lives of thousands and compelled transatlantic partners once again to intervene militarily.

Yet the topic of Kosovo had been excluded in Dayton, in order to avoid overloading the negotiations with Milošević. The subject of Kosovo was simply not negotiable in 1995.

The biggest mistake we made, though, was something else. We made the agreement, dispatched a high representative, and sent peacekeeping troops. But in the period thereafter, we abandoned Bosnia and Herzegovina politically. Not many heads of state or prime ministers found it necessary to visit Sarajevo and to personally engage the various ethnic group leaders.

SUSTAINABLE PEACE AS A GENERATIONAL TASK

The effects of the Yugoslav Wars can be felt even today in all seven states on the territory of former Yugoslavia—Serbia, Slovenia, Croatia, Bosnia-Herzegovina, Macedonia, Montenegro, and Kosovo—in all areas of life.

The genocides and war crimes of the years 1992 to 1995 left deep scars. As early as May 1993, the United Nations had established an ad-hoc court based in The Hague to prosecute the war crimes. The International Criminal Tribunal for the former Yugoslavia is where General Ratko Mladić was indicted in absentia as a war criminal—for genocide, crimes against humanity, and numerous war crimes. While we were still negotiating in Dayton, namely on November 17, 1995, the indictment was extended to a new count: the attack on Srebrenica. Sixteen years later, in May 2011, Mladic was arrested in Serbia and handed over to The Hague. The media rejoiced about the capture of the "butcher of the Balkans." In November 2017 he was sentenced to life in prison.

The former adversaries have still not fully reconciled. To guarantee a voice for every minority group in Bosnia, a state with fewer than 4 million inhabitants, there are a total of 130 ministers, who often work against each other. Although the military intervention and the peace negotiations in Bosnia and Herzegovina were a great success story, the efforts to turn Bosnia into a viable, functioning state were considerably less effective.

In retrospect it is clear to me that the Bosnian warring parties should have been brought back to the negotiating table every couple of years in order to facilitate and provide support for the country's development: Dayton II, Dayton III, and so on. The transatlantic partners, we Europeans in particular, made the mistake of looking away and turning attention to other problems.

Today, of course, more than twenty years later, we can say with some degree of pride that the shooting stopped and never started again! But the country has not really been healed. We are dealing with a patient who may well end up back in intensive care at any time.

Unfortunately, we often stop a bit short. We tend to say, "Now we have achieved something, so we're done now." But mastering crises like these requires diligence and a long-term commitment. After World War II the occupying powers could have said, "Now that the warmonger Germany is occupied, we will take away everything that is militarily relevant and leave the people to their own devices. Let them figure out what to do with their screwed-up history!" Wisely, they did not choose this path. Instead, they chose a long-term commitment.

Chancellor Angela Merkel deserves praise for initiating a series of Balkan conferences starting in Berlin in 2014 and meeting annually in different cities to continue what has been christened the "Berlin Process." This process shows how the EU states are turning their attention back to the Western Balkans, because, after all, it also concerns the prospects for EU membership. Slovenia already joined the EU in 2004, and Croatia in 2013. Accession negotiations are underway with Montenegro and Serbia. Bosnia and Herzegovina as well as Kosovo have applied for membership, as have Albania and North Macedonia. Unfortunately for these two—Albania and North Macedonia—the EU was not sufficiently united in 2019 to offer accession talks, which was a big mistake, in my view.

The Western Balkans are still—please excuse the tired trope—a minefield! And even though I am tiring of this argument, the last thing on Germany's wish list right now is another war in Europe— and the next 500,000 refugees seeking asylum in Western Europe.

It is in our interest that sustainable peace and calm be finally restored to Southeastern Europe. And that is possible only with a long-term effort. Sustainable peace is a generational task and— unfortunately—has a high price. And if the EU cannot even create peace and stability in its own backyard—Southeastern Europe— how can it act with credibility in other areas of the international arena?

THE EU'S GREAT FAILURE IN SYRIA

I am relating all of this as background for the current war in Syria. It is hard to find an area in which the EU failed as obviously as it did in the Syrian conflict.

Syria is different from Bosnia, of course, but Syria abuts the same Mediterranean on which the EU states Greece, Italy, and Spain border. On land, Syria shares a border with Turkey, a member of NATO and candidate for accession to the EU.

Syria is thus our neighbor. This became clear to all when people started fleeing from the escalating conflict: They did not seek asylum in Moscow, nor in front of the White House in Washington. They tried to get into the EU. For Syrians, this is their neighborhood, the safe haven nearby.

It would have been Europe's historical and political mission to lead an international effort, to push tirelessly for a ceasefire and a peace agreement, and to get involved in a regional peace framework or security architecture. We have not managed to do any of this. We have not even made a serious effort.

Never before have we Europeans been so strongly affected by a conflict beyond our own continent, and never have we done so little to resolve it.[9] With the war in Syria and the subsequent strengthening of the Islamic State, terrorism has returned to our continent. This became apparent in the attacks in Paris, Brussels, Nice, and Berlin. The war has resulted in the flight of hundreds of thousands of people and created a stress test for the internal cohesion of the EU. As a reaction to the influx of refugees, an "axis of fear" emerged across many EU states, made up of populist and illiberal forces that stoked resentment and preached a new nationalism. This axis of fear has perverted the political climate nearly everywhere, weakening the democratic consensus and thus endangering the future of the European project. What is at stake here is the very idea of Europe.

From the outset of the Syrian tragedy, the EU member states

did not translate their words into action. While European governments, including Germany's, called for Assad's ouster, the strategic resolve to pursue this goal was entirely lacking. Opponents
of getting involved in Syria had warned beforehand that doing so
would contribute to radicalizing the belligerent parties and to the
regionalization of the conflict. In Berlin there was talk of a "conflagration" that could be sparked by Western intervention. This had
the effect of suppressing any serious discussion about no-fly zones
or other options to protect the Syrian population. "Anything, as
long as we don't have to act ourselves" appeared to be the motto of
convenience.

The conflagration—entirely without intervention by the West
and certainly also because of our inaction—has long since become
reality. We see a disintegrating country in the heart of the most
unstable region on the globe. Syria became the deployment zone
for jihadists from all over the world. The regional proxy war being
waged in the country, with its religious and ethnic components,
has effects far beyond the Syrian borders. It threatens to have severe
consequences—for the future of all neighboring countries and for
the already dangerous struggle for supremacy in the Middle East.

Guilt and responsibility can also come from inaction. And inaction can actually turn out to be more costly than action.

Considering the many thousands who have died, I share the
desperation and frustration of everyone who feels reminded of
what happened in the Balkans in the 1990s. In Bosnia, too, we did
too little for too long. It is clear that the challenge of rebuilding is
growing with every month that this butchery and murdering continues in Syria. And I do not just mean the material rebuilding.
Patching streets, erecting buildings, repairing bridges—all of this
is relatively easy. But rebuilding in the sense of reconciliation—
creating a coexistence of different religious, ethnic, and other kinds
of groups that are still mowing each other down today, and rebuilding a peaceful community—is, as we know from Yugoslavia, a generational task. And the longer the war lasts, the more difficult it

becomes. Therefore, the argument that we must allow the war in Syria to bleed itself out is not only morally irresponsible, but also completely wrong politically.

Admittedly, a negotiated peace like the one we attained for Bosnia in Dayton in November 1995 is not yet in sight for Syria. And the situation in Syria is considerably more complicated than it ever was in Bosnia.

Ultimately, the conclusion of the Dayton Accords, which finally ended the war in Bosnia in 1995, was possible only because Milošević and the Bosnian Serbs suddenly developed an interest in a negotiated solution, because the situation on the ground had changed in such a way that they no longer saw any chance of a military victory.

This is the decisive point for Syria as well: From a position of strength, to which Assad has apparently been restored by now, his regime will not be willing to make meaningful concessions. As long as Assad is convinced that his situation will improve over the further course of the conflict, or that he may even be able to win the war, he will continue to fight. If the international community wants to achieve a political solution, it would need to change this calculus.

But even excluding the option of military intervention, we must still ask, what are we willing to contribute to the postwar order, whatever it may be? Without stationing an international peace-keeping force in Syria, no political, negotiated resolution will last for long, just as it did not last in the Balkans. Do we want to merely comment on this process from our armchairs as we watch it unfold on TV? And if not, are we strategically prepared in Europe (and in NATO) for regional wars in the Middle East?

SANCTIONS INSTEAD OF SOLDIERS

Let me be clear: Between intervention and inaction there are, of course, countless political and diplomatic steps and instruments that can be—and should be—used. Expanding the number of options is a core objective of all diplomacy. Excluding anything from the outset, be it sanctions or the application of military force, generally only helps one's opponent.

Sanctions are one of the instruments between military force and hard diplomatic language. They are supposed to exert political pressure and thus induce compliance. But is a ruler who bombards his own people with chemical weapons impressed by economic sanctions? According to the latest estimates, 500,000 people have lost their lives since the beginning of the war in Syria. The sanctions that we Europeans and the United States imposed were not able to prevent that.

Supported by other states, the United States and the EU pulled out all the stops in the sanctions repertoire: arms embargo, ban of exports to Syria, travel bans, freezing the assets and economic resources of Assad and high officials, locking out the accounts and assets of the entire Syrian government, prohibiting every kind of business transaction, an oil import ban, and so on.

Sure, with these sanctions we condemned the violence of the Syrian regime, and moreover, we supported the Syrian population with humanitarian aid. Yet none of this has stopped the brutal violence.

Incidentally, on her first visit to Washington as German chancellor in January 2006, Angela Merkel gave President George W. Bush a little lesson on the subject of sanctions. There was a great deal of suspense about how the first conversation between Merkel and Bush would go. They spoke English. After ten minutes, Bush addressed a topic that was under intensive discussion at the time because of the Iran nuclear negotiations: "What do you think about sanctions against Iran?"

Merkel responded:

Well, here's the thing about sanctions. One has to know who they will affect. Where I grew up in the former GDR, we were happy when the Americans imposed sanctions against the Soviet Union, because we were not exactly fans of the Soviet regime. However, this caused great indignation when, as a consequence, there were suddenly no more bananas in the local stores in my hometown, Templin. Then we asked: So what have *we* done wrong now? Why are *we* being punished?

George W. Bush understood: "Smart sanctions."

"Smart sanctions" or "targeted sanctions" are the catchphrases, meaning do not punish the civilian population indiscriminately, but impose sanctions directed at individuals, companies, and organizations whose behavior one wants to influence.

The UN Security Council had imposed smart sanctions for the first time in 1999, against the Taliban in Afghanistan. From 2002 on, targeted sanctions were imposed against Osama bin Laden, and smart sanctions have been used as diplomatic instruments repeatedly ever since. They were also used on Syria but, unfortunately, without any major effect to date.

One reason for this is the conflict in Syria is no longer a plain old civil war. What is raging there has long since become a geostrategic conflict, a war that has become enmeshed with the Kurdish separatists' war of independence in Syria, Iraq, and Turkey; a war that reflects a political power struggle between Saudi Arabia and Iran, and between Russia and the United States; a war that created the unrest and chaos that fostered the development of a brutal Islamist terror group that calls itself the Islamic State, conquered a territory, and brazenly proclaimed a caliphate in 2014; a war which only tangentially still resembles the efforts of the people to cast off a brutal dictator.

The goal propagated in the West, namely to precipitate the fall of Assad, has clearly not succeeded. On the contrary, the Syrian regime has actually cemented its structural dominance. For a long time, the Syrian opposition hoped for more extensive support from the West, the Gulf states, and Saudi Arabia, which could have helped it compensate for the material superiority of the Assad regime, which is supplied by Moscow and Tehran, and receives massive support from Hezbollah, the Iran-backed Lebanese militia group. To put it bluntly, the only ones who received hardly any foreign support at all were the leaders of the more moderate Syrian opposition. That these forces would melt away was thus to be expected—and herein lies a tragedy of our failure. The situation in the Balkans was similar, where the Bosnian government in Sarajevo struggled so long, to no avail, for the lifting of the arms embargo, which clearly played into the hands of Belgrade and the Bosnian Serbs.

"ASSAD MUST GO!" IS NOT A POLICY

We all remember how in 2011 the calls grew louder, not only in the United States but from European politicians as well: Bashar al-Assad must go. Such calls went down well, because it was already common knowledge that Assad led a repressive regime, applied persecution methods reminiscent of genocide, and did not even shrink from using chemical weapons against his own citizens.

In this first phase, President Obama drew a red line in the sand, threatening that if Assad were to cross the line by using chemical weapons, Obama would retaliate.

What did the German political strategy look like at the time? In this country it was announced just as pompously that Assad had to go, but we were relieved when we were spared the call to participate in an intervention. There was relief when the British parliament rejected intervention and Obama responded by halting his "red line" plans. And because all of this allowed Germany to save face, it was a relief when the Russians offered to make sure that Assad destroyed all of his chemical weapons. In short, in Germany we were delighted not to have to take action.

The European Union displayed incompetence as well. In all

these years, it has not made a single credible attempt to initiate peace negotiations. We Europeans stared at the conflict and waited until the usual suspects initiated peace negotiations in Geneva.

The most appropriate comment on this came from my friend, the veteran Algerian diplomat Lakhdar Brahimi: Simply calling for Assad to step down does not a strategy make. Brahimi had been appointed United Nations special representative for Syria in 2012, after Kofi Annan resigned his mandate for lack of progress. A year and a half later Brahimi, too, resigned from the post, because he no longer saw any prospect of success for the Geneva peace talks. Assad refused to participate. The opposition was present at the negotiating table but had lost practically any influence now that the war was so dominated by the Islamists.

In Doha in May 2013, I had the opportunity to talk with the prime minister of Qatar. His frustration about (to put it bluntly) the ineptitude of the international community as a whole and about (diplomatically put) the low visibility of the European Union was immense.

By now the idea is becoming more and more popular, in European capitals and Washington alike, that the regime led by Assad may be the lesser evil. Assad is tolerated in concert with Russia against the Islamic State, at least for the moment. Thus political failure becomes moral failure as well.

No one will be coming out of this war with their hands clean.

COUNTLESS CONFERENCES, TO NO AVAIL

Now of course, after more than seven years of war, people are pointing out the complexity of the conflict and that it will take a long time until all conflict parties can think rationally again and be at all able to negotiate for peace. This is true. But to be fair, we have not seriously tried to negotiate, not even directly after the conflict broke out.

The first step for the European Union would have been to proactively and resolutely seek dialogue with the Russian Federation, the United States, and the Arab countries. In short, the EU should have established a contact group with the United States, Russia, and others, as it did back in the Bosnian War. A contact group is an informal group of states that work together in promoting and leading negotiations to resolve conflicts.

Now some of those who have followed the Syria conflict over the years may protest: But such meetings took place nonstop!

And it is true that there were conferences, meetings, and gatherings of all kinds. In February 2012, for instance, after Russia and China had vetoed a UN Security Council resolution condemning the violence in Syria, French President Nicolas Sarkozy started an initiative outside the UN Security Council. Under the name "Friends of Syria Group," it pursued the goal of seeking a resolution for the Syria conflict.

The first time this group met, U.S. Secretary of State Hillary Clinton proposed that Turkey, Qatar, Saudi Arabia, and Jordan could set up a no-fly zone to protect Syrian civilians. The Syrian National Council made a prominent appearance at the meeting and submitted a seven-point list of demands, including, among others, that the Syrian regime end its violence and step down. If this demand was not met, the council continued, the Friends of Syria Group should not prevent any countries from supporting the Syrian opposition through such means as military advice, training, and arms shipments. But this was clearly not a peace plan and therefore not terribly constructive, either.

Subsequent meetings with up to 114 participants and just as many conflicting interests were similarly unsuccessful. For instance, there was one meeting in Riyadh, Saudi Arabia, for which thirty-four Syrian opposition groups and individuals had formed a negotiating committee. There was a conference of conferences, in order to bring as many actors together as possible. There were meetings of various foreign ministers, for the first time also including Iran.

In 2017 Kazakhstan, at the urging of Russia, Turkey, and Iran, extended an invitation to engage in peace talks in Astana, now called Nur-Sultan. This time the rebels did not participate. By this time, they had fallen apart into so many splinter groups that the question had been who to actually invite in the first place. In any case, twelve Syrian rebel groups had already announced in early January 2017 that they would be freezing all conversations about plans for peace negotiations because of ceasefire violations. But even the three participants in Astana were not pulling in the same direction. Their attempts came too late, because it was no longer possible to reconcile the competing interests of all participants.

THE CONTACT GROUP PRINCIPLE

All of these formats had little to do with the principle of a contact group. A contact group is characterized by the fact that all members feel committed to pursuing a common objective and refrain from separate activities that run counter to this objective. That is why one key to the success of a contact group is that there is agreement from the outset: From now on we will all do only what has been mutually agreed.

For Syria a contact group could have been set up early, in 2011 or 2012, with members from Turkey, Iran, Russia, the United States, and the EU, perhaps along with Saudi Arabia. But even the group that successfully negotiated the nuclear deal with Iran could have served as a model: the permanent members of the UN Security Council plus Germany, perhaps along with Saudi Arabia, Iran, and Turkey.

But such a contact group does not just appear out of thin air. Foreign policy peace processes, when they are successful, have many parents. However, the truth is that the process must be led by one person—someone who all parties believe will honestly listen to and integrate the others.

In the case of the Balkan wars in the 1990s, it was Richard Holbrooke who was able to integrate Russia, the EU, Germany, France, the United Kingdom, and NATO so that everyone could say afterward, "We participated actively in the successful deal." In reality it was the American delegation that called the plays and also scored the points. Most of the others sat on the bench but were allowed to bask in the glory of the trophy.

Holbrooke's determination, occasionally bordering on brutality, his endurance, his diplomatic brilliance in negotiations, and his legendary political instinct made it possible, after a 21-day negotiation marathon in Dayton in November 1995, to lay the foundation for peace in Bosnia and Herzegovina. Henry Kissinger fondly described the bulldozer Holbrooke thus: "When Richard wants something from you, it's best to say yes right away. If you say no, you'll eventually get to yes, but the journey will be very painful."

That is the truth behind the headlines: We need personalities who can lead and manage these things. That requires leadership skills.

In this way we were successful in Bosnia and later in Kosovo, too. And this is how the negotiations with Iran over the nuclear deal were conducted, where the EU played the coordinating role, but success was achieved only when Secretary of State John Kerry brought to bear the entire weight of the United States.

A contact group requires that there must not be too many members, and they have to be the right ones. One of the reasons why such a contact group was not formed for Syria was that the United States did not want to sit at a table with Iran as long as they were still fighting about the nuclear deal. And, to be fair, it would have been very, very difficult to bring Iran and Saudi Arabia together to the same table. But would it have been completely impossible? Well, we never even tried.

In any case it would have been sensible for the EU to prove its serious commitment to the matter by at least appointing a very high-ranking representative as a special envoy for the Syria crisis—

for instance, someone of the caliber of a former French president, a former British prime minister, or a former German chancellor—someone who could have negotiated at eye level.

Syria thus remains a stain on the history of EU foreign policy, a stain of incompetence. Part of that failure is our specifically German inability to threaten the use of military force. We prefer to leave that to others, but to no good end.

SEVEN

THE UNITED NATIONS

Who Provides for Global Order?

WORLD PEACE IN A GRAY ZONE

On April 7, 2018, there was a suspected poison gas attack on the Syrian city of Duma in Eastern Ghouta. At least 42 people were killed and more than 500 treated in hospitals. One week later, the United States, France, and Great Britain reacted with air strikes on three targets that the U.S. Department of Defense believed to be associated with the Syrian chemical weapons program. The air strikes, U.S. President Donald Trump declared, constituted retaliation for a chemical weapons attack against the Syrian population, launched by the Syrian government under Bashar al-Assad: "We are prepared to sustain this response until the Syrian regime stops its use of prohibited chemical agents."[1]

America under Trump had already flown an attack around a year before. That one targeted the Syrian air base Shayrat, also in response to a poison gas attack with dozens of casualties for which UN experts held Assad responsible.

Again, Syria criticized this most recent attack by the United States, France, and Great Britain as a clear violation of the prohibition of the use of force under international law, which expressly forbids the members of the UN from threatening or exerting violence against each other, and allows exceptions only in the case of self-defense or with authorization by the UN Security Council. The regime demanded that the international community condemn this aggression. Russia, too, condemned the Western intervention, demanding an emergency meeting of the UN Security Council, at which the "aggressive actions of the U.S. and its allies" were to be discussed.

The German government, in contrast, backed the Western attacks, and NATO endorsed them as well. The events in Duma had demanded a "collective" response from the international community, declared NATO General Secretary Jens Stoltenberg. The United States also declared that its actions were justified, although the UN Security Council had not given any authorization for the attacks.

So, which is it? Were the airstrikes a war of aggression and a violation of international law? Or were they legitimate and an appropriate reaction to the deeds of a "monster," as Trump put it?

The truth probably lies somewhere in between. In short, these actions took place in one of those famous "gray zones." It is not really allowed, but it is not actually prohibited either.

For nonlawyers who would like jurisprudence to be clear and consistent, such explanations may seem bewildering. But international law is full of gray zones that have to be navigated anew over and over again. In an article in the *Frankfurter Allgemeine Zeitung* of November 9, 2017, Claus Kreß, an international law professor in Cologne, offered this explanation of these gray zones that can be summarized as follows:

> While at the end of World War II every act of aggression was still roundly condemned for violating the supreme commandment of international law to safeguard state sovereignty, over the course of the

decades a new guiding principle emerged: The protection of human rights under international law. As a result, genocide was declared the "crime of all crimes," the prevention and termination of which was also the responsibility (to protect) of the international community. Human rights—first and foremost, the right to life—were thus defined as at least as worthy of protection as (only) state sovereignty had been up to that time. So "humanitarian interventions"—and thus interventions into the self-determination of states—suddenly became possible, even "if these—as in the case of Kosovo in 1999— [were] conducted without authorization by the UN Security Council." After all, how can the protection of sovereignty claim priority "when an entire civilian population becomes the victim of the brutal use of force by its own government"? Anyone who wants to put a stop to the brutal, cruel actions of dictators and instigators of civil war must be able to fulfill his "responsibility to protect," even if an official UN mandate is lacking. What is also clear: Today the International Criminal Court would hardly prosecute anyone for conducting an emergency humanitarian intervention without a UN mandate.[2]

Yet, how these two ideas—the right to protect and the principle of sovereignty—can be reconciled with each other remains an unresolved question. And it can be answered only case by case, so that it is always a political decision.

Many in Germany do not want to take on this decision and the political responsibility it entails. Whenever world peace is concerned, all eyes turn to New York—more specifically to the United Nations, whose core mission is international peacekeeping. Germans think of it as a kind of world police, meant to take on all conflicts; accordingly, they have left the field of conflict resolution up to the UN. Just as they call "110" in case of an emergency, Germans make a mental call to the UN Security Council in any geopolitically tricky situation. Yet in so doing, they often overestimate the possibilities of the United Nations.

Created by the "Declaration of the United Nations" in 1942 at the initiative of the United States, Great Britain, the Soviet Union, and China, and immediately joined by 22 more countries, today the

United Nations incorporates 193 member states, or nearly all countries in the world. They are all bound to the UN Charter, which took effect on October 24, 1945, and defines how wars and violent conflicts between states are to be prevented or ended.

This sounds like world government, but in reality it is far from it. Instead, the Charter of the United Nations is a treaty under international law, which obligates all signatories to resolve conflicts peacefully. It can work only if all of the member states trust that every other one will follow the rules, and that someone will intervene if they do not. But the question is, who decides whether to take action, and how?

The UN Security Council was designed as the central and most powerful body of the UN. It has five permanent members, China, France, Great Britain, Russia, and the United States, as well as ten nonpermanent members, each of which is elected for terms of two years. In June 2018, Germany was elected to the Security Council for another two years, beginning its term as a nonpermanent member on January 1, 2019. The members consult and decide about everything they regard as a threat to international peace and security. According to Section 7 of the UN Charter, decisions of the Security Council are binding under international law: the Security Council is the only body that can make decisions that apply globally and that are therefore binding even for nonmembers.

A distinctive feature of this body is that each one of the five permanent members of the Security Council can block any resolution with a veto. This has substantial (even paralyzing) consequences: During the Cold War, the Soviet Union and the United States obstructed the Security Council for decades by reciprocally exercising their veto rights. But this has continued even after the end of the Cold War—for example, over Kosovo in 1998-1999, over Ukraine since 2014, and over Syria since 2011.

Moreover, as the United Nations does not have its own police or army, member states must decide whether to volunteer their soldiers and weapons as incidents arise globally—mostly for "peacekeeping" but sometimes also for coercive measures against individual states.

Therefore, this body Germans are so fond of idealizing as the global police is restricted in its capacity to make decisions and to act, for multiple reasons. Once that has been understood, the expectations placed on the UN can be measured out more accurately: It is seldom possible for the UN to truly resolve or even prevent conflicts. Usually, the best that can be expected is to increase the chances for a conflict to be ended peacefully—or at least more peacefully than in a world without the UN rulebook.

YET, MANY SUCCESSES

In practice, the missions authorized by the Security Council have not been without success. When this book went to press, a total of seventy-one peace missions had been authorized, which were or are active in nearly all parts of the world—from A as in Afghanistan to Y as in Yemen. Among these, fourteen UN missions are still in progress; the oldest date back to 1948 (Israel, Palestine) and 1949 (India, Pakistan), the most recent ones began in 2014 (Central African Republic) and 2017 (Haiti). There have been over 2,400 resolutions—on the accession of new countries, the situation in crisis regions, hijackings, aid missions, land mine action plans, or preventing terrorists from acquiring weapons.

By setting up the criminal tribunals for the former Yugoslavia (1993) and Rwanda (1994), the Security Council has further ensured that genocide, crimes against humanity, and war crimes can be recorded and prosecuted. In 2002 this culminated in the creation of the International Criminal Court in The Hague—albeit against the resistance of the United States, China, India, and other states that did not want to relinquish sovereignty in even this one important point.

In the 1998 Rome Statute, the founding document of the International Criminal Court, the EU states closed ranks to support this new institution. Its objective is to punish the most serious international crimes, including genocide, through an independent international court.

The United Nations has thus continued to develop its instruments over the decades since its founding, including pure peacekeeping, or the dispatching of peace troops to monitor compliance with a peace treaty; peace enforcement, when peacekeeping soldiers help to enforce a peace agreement; and post-conflict peacebuilding, or the rebuilding of sustainable structures after hostilities have ceased.

The security policy topics to which the UN dedicates its efforts are no longer limited to wars and violent conflicts, either, but range from feeding the growing world population (the focus of the UN World Food Programme) to the protection of children (by the relief organization the United Nations Children's Fund, or UNICEF), all the way to the management of refugee crises (in the framework of the refugee agency United Nations High Commissioner for Refugees, or UNHCR)—that is, "peace operations" of every conceivable kind.

At the same time, the weakness of the United Nations is a constant subject of criticism, of which there are four central points.

FIRST CRITICISM: ABUSE OF THE VETO

The first issue with the United Nations is the already mentioned veto power enjoyed by the permanent members of the Security Council. As of April 2018, the most vetoes had been cast by Russia (or the Soviet Union, respectively) with 112, followed by the United States (80), Great Britain (29), France (16), and China (11).[3] Some vetoes were directed against new members joining the UN. China, for instance, opposed Bangladesh's membership in 1972; the country joined nevertheless, but not until 1974. Other vetoes, however, were used to directly block peacebuilding measures: In 1999 the extension of a peacekeeping mandate in Macedonia was blocked; China had vetoed the extension to punish Macedonia for establishing relations with Taiwan.[4]

Often the mere threat of a veto is sufficient to keep some conflicts from ever making it onto the Security Council's agenda, because one of the five great powers holds a protective hand over the offender. The United States does this frequently for Israel, the Russians for Serbia, Belarus, and the Arab countries, the Chinese for Zimbabwe, Myanmar (Burma), Pakistan, and others.

Through the permanent blockades caused by vetoes in the Security Council, individual states or groups of states have felt compelled to intervene in global conflicts without an explicit mandate from the Security Council—as in the case of the 1999 NATO airstrikes to protect Kosovo, in which Germany also participated.

That was a difficult decision, and one in which I—as then state secretary at the German Foreign Office—was directly involved at the time. Foreign Minister Joschka Fischer and especially his party, the Greens, faced a crucial test. Did the party of the peace movement, just a few days after joining its first governing coalition, dare to break a taboo, abandon its pacifistic ideals, and become a "war party"? Or would it adhere to its fundamental convictions and watch as Slobodan Milošević massacred part of his own population for a second time?

There had been a whole string of UN resolutions on Kosovo, but no explicit authorization for the use of military force to prevent the Serbian attacks and massacres. Authorization was not possible because it was opposed by the Russian Federation, which held a protective hand over the Serbs and threatened, once again, to use its veto.

So if Germany—for the first time in postwar history—were to actively participate in a military operation, this would not even be sanctioned by an official UN mandate? How terrible! Yet the decision was finally made: The goal of preventing a humanitarian disaster was considered so important and serious that nobody wanted to be guilty of inaction with such fatal consequences. And we Germans did not make the decision alone, but together with our European and transatlantic partners.

It was a success in the history of the EU that we managed to take this decision together in 1999, even if it was facilitated by the fact that all NATO members—and thus also the United States, Canada, Norway, and the entire EU—believed it imperative to protect the population of Kosovo. For this we had to enter a gray zone of legality. Of course, in Moscow this was taken to be a military and legal violation—just as the airstrikes against the Syrian dictator Assad would be almost twenty years later.

In the case of Kosovo, bombing began on March 24, 1999. The U.S. military had predicted that Milošević would raise the white flag after a few days. But at the end of March there was no sign of surrender. After several weeks, the generals posed the question, "We bombed all relevant targets. Whom or what else can we still bomb?" So the same targets were hit once again. The war lasted seventy-eight days instead of five.

This massive miscalculation of military effectiveness gave us plenty to think about. I still believe that the decision to use military force to deter Milošević was correct nevertheless. The fighting did not actually end until June 10, 1999, with UN Resolution 1244, which was then passed with the support of Russia. This resolution tasked NATO with ensuring public order and peacekeeping with the Kosovo Force (KFOR), in which Germany was also involved— and still is, incidentally. With that, peace finally came to Kosovo. There has been no more shooting, but the political problem is still not resolved.

In 2008, Kosovo declared independence, which has been recognized by more than 110 of the 193 UN member states so far, among them the United States and the majority of the EU states. About eighty countries do not recognize Kosovo's independence, including the veto powers Russia and China as well as the EU states Greece, Cyprus, Spain, Romania, and Slovakia. There are a variety of reasons. Officially, the UN principles of nonintervention and territorial integrity—according to which, the international recognition of Kosovo was a violation of Serbian sovereignty under international law—are often cited. Yet this official justification often conceals other, specifically national concerns. For instance, if the Kosovars are allowed to detach from Serbia, can the Catalonians leave Spain? Madrid's worry about setting a precedent became stronger in spring 2018, and such worries are certainly understandable. Unfortunately, the questions about how far the right to self-determination extends, to whom it extends, and to what extent every state may insist that its territorial integrity be respected are not really clearly and conclusively answered in international law.

The continuing dispute does not make things any easier for the small country of Kosovo. Nevertheless, there are huge differences between pre-2008 and today: Kosovo may not yet be a member of the United Nations, but one can cross the border from Kosovo into Serbia and back; business is being done; children are going to school; and there is once again a university in Pristina, of which I am even the proud recipient of an honorary doctorate.

Of course, the fact that people in Serbia still like to consider Kosovo a part of Serbia called the Autonomous Province of Kosovo and Metohija complicates the development of a more harmonious coexistence between Belgrade and Pristina.

But has German history not had its own share of similar sentiments? In the postwar era, many Germans had a hard time accepting that the historically German territories of Pomerania and Silesia were lost. In the Potsdam Agreement of 1945, the victors of World War II had placed the regions west of the rivers Oder and Neisse under provisional Polish, or rather Soviet, administration. In 1950, East Germany recognized the Oder-Neisse line as the German-Polish state border, while West Germany did not sign off on this "factually inviolable" eastern border until the Treaty of Warsaw of 1970—albeit with a caveat in case of changes in the framework of a future peace settlement.

Shortly before reunification, there were still worries that a unified Germany could lay claim to these former territories. Not until the "Two Plus Four Agreement" on October 3, 1990, was today's border between Germany and Poland finally enshrined in the German-Polish Border Treaty.

This was certainly the right decision, painful as it was for some. In 1960, recognition of this border was not possible politically, but it was by 1990. Therefore we can hope that the Serbs, too, may someday be capable of doing what they could not in 2008: coming to terms with an independent Kosovo. And sometimes it helps to exclude particularly contentious issues: In 2007, as the Kosovo negotiator for the EU, I proposed dealing with the relationship between Serbia and Kosovo according to the German model of the 1970s, namely normalization without formal recognition: Simply exclude from the negotiations what cannot be resolved at the time, but achieve what can be accomplished at the time. Perhaps all will eventually work out in the end. Time helps. Agreements under international law do not happen overnight.

Another, second war—albeit on a different occasion and under completely different circumstances—happened without an explicit mandate from the UN Security Council: the U.S. intervention in Iraq in 2003, suggesting that the superpower United States was elevating itself above the United Nations and intervening in international conflicts at will. This impression is not entirely correct: The United States never once argued that it did not need the legitimation of the UN; instead, it cited legal precedents set in previous UN resolutions on Iraq and interpreted these as at least an indirect authorization for intervention.

SECOND CRITICISM: UNJUST COMPOSITION OF THE SECURITY COUNCIL

A second flaw of the United Nations is its composition: The UN was founded as a general assembly of all states, large and small. The whole world is gathered there. In keeping with the adage "Too many cooks spoil the broth," some believe that this is the greatest difficulty when trying to establish a global organization with the capacity to make decisions and take action. Yet the greatest difficulty is not in the universality of the UN itself, but in the composition of its most important body: the UN Security Council.

This composition is based on the context in which the United Nations was created: It reflects the balance of power in the immediate postwar era. The United States, the Soviet Union (now Russia), China, Great Britain, and France, as the victorious powers of World War II, are the permanent members of the Security Council, and each has the veto power.

The five permanent members of the Security Council, known as the P5, consider themselves to be in control of the situation in the world. The consequences of this attitude are regularly felt by the ten nonpermanent members, who are even sometimes disparagingly called "tourists" in the council.

The current power structures at the beginning of the twenty-first century are not accurately reflected in the Security Council. Important states with large populations or global political importance, like India, Brazil, and even Japan, are not represented. Reform is thus well overdue. The ones who do not regard reform as particularly urgent are, of course, the five veto powers.

Their veto is not the only reason the P5 are able to dominate the Security Council. The mere fact of their constant presence makes it easy for these five states to determine the body's agenda.

Therefore a debate about the need to fundamentally reform the UN Security Council has been underway for years. The question of who should be a permanent member and who cannot is discussed passionately. A permanent seat on the UN Security Council—especially when it comes with the right to veto—grants a privileged status. Any country that wants to be a great power is not happy to have its status reduced to that of a tourist or a mere spectator.

Since the 1990s, Germany has made repeated attempts to become a permanent member itself. In July 2005 the countries known as the G4—Japan, India, Brazil, and Germany—submitted a reform plan that proposed a permanent seat for each of these states. In summary, they argue that Germany and Japan are the main donor countries to the United Nations after the United States; India is an emerging nation of billions of people; and Brazil is the largest economy on the South American continent. The unsurprising result? The African Union rejected this proposal because it did not include a single country in Africa—a continent whose population will soon reach three billion. As a result, the required two-thirds majority in the UN General Assembly was not reached.

Discussions about reform and enlargement have gone on for many years. It is like tilting at windmills, because those who are already represented do not want to cede their seat or see their influence reduced in a larger body. And those who want to get in cannot agree either. For instance, who would represent Africa on the Security Council? Nigeria, Egypt, or South Africa? It is a difficult question.

And Germany's hope of joining the Security Council as a permanent member? In my opinion there is no chance. During my term as ambassador in Washington, I was occasionally instructed to approach the White House and lobby for this request. One day I explained to National Security Advisor Condoleezza Rice why it was essential for Germany to join the UN Security Council. Rice responded, "That is nothing really new. I would like to explain the United States's position."

And then she wrote a few numbers on a sheet of paper: "The situation today: China = 1 seat. U.S. = 1 seat. Russian Federation = 1 seat. Europe = 2 seats (UK + France)."

She drew a large circle around the numbers and started a new list next to it: "You Germans now want to push through the following: U.S. . . . . , Russia . . . , China . . . , still one seat each. Added to this: Brazil, Japan and India, also one seat each. And Europe . . . 3 seats?"

She turned to me: "Europe, whose two seats are actually one too many already, should then have three? How should I explain that to the American senators whose approval we need? That is absolutely futile. In reality Europe should actually have only one seat—that would be fairer!"

At which point I proposed to change the subject. In other words, since our British and French friends already occupy two seats, it is unrealistic to believe that Germany will get an additional seat.

Since Paris and London are not going to make way for us, we have to concentrate on more realistic objectives. My proposal would be for the German government to continue lobbying intensively for the reform and expansion of the Security Council, which is indisputably overdue. The strongest argument must be that half of humanity is not represented: India, Africa, South America. Germany should therefore, above all, explicitly call for the increased legitimacy of the Security Council, that is, better representation of all regions of the world. Then Germany should make itself available for permanent membership if this is expressly desired by all other states. And as a consequence of further European integration, Germany should push strongly for a permanent seat on the Security Council for the EU. This will certainly take some time. But it would be a splendid goal, which the Germans could represent sensibly and honorably. Chancellor Merkel's suggestion in June 2018 to "Europeanize" the nonpermanent seats of EU members is a step in the right direction. Germany can actively set a good example starting in 2019-2020 by fully coordinating its positions in the Security Council with its fellow EU members.

THIRD CRITICISM: A TOOTHLESS TIGER WITH A MONOPOLY ON THE USE OF FORCE

The third weakness of the United Nations is that it lacks armed forces of its own—and thus has to rely on the goodwill of its member states.

The Germans are particularly fond of pointing to the UN's

monopoly on the use of force—the abovementioned principle, anchored in the UN Charter, that force can be used only for self-defense or when it is authorized by the UN Security Council. In theory, this is both good and right. If the UN Charter were to be implemented in its entirety, then the UN's claim to a monopoly on the use of force certainly could be applied more comprehensively. According to the original plan, the United Nations would establish its own military forces, over which the Security Council would then dispose; the charter speaks of a Military Committee. The original idea was that the Security Council would be able to prevent or end crises and wars using its own military. However, this part of the UN Charter was never implemented. Unfortunately, without its own armed forces, the UN's monopoly on the use of force remains mostly wishful thinking.

Enforcing the UN's monopoly on the use of force is further hampered by the change in the nature of wars, discussed in the opening chapter, and by the resulting conflicts about the basis for military intervention under international law. Indeed, the many new conflicts arising within states continually raise the question of whether the need to end a conflict through force legitimizes the violation of state sovereignty rights.

In practice, the states involved frequently dodge this confrontation: For instance, they simply deny that they actually used military force. Or they point to self-defense.

In the case of the annexation of Crimea, Russian soldiers were involved in one way or another. Simply put, the Russian military was deployed. Moscow, however, said, "We have nothing to do with that. It may be that people in uniforms were active there, but they are volunteers." This, Russia claimed, was something completely different than an intervention in a sovereign state. But is it really?

Second example: In the "little war" between Russia and Georgia in 2008, when South Ossetia and Abkhazia were separated from Georgia, the Russian side asserted that the Georgians started it by attacking the Russian minorities. Accordingly, military support from Russia merely assisted in their self-defense. And under the UN Charter, self-defense is allowed. But is Russia allowed to defend the Abkhazians in Georgia? What about Georgia's sovereignty? Is Moscow allowed to decide what happens in Georgia?

In other words, the UN's monopoly on the use of force is the theory, but practice is all too often very different. Where, for instance, is the UN Security Council resolution that would allow a no-fly zone to be imposed in Syria to stop airstrikes on the civilian population? As long as this fails to materialize, Russian planes continue their bombing with the authorization of the Syrian government. The very same Russians who are blocking the necessary UN resolution explain, "We were invited. We are supporting a sovereign state. This is allowed."

In this way facts are withheld, events distorted, and falsehoods spread as the truth. Military means are applied in secret, or even openly, without the Security Council having approved them at all. We have to live with these circumstances, unfortunately.

And even when it all does work, when there is unity in the Security Council on the need to send peacekeeping troops, the conflict in question is not necessarily contained. First, the mandate for such a mission must be formulated. Once that is done, suppliers of troops must be found, and soldiers recruited for the mission. And then the commanders of the peacekeeping troops must lead these forces on the ground through the crisis region. The result is often a rather inadequately equipped UN mission facing expensive high-tech deployments by its adversary. This means that UN peacekeeping is not possible without the active support of capable UN members—and it must be well coordinated and conducted in the spirit of the UN Charter.

FOURTH CRITIQUE: EMPTY WORDS

And finally, the weakness of the UN is also due to a lack of assertiveness—especially when UN decisions run counter to the interests of important states, without the support of which nothing can happen. That is why many of the General Assembly's decisions end up going nowhere. To name one example from recent history: The Treaty on the Prohibition of Nuclear Weapons, contained in a General Assembly resolution of July 2017 that was signed by 122 member states, was not approved by any of the nuclear powers—not one of them will comply with it. It was rejected by NATO as well. The nuclear powers felt that the treaty did not take their interests into consideration sufficiently. These interests cannot simply be prayed away. This is hardly the way to achieve complete nuclear disarmament.

I am writing this as a member of the "Global Zero Commission," which is attempting to support the vision of a world free of nuclear weapons through step-by-step operational suggestions.

In this context the Treaty on the Non-Proliferation of Nuclear Weapons (NPT for short) has to be mentioned. It was passed in July 1968, became effective on March 5, 1970, and is based on a dual promise: The states that do not possess nuclear weapons promise to permanently renounce any nuclear ambitions, and the nuclear powers promise to strive for comprehensive disarmament. This treaty was initiated by the five nuclear powers, the United States, the Soviet Union, Great Britain, France, and China, and signed by 191 states, including Germany.

The NPT has been focused—for half a century—on the fulfilment of these contractual obligations. These have not been taken seriously enough so far, especially the obligation for the nuclear powers to disarm. Bilateral agreements on the reduction of armaments have been achieved between the Soviet Union (or Russia) and the United States—including the Strategic Arms Limitation Treaty (SALT), as well as START and INF—but the other nuclear powers did not participate. And unfortunately, new nuclear powers have emerged in disregard of the NPT—such as India, Pakistan, Israel, and recently, North Korea. The NPT has thus hardly proved effective.

Only for chemical weapons has a comprehensive ban been achieved, and one that seems to work pretty well. So why should the idea of a world without nuclear weapons be so absurd? A world without nuclear weapons—Global Zero—remains a good vision, but unfortunately it is very difficult to realize. We have a very long way ahead of us.

TRUST AND DISTRUST IN NORTH KOREA

The current case of North Korea is also an example of the power-lessness of the UN, where the appeals and warnings from New York to end the North Korean nuclear weapons program have long rung hollow with Supreme Leader Kim Jong-un. How can this problem be resolved? Can it be resolved at all? What leverage is there when the previous sanctions imposed on North Korea by the Security Council succeeded in persuading Pyongyang to temporarily aban-don its warmongering rhetoric and cease its nuclear weapons test-ing, but fell far short of complete denuclearization of the Korean peninsula? By 2020, Trump and Kim had met three times, and had exchanged messages and letters. But no concrete steps toward full denuclearization have been taken. The prospects of future negotia-tions are anything but clear.

Moreover, it is important to note that North Korean nuclear disarmament is hardly a new issue. There has been a nuclear program in North Korea since the 1950s—at that time with the friendly support of the Soviet Union—which was initially supposed to help modernize the country's energy sector. But the technology that Moscow supplied to the North Koreans for this, the gas-cooled graphite reactor, yielded such large amounts of plutonium that military use was possible as well. Not until 1985 did Moscow link the provision of this technology with the condition that North Korea sign the NPT.

In 1993 a crisis erupted when North Korea announced that it would withdraw from the treaty. Negotiations ensued, in which Europe participated. The technology that North Korea used up to that point was to be replaced by light water reactors supplied by the United States. The EU declared that it was willing to share the costs. There were moments when it looked as if everything would turn out well. The "Agreed Framework" negotiated in Geneva in 1994 stipulated that North Korea would "receive two light water reactors, and until their completion, 500,000 tons of oil per year."[5] There was even a temporary rapprochement between North and South Korea. In spring 1995 the United States, the EU, South Korea, and Japan founded the Korean Energy Development Organization (KEDO), which was to ensure the transfer of the reactor and the oil delivery.

However, these agreements never came to fruition, for all sorts of reasons. In 2002, North Korea surprised the world by admitting that it was continuing work on a secret nuclear weapons program. In 2003 it actually did become the first, and so far the only, country to leave the NPT.

George W. Bush added the country to the axis of evil and talked publicly about a military intervention. Since the Korean War, American soldiers and weapons have been stationed in South Korea, and a large U.S. fleet cruises off the shores of the divided Korean peninsula. North Korea had previously used this presence as an argument against relinquishing its nuclear program, claiming that the country needed nuclear weapons to sufficiently guarantee its security. There is some logic in this assertion.

In 1994, Ukraine had renounced the possession of nuclear weapons. The international promise made at the time to respect the territorial integrity of Ukraine, the Budapest Memorandum, was violated by Moscow through the annexation of Crimea in

2014. This raises the question, would this have happened if Ukraine had still been a nuclear power? Another example is Qaddafi, who, bowing to international pressure, gave up his nuclear program in 2003—and we know how he ended up. Not exactly encouraging examples for North Korea's leader.

It can only be welcomed that direct talks between North Korea and the United States have begun. But can the zigzag course of President Trump, who initially mocked Kim Jong-un as "rocket man" and then called him an "honorable man," really lead to success?

It has to be acknowledged that Trump's course of maximum pressure—ever stricter economic sanctions while building up a plausible war scenario—resulted in Kim Jong-un relenting in spring 2018. The meeting between the ruler of North Korea and South Korea's President Moon Jae-in was praised by UN General Secretary António Guterres, who called it a "truly historic summit." For this reason, Trump supporters even demanded the Nobel Peace Prize for the U.S. president. Although this is not the first time that North Korea has struck such a tone, Kim did promise to completely dismantle his nuclear weapons program and end hostilities with South Korea. China certainly contributed as well. Chinese president Xi Jinping had supported the sanctions passed by the UN Security Council, thus increasing the pressure on North Korea, which relies heavily on economic cooperation with its Chinese neighbor.

It remains to be seen whether, and to what extent, the joint statement signed by Donald Trump and Kim Jong-un in Singapore on June 12, 2018, will actually serve as the basis for a verifiable denuclearization process and a Korean peace process.

So far, U.S. concessions (for instance, the cancellation of a joint military maneuver with South Korea) have prompted no more than a promise by North Korea to promote the nuclear disarmament of the Korean peninsula. Moreover, there is reasonable doubt that Kim Jong-un will keep the promise he made in Singapore. After all, satellite images supposedly show that North Korea, rather than disarming, is continuing to fine-tune its nuclear capacities.

Precisely because the decisionmaking power of the United Nations has reached its limits so often, other more informal formats for international policy are growing in importance. These include not only bilateral summits like the one in Singapore, but also bodies like the G7, G8, or G20 and more informal cross-border civil society campaigns.

THE G20 AND OTHER INFORMAL GATHERINGS

The United Nations is often criticized for its lack of success or for its inefficient operation. The critique of the G7, G8, or G20 summits frequently has a different basis: a lack of legitimacy.

"The richest of us all sit together and tell the rest of humanity what is good for them. This is colonialism 2.0," said a Berlin correspondent.[6] Free trade, climate protection, aid for Africa—these issues affect everyone, he argued, and that is why they belong in a forum where all are assembled, "namely in the United Nations. There the poor have a voice as well."

In an ideal world, if there were still any problems to address, democratically elected governments would meet at UN headquarters in New York to seek optimal solutions through peaceful communication. But in 2020 we live in a world where it is rarely possible to pacify even a relatively small state like Colombia, let alone to stop a war in Syria that has escalated into a regional conflict. How, then, would it be possible to solve such complex issues as economic crises or trade disputes and "trade wars" in a group of about 200 members, many of which do not even possess any democratic legitimacy?

For this reason, I agree with the following response: "For anyone who wants to promote climate protection, strengthen the stability of the financial system, or shape globalization, such informal meetings [as G20 summits] are an absolute must."[7]

Geopolitically, the G20 format is currently the only one in

which the truly large and significant countries—such as the United States, Russia, and China, to name the three most important ones—actually convene with other relevant partners at the highest levels of heads of state and government. Twenty or thirty years ago, leaders had to wait for the next "working funeral," that is, for the next state funeral that might offer such an opportunity. We should be glad that the heads of state now meet regularly in order to consult about how they can respond to the most urgent global issues.

In contrast to the United Nations, G20 summits are attended not by ambassadors acting on instructions from their capitals, but rather by the Trumps, Putins, Xis, Merkels, and Macrons themselves. That is why such meetings are of particular value.

Until 2014 the main format was the G8, which included the large Western industrial nations along with Russia. Unfortunately, this format was discontinued when Russia intervened in Ukraine, and Moscow was excluded from these meetings as a consequence. I believe it was a mistake to suspend or abandon the G8 format. How can we negotiate if we are not talking to each other? And another thing was clear to me: When you throw someone out, you must know under what conditions that someone can be let back in without losing face.

At that time, in 2014, the upcoming G8 summit was supposed to be held in Russia. I had proposed that, instead of canceling the summit altogether, the other members should inform Putin that they wanted to discuss only a single agenda item with him, namely Crimea. Then the ball would have been in his court, and he would have had to either cancel the summit himself or accept the dictate from the other seven members of the G8. At that time, unfortunately, this suggestion fell on deaf ears. Now the G20 is the only remaining multilateral framework in which the Western world can at least have a personal dialogue with Putin. Strictly speaking, the door to the G8 can be reopened only if either the West retroactively accepts the annexation of Crimea by Russia—or Putin, for his part, rescinds this annexation. Both of these are highly improbable, and possible only if one party or the other loses face. So, unfortunately, the G8 format is dead for all practical purposes.

To come back to the Dayton negotiations one last time: The contact group that accompanied the negotiations was an informal club, thrown together from scratch and legitimized by no one. Five states—the United States, France, Great Britain, Russia, and Germany—came together in order to move forward the negotiations on Bosnia. In the end the UN Security Council consented, happy that a peaceful solution had been reached, rather than taking the position that "We will not acknowledge this peaceful agreement; the contact group should never have existed because that was a job for the UN Security Council."

For topics such as the reliability of the global financial system and the flow of refugees, but also for problems like terrorism, corruption, and the question of African development policy, overarching solutions are needed. For these solutions to be achieved, heads of state and government must be able to talk with each other informally.

That is why we need the G20 more urgently than ever. I am all for civil society becoming more strongly involved in political discourse, but not by simply saying no. Categorically rejecting the principle of the G20 is the opposite of constructive. Fortunately, though, there are all kinds of examples in which the involvement of civil society is considerably more constructive—and has even made an effective contribution to solving global problems.

Up until a few years ago, international policy issues were a task reserved exclusively for governments. This is no longer the case. Today, Amnesty International, industrial federations, Human Rights Watch, Doctors Without Borders, and other groups play important roles similar to those of government bodies.

Years ago, for instance, the idea of a global ban on land mines was promoted so effectively by private groups that the ban ultimately became reality. In 1992, six nongovernmental organizations (NGOs)—Handicap International, Human Rights Watch, Medico

International, the Mines Advisory Group, Physicians for Human Rights, and the Vietnam Veterans of America Foundation—started a mobilization campaign to combat the humanitarian crises caused by land mines. First, they built up public pressure by recruiting other organizations outside of the government to contribute their support. This is how the "International Campaign to Ban Landmines" (ICBL) was founded in 1995 as a network of over 1,200 NGOs in ninety countries. Because of what Geneva stands for, the organization selected the city as its headquarters.

The second step was to seek out coalitions with like-minded governments. In December 1997, several countries convened in Ottawa, Canada, to sign the "Mine Ban Treaty," also known as the Ottawa Treaty. The event had been prepared with a modern media strategy, at a time when the internet and digital communication networks were in their infancy. By enlisting the participation of Diana, the late Princess of Wales, and a professional photo campaign by the tabloid press, it was able to reach a broad audience.

The strategy led to an unprecedented success, namely an international, legally binding ban of a conventional type of weapon, land mines. It became effective on March 1, 1999. Not only due to this result, but above all because of the way the campaign itself was conducted, the ICBL and its coordinator, Jody Williams, were awarded the 1997 Nobel Peace Prize for this new approach to international decisionmaking.

But even if countless citizens are today involved in NGOs and support them with donations, this also raises a question of democratic legitimacy. How transparent and accountable are the internal decision processes of these organizations? Who is elected to leadership positions and according to what process, if elections take place at all? Are there possibilities for democratic control? Who monitors compliance with rules and the proper handling of finances?

THE WORLD IS BECOMING HYPERPOLAR

The rise of NGOs and other non-state actors on the world stage also brings us right to the next questions: When has the point been reached when non-state actors should have a say at the United Nations? And how could this be organized? These are difficult organizational and structural questions, to which international policy must dedicate itself in the coming years, to say nothing of the fact that many UN member states—and not only those with authoritarian rules—are rather skeptical about opening up to civil society organizations.

Currently the power of large corporations is a frequent topic of discussion. But the influence of smaller actors is also growing inexorably. If we link the growing importance of NGOs with the technical innovations that are spreading through the world at lightning speed, the possibilities are dizzying: Pandora's box has long since been opened. What if non-state actors, with the help of modern technologies that are no longer subject to state control, were to interfere in the political arena—be it through hacking, by manipulating elections, or by paralyzing the cooling water circuit of a nuclear power plant through a cyberattack? What would happen if a group succeeded in crippling the traffic light systems in large cities? What kind of economic losses might that cause? How can a cyberattack against a country's health care system be prevented? Who can be prosecuted by which court if, as the result of an international cyberattack, the electrical systems of hospitals failed and patients died?

Today, modern technologies have given the interested citizen, but also the individual terrorist, instruments with so much potential power that they can no longer be harnessed effectively by the state. To confront the security risks of cyber technology on a level above governments and across organizations, we need bodies where experts can meet and exchange ideas in a cooperative environment.

The Munich Security Conference (MSC), which was founded in 1963 and whose chairmanship I assumed in 2008, is one such place. Originally it was a bilateral U.S.-German defense seminar called Wehrkunde, where primarily security policy and military experts assembled. It is organized privately and is not a government event. In the decades of the Cold War, it focused on a single question, namely the credibility of Western deterrence strategies toward the Soviet Union. Ewald von Kleist, founder of Wehrkunde, believed that the Germans should participate more intensively within NATO if they were not to become the mere object of superpower strategies. With Wehrkunde, he created a forum for this discourse. Today we deal with a plethora of security policy challenges, from nuclear strategy and nonproliferation to combating terrorism, to the conflicts in the Middle East, all the way to issues of health, cyber, climate, and energy security. The MSC has thus become a central platform for international foreign policy. No resolutions are passed here, and no communiqués are published. We simply seek solutions and answers, and conduct often passionate debates. And this is precisely why our participants include presidents, prime ministers, ministers, and national security advisers. They come to Munich each year to meet with each other and with CEOs, professors, and generals.

The attendees in 2018 and 2019 were more than thirty heads of state and government, among them the German chancellor, the British prime minister, the emir of Qatar, U.S. Vice President Mike Pence, the president of Egypt, Prime Minister Benjamin Netanyahu of Israel, and a member of the Chinese politburo, as well as the prime ministers of France and Turkey. Over one hundred other ministers from all over the world participated as well. The many foreign ministers included those of Germany, Russia, Iran, and Saudi Arabia. UN Secretary General Guterres, EU Commission President Jean-Claude Juncker, and NATO Secretary General Stoltenberg were also included in my total of around 500 guests. This is why the former NATO ambassador to the United Nations, Ivo Daalder, once called the Munich Security Conference the "Oscars for security policy wonks."

When organizing such an event, the question is whom to invite. If the war in Syria is on the agenda, then of course the Iranian government should be invited, as well as a representative of the Syrian opposition. But invitations must also be extended to Reporters Without Borders and Amnesty International. Moreover, security is no longer a purely military issue, about which primarily generals should have their say. Anyone who wants to talk about global security today cannot exclude the topics of financial crises, resource crises, climate change, and artificial intelligence.

For this reason, today's participants at the Munich Security Conference not only hail from a wide range of geographical locations, but also reflect a very broad definition of security. The gatherings still include many ministers of defense, but also many CEOs, high-tech entrepreneurs, trade association leaders, human rights activists, environmentalists, and other leaders from global civil society. Today most of the debates are broadcast live to the public, on TV and online. An audience of millions can now follow the debates and even participate actively via social media.

Because of the great thematic diversity, the plenary of the Munich Security Conference is complemented by side events on a wide variety of topics, including, for instance, regional crises. In addition, we hold MSC events on particular topics at selected locations all over the world. For instance, in November 2016, we hosted a Health Security Roundtable in Beijing to discuss strategies to mitigate global health security threats, including debates about pandemic prevention and the lessons learned from the Ebola outbreak in West Africa. And at the Cyber Security Summit in Tallinn, Estonia, in May 2018, the agenda included topics such as the danger of digital interference in democratic processes, the protection of critical infrastructure, and the effectiveness of norms in cyberspace.

Since 2009 the Munich Security Conference has organized annual Core Group Meetings in different capitals. High-level participants made up of ministers, CEOs, legislators, and other decisionmakers are given the opportunity to discuss important international security policy issues in a more intimate setting with public figures from the region where the meetings take place.

The fact that the University of Pennsylvania singled out the Munich Security Conference as the world's "Best Think Tank Conference" for three years running between 2015 and 2017 is evidence that it is not only my staff and I who believe our concept to be a good idea. And in 2018 and 2019, the MSC was ranked among the very best once again.

All of our meetings serve the objective of strengthening institutions and rules in a world that has become more dangerous and less orderly, in order to preserve and restore a "rules-based global order." Considering the increasing complexity of the world, this task is not getting any easier, but ever more important. It would not be enough to simply dump it at the doors of the United Nations headquarters and hope for the best.

EIGHT

EUROPE

Only Strong Together

WITHOUT EUROPE, EVERYTHING IS NOTHING

The war in Syria and its consequences for Europe should have shown us that we cannot simply keep out of conflicts beyond our borders. But are we prepared to act accordingly? What has to happen so that we, the EU, are taken seriously in Moscow, in Beijing, and in Washington, D.C.? We can no longer dodge these and other unpleasant questions.

Europe faces new challenges and expectations—especially if we are ever less able to rely on a United States that is willing (and able) to show up whenever there is an emergency that affects our interests.

For German foreign policy, one truth remains: Without Europe, everything is nothing. To respond to the uncertainties of the present by retreating back into nineteenth century nationalism would bring neither peace nor prosperity. There is no foreign policy interest for Germany more important than the creation and preservation of a stable Europe. In the past decades, we have benefited immensely from a peaceful Europe—politically and economically integrated in the European Union, with our security anchored in NATO. Yet, to keep things this way, Germany will have to do considerably more than in the post-Cold War past.

For Germany, European integration is not only an irreplaceable peace project, but also a strategic necessity. If the German Federal Republic lives in harmony with all of its neighbors today, without any territorial or other classic types of disputes, this is not least because of an EU in which the small members are not pushed around, let alone hassled or threatened by the large ones. The EU is the key condition for the fact that many of our smaller neighbors define reunified Germany not as a threat, as they did for the last 130 years, but as an asset—at least in principle, occasional conflicts notwithstanding.

Yet the European project is more endangered now than it has been for decades. It has again become fashionable to seek salvation by fleeing into nationalist, or even nationalistic, sentiment. From France to Finland to Germany, national-populist parties have spread throughout Europe. Yet their promises represent a flight from the twenty-first century back into the disastrous nineteenth and twentieth centuries. It is conceivable that Europe could fall back into chaos. But even if this "worst case" does not materialize, an EU in a state of perpetual disagreement, stumbling from one crisis to the next, would be an existential burden for all of Europe.

While most Americans can recite the roster of American presidents, most Europeans would react with a shrug if they were asked to name the presidents of the EU Commission. Listing the chancellors and presidents of the German Federal Republic, by contrast, would rouse the sporting ambition of most educated Germans. And the French would certainly know the names of their presidents.

But the leaders of the EU? If you would like to give it a try, there have been twelve presidents of the EU Commission since 1967. Or could you name the first and only president of the EEC, the European Economic Community? He was a German named Walter Hallstein, and he served from 1958 until 1967.

When Jean-Claude Juncker, the outgoing president of the European Commission, gave his speech on the state of the European Union each year, most EU citizens did not even know that there is such a speech, let alone listen to it. Maybe Ursula von der Leyen, chosen in 2019 to follow Juncker, will have a better chance—at least in her native Germany.

When the president of the United States gives his State of the Union Address, in contrast, it receives global news coverage. This is not because of the timing, as the last Tuesday in January is not really a less arbitrary choice than the European date in September. And neither is it because the American president speaks to a nation of over 300 million people, for the European president addresses over 500 million citizens of the EU.

It presumably also has little to do with the lack of importance of Europe's military, which, unfortunately, corresponds neither to Europe's size nor to its economic power. It is primarily because the national governments consider themselves more important than the EU. And far too often, "Brussels" has to serve as the nations' scapegoat. The Brexit debate in the United Kingdom is the perfect example.

"THOSE PEOPLE IN BRUSSELS": THE EU SCAPEGOAT

When you listen to elected political leaders today, there is a recurring narrative that remains astonishingly similar in all twenty-four official languages of the EU: If something does not work, it is the EU's fault. If there is good news to report, then it is framed as national victories, ideally ones that were won against Brussels or the other EU states. Brussels is the most popular excuse for any political failure. The fatal consequence of this national narrative of success is that, to some degree, Brussels becomes the victim of collective European political bullying.

Reservations against the EU are nothing new historically: In the 1950s, the German Social Democratic Party feared that European integration could become an obstacle to potential German reunification. Today we know that unification would not have been possible without Germany's integration into the European community and NATO. France's President Charles de Gaulle opposed the EU in the 1960s because he feared for the sovereignty of *la Grande Nation*.

The United Kingdom was even more worried about its status as a world power, joining the union reluctantly in 1973—and only because the looser association of states founded at the same time, the European Free Trade Association (EFTA), never really got off the ground. Complaints about European "paternalism" always formed the background against which British policy toward the organization was made. In coming years, after Brexit has been implemented, we will see what kind of position the United Kingdom will occupy in the world. Fears are growing in London that the country's importance could shrink rather than prosper.

The Visegrád states of Poland, the Czech Republic, Hungary, and Slovakia, which banded together in 1991, initially pushed with all their might to be admitted to the EU and NATO. More recently though, especially in Hungary and Poland, nationalist forces have come into power with demands for populist isolation.

Because of the new nationalistic sentiments, there are concerns that the European Union might erode. However, to paraphrase Mark Twain explaining to journalists who arrived to report on his supposed demise, the reports of the EU's death are greatly exaggerated.

Even today, the European idea is still a magnificent idea. I would even go a step further: If the idea of European integration had not been advanced by Robert Schuman, Alcide de Gasperi, and Jean Monnet—three of the founding fathers of the EU—it would be all the more urgent to invent and propagate it today—and the reasons are twofold.

THE PEACE PROJECT EU: STILL NECESSARY

The original impetus for European integration was to end fratricidal wars in Europe, especially between Germany and France. No more war! That was the European motto of Helmut Kohl's generation. This is what motivated the generation of the founders who instigated and propelled European unity forward, up until German reunification.

The idea "No more war!" is by no means obsolete. On the contrary, nearly every day, we experience how thinly the coat of peace has been applied to Europe since World War II.

Indeed, it is not all that long ago that grueling fratricidal wars occurred right in our neighborhood, in the former Yugoslavia, with hundreds of thousands dead. With the same quality of hate and bloodlust, we had lamented in Europe in previous centuries.

Even today, with the two decades of the twenty-first century over, the danger of war in Europe is anything but eliminated. Tensions are simmering under the surface. We are still far removed from permanent stability in the Western Balkans. And shooting continues in Ukraine, a two-hour flight from Frankfurt!

Of course, European unification is a great success: twenty-eight member states in the EU, twenty-nine in NATO, and right in the middle, a reunified Germany. Isn't this a dream come true?

On the one hand, yes. On the other, we see crises and instability in parts of Europe—ethnic discord, territorial conflicts, massive economic problems, and fear of intervention from abroad. Many of the "in-between" states located between the EU and Russia—from Belarus and Moldavia to Georgia and Ukraine, all the way to Azerbaijan and Armenia—are still not securely anchored in a comprehensive and durable European security order.

And even within the EU, there are unresolved issues, not just as a consequence of Brexit or, for example, the Catalonia crisis in Spain. Conflict prevention remains essential in Europe. European integration, peace, and stability require constant and regular care. There is no autopilot!

Signs of deterioration are the root of the second essential argument for the necessity of a European Union: The nation-state has outlived its function as a driving force. I do not want to be misunderstood; the nation-state in Europe is not obsolete—in fact, it continues to fulfil important functions. But it is running up against its limits everywhere.

Today the prosperity of Germany is determined as much by events in Shanghai or New York as it is in Berlin. Pandemics, terrorism, climate change, environmental catastrophes, nuclear proliferation—the nation-state alone can do only so much against these kinds of threats. The challenges of today and tomorrow may be acutely felt by citizens, but to a large extent the causes are located outside their national borders—and thus beyond the grasp of the nation-state.

When I, as German ambassador in London, was asked to address the EU Committee of the British House of Lords about the future of Europe, an appalled British lord reproached me, "Dear Ambassador, we do not need the EU; we have the Commonwealth!"

He, like other Brexit supporters, is on the wrong track. I asked him, "Do you really believe that, just because of the Commonwealth, the prime minister of India will grant you or the British government more than a courtesy visit?" He understood the question: If the EU showed up in Delhi, representing the largest trade and export market in the world with its 500 million people, India would listen.

A current example: While I am writing this chapter, in the fall of 2019, a dispute in the transatlantic relationship is brewing about Trump imposing tariffs on steel and aluminum imports from the EU. Nobody knows how the dispute will continue to develop. But one thing is clear: In the long term, such tariffs will have a substantial impact on the European economy and then on the global economy as well. It is a short-sighted approach, motivated by Trump's domestic politics and campaign tactics. But the point is not whether his policy is reasonable or whether it is lawful. The question is, what can we do about it? The EU Commission reacted by announcing reprisals, which would allow for measures like duties on American whiskey and Harley Davidson motorcycles. Trade policy for EU members is made by the EU, with the commission speaking and acting for all member states. As a result, such announcements carry significant weight. The EU has real power in trade policy because it speaks with one voice—the voice of the EU Commission. And this voice is powerful.

THE EU UNDER PERMANENT CONSTRUCTION— BUT NOT BECAUSE OF ITS SIZE

No question about it: The European Union is a permanent construction site. And one builder or another is always throwing away his shovel in frustration. This started back in 1954, when the European Defence Community (EDC) failed to materialize because France refused to ratify the EDC Treaty signed in May 1952. Not until the 1990s was there another attempt launched toward founding a joint European security and defense policy. And we still have a long way to go. The Britons might prefer not to remember, but there was a time when they wanted to join the EU but were not allowed to: In 1963, French President Charles de Gaulle prevented British accession to the European Community. The British were accepted ten years later. Six years after that, Margaret Thatcher, the British prime minister, pushed through the "U.K. rebate," a reduction in the British contributions to the shared budget—much to the displeasure of many other EU members. That by itself would naturally be reason enough for many members to be less than accommodating of a particularly generous Brexit deal. In 1992 the Maastricht Treaty on a common currency was rejected by 50.7 percent of Danes in a referendum. Here, too, the consequence was an exemption for Denmark.

Not even the institutional EU reform around the turn of the millennium was free of conflict, for it entailed shifts in power. As the example of the UN Security Council reform in the previous chapter illustrated, nobody likes to surrender privileges, and nobody likes to forfeit their influence to shape policy. Thus, infighting ensues.

Two major efforts to reform and strengthen EU institutions happened in 1999 and 2003, with the Treaty of Amsterdam and Treaty of Nice, respectively, but the institutional structure of the EU still needed improvement with regard to democracy, transparency, and efficiency. The next attempt—this time a constitutional treaty was painstakingly negotiated—failed in 2005 due to negative referendums in the Netherlands and France.

The Treaty of Lisbon, in which the influence of the European Parliament—the legislature arm of the EU—and the common foreign and security policy were to be strengthened, was the next attempt at reform. After all, the EU had undergone an enormous expansion in 2004, with ten new states joining at the same time. The previous procedures allowed fifteen heads of state to assemble around the conference table, but twenty-five were definitely too many, especially since the next candidates for accession were already in line. But the road to the treaty was rocky and winding.

The Lisbon Treaty was signed in 2007 and took effect in 2009, but not before teetering on the brink: Initially, the Irish population rejected it in a referendum. Then there was a second referendum in 2009, with a positive result. In Germany there was no referendum, but there were constitutional challenges: The Federal Constitutional Court ruled that the treaty was constitutional in principle but insisted on having certain details rectified.

Since 2014, as stipulated in the Lisbon Treaty, decisions in the European Council must be approved with a "double majority." This means that 55 percent of the states must agree, and these states must also represent a 65 percent majority of the European population. This voting procedure, called qualified majority voting, applies to most areas of decisionmaking but not to foreign and security policy. More on that later.

The Treaty of Lisbon also introduced the "European Citizens' Initiative," with which a million people from different member states can force the European Commission to deal with a given subject. This has been attempted several times since 2012, for subjects ranging from regulations for the disposal of plastic waste, to roaming fees, to unconditional basic income. So far, no initiative has been successful, with most attempts failing to obtain the required signatures. But we have to try out new political instruments like these and learn how to use them. In any case, these methods offer a great new opportunity for a European unification project with even stronger democratic legitimacy.

EASY PREY: THE CACOPHONY OF
EUROPEAN FOREIGN POLICY

I do not share the concern some express about the future of the EU. Gloomy prophecies that the EU will disintegrate have not come true before, and the EU will survive the next crises as well. They are part of a maturation process that advances unification and will make the organization stronger. Seventy years after peace was proclaimed, the EU is now turning to issues of internal and external security. The priority now is to figure out how the EU can position itself politically and militarily so that it is recognized and respected as a security policy actor on the global stage.

Representing our interests works best when Europe speaks with a single voice and takes action as one. This is why continuing to use the consensus principle for foreign and security policy decisions is such an obstacle. Any decision can be thwarted by every individual member country. How then can we improve the effectiveness of European foreign policy?

We could continue the cacophony of European foreign policy forever, of course. Scenarios like the following would run on an infinite loop: On Monday the French foreign minister takes a trip

to Saudi Arabia to tell his counterpart there about the French position on the Middle East. On Tuesday the Danish foreign minister
comes and gives his opinion and advice. Wednesday the German
foreign minister arrives with views and recommendations that are
slightly different from those of his French and Danish colleagues.
By the time the foreign minister of Austria arrives on Friday, the
Saudi minister will have stopped listening at all. But what if the EU
were to show up with a clear plan and speak with one voice? This
would be a major step toward real EU crisis politics. This is where
the focus should be.

In 2017 the United States and Europe were arguing about sanctions against Russia. The U.S. Congress was about to pass a law
with new, additional sanctions, which might potentially have affected the interests of certain European energy companies. German
Foreign Minister Gabriel agreed with Austrian Chancellor Christian Kern and expressed their indignation publicly: We will not let
Washington dictate European energy policy. He said that he hoped
other EU member states would react in the same way and approach
Washington.

Only very few fulfilled his request, however, because many of
his colleagues have very different ideas about European energy
policy than Germany and Austria, as well as their own external
energy policies. In Poland, the Baltic states, and Ukraine, for example, there is concern that the Nord Stream 2 pipeline from the
German Baltic coast to St. Petersburg threatens to make Europe
even more energy dependent on imports of Russian gas—and thus
on Moscow.

The question here is not whether Nord Stream 2 is good or not.
The question is whether we want a common EU policy or not. Calling for a European foreign policy does not mean allowing members
to pick and choose among different points along the foreign policy
spectrum. A common foreign policy worthy of the name must include a common external energy policy.

Another foreign policy topic that will require more unity from

Europeans in the future is how to deal with an ever more asser-
tive China. Significant doubts have arisen as to whether China will
become a "responsible stakeholder" in the existing liberal world
order. The dubious legality of Beijing's behavior in the South China
Sea and Xi Jinping's pet project for a new silk road (the Belt and Road
Initiative, or BRI, also christened "One Belt, One Road"), which
is riding roughshod over international standards for transparency
and accountability, are just a few of the many reasons. Yet the "One
Belt, One Road" project, in particular, has shown how easy it is for
China to divide the supposedly united Europeans. In fact, seven-
teen Central and Eastern European (CEE) states have joined China
in the framework of the 17+1 Group—formerly 16+1—a platform
to facilitate cooperation between China and CEE countries, particularly in the economic realm—in hopes of receiving increased
investment from Beijing. However, Europeans will succeed in asserting their interests and standards in negotiations with the new
economic superpower only if they speak with a single voice. And
expressing criticisms toward Beijing will certainly not get easier as
individual European states become ever more dependent on China.

Once again, the idea of Europe is magnificent; awarding the
Nobel Peace Prize to the EU in 2012 was no mistake. In addition to
disunity, however, the EU also has the problem that joint projects, of
course, work only when they are based on rules, and these rules must
be, first, well designed and transparent, and second, complied with.

Unfortunately, some of the major projects to design Europe—
like the Schengen Area, which eliminated border controls between
EU members, and the euro, the common currency—were conceived
as fair-weather projects, trusting that there would be no rain.

As we were compelled to realize in 2009, the financial crisis and
the euro crisis have brought plenty of rain clouds, and the refugee
and migration crises since 2015 have also caused heavy storms for
the Schengen system. And on top of it all, we discovered that we did
not have a reliable plan B for such rainy days—no crisis plan and no
emergency plan to trigger the needed rescue operations.

We survived these crises, although they still have not been overcome completely. But for the future, it is clear that we need projects that are more resilient. While this is certainly not impossible, it will cause new confrontations within the European Union. And first of all, it requires restoring trust, both internally and externally.

Economic growth would certainly help. After all, we only have growth to distribute when there is growth at all. And the way it is, many of the poorer members, who receive more from the EU than they pay into the budget, regard the benefits of EU funds as a basic element of their membership. Or, to put it more simply, they joined above all because they expected some financial aid. Growth means prosperity, which means jobs, which mean less youth unemployment. Providing for this virtual circle is a major generational task for the EU. Yet with the economic downturn caused by the coronavirus pandemic, it is unclear whether and when the EU economy will be able to return to the path of growth that it had entered in 2016.

Furthermore, we need better mechanisms to improve financial stability. Ultimately, we must ensure that net contributors do not run the risk of having to take on the old debts of their European neighbors and partners. On the other hand, we can increase solidarity by creating instruments that reduce the risk of liability. Another element of this system could perhaps be a European finance minister, an idea that has been discussed for some time. At the same time, Germany and the other net contributors should be ready to conduct this discussion about more stable structures proactively, not defensively. This does not mean, for instance, that Greece has to achieve Bavarian levels of prosperity tomorrow. Neither does it mean that the per capita income in Bremen, Germany, must be as high as it is in Munich. But the differences must not mushroom into a political time bomb.

There is also an urgent need for action in the area of internal security. We have the Schengen Area, but there is still insufficient cross-border cooperation between the police and intelligence services. Whether or not European citizens believe the EU's promise that it will provide for their security and stay in control will be decided by whether European member states are able to effectively combat terrorism despite their open borders. This why it is not enough to increase cooperation among police forces in the EU by incremental steps. Why is the discussion about a European intelligence and security organization—similar to the United States's Federal Bureau of Investigation (FBI) and building on the existing structures of the EU's law enforcement agency, Europol—not much higher on the agenda?

THE GERMAN-FRENCH TANDEM: TUNED UP?

In this and other very important questions, Germany has no better partner than France, especially under President Macron. Even before his election, Macron introduced a number of major pro-European ideas and visions—ranging from the reform of the eurozone to a common European defense budget. Germany will not always have the same opinion as France. But it is unacceptable that every French idea to change something is immediately talked to death. We have a unique opportunity in coming years to carry Europe forward with a stronger Franco-German duo—the *couple franco-allemand*, as they call it in Paris.

Before meetings of the European Council in the 1980s and early 1990s, Helmut Kohl and François Mitterand wrote joint letters that served as a foundation for the European agenda and European decisions. This would not work anymore, as the EU has become a completely different organization. But we still need this Franco-German engine nevertheless. It would be good for the European reform process if it were accompanied and actively shaped by an invigorated Franco-German relationship. This is why it is so important that a new edition of the Élysée Treaty of 1963 has been negotiated to, more than fifty years later, restructure and redesign the importance of our friendship for a whole new age and under completely different global framing conditions. The bilateral "Treaty of Aachen" presented in early 2019 is an important step. It is a great idea and stands symbolically for the necessity to reinforce and refresh old connections.

I am often told that Germany, like every other EU member, would like to be a completely normal country and pursue its national interests. But how can it be that in Germany, which benefits disproportionately from the EU, both politically and economically, it takes so much effort to raise support and enthusiasm for the EU? Sure, the European debt crisis, questions of expansion, and refugee discussions cost energy and do not exactly generate euphoria. But it is also true that we talk much too little about the everyday advantages Germany enjoys thanks to the EU, the euro, and the EU internal market.

German news and talk shows spend a great deal of time on subjects like the commuter allowance and splitting the income tax for married couples, and much less time on topics like foreign policy, European defense, the war in Ukraine, and equipping the German Army with what it needs. Within the Bundestag, Germany's parliament, committees on foreign policy and security policy are no favorites either. Successful party careers are more likely to be cemented with a social, financial, or economic portfolio. Visionary addresses about world order and peace are rare in Berlin. For that, it takes an American politician on the scale of then presidential candidate Barack Obama, who attracted an audience of 200,000 to hear him speak at Berlin's central Tiergarten park in 2008.

Anyone who wants to be heard in the world must also concentrate on the world—and be an active listener. And this listener must acknowledge how much he or she benefits from transnational communication and cooperation, even in times of crisis. The fact is, even during the euro crisis, no country benefited as massively from the common currency as Germany.

That Germany is a global export champion, is experiencing historically low unemployment, and regularly reaps enormous gains in prosperity is certainly due to the diligence of German workers and the skills of German engineers, but it is also based on the way the euro is designed. Without the euro, the deutsche mark might be valued at twice the price of the euro today—and so Germany would sell much less because our goods would be twice as expensive.

Germany benefits from the Schengen Treaty as well. It is only because inter-European traffic in goods and merchandise can be handled so smoothly that the just-in-time manufacturing of German machines is possible, with component parts made in Poland, the Czech Republic, or Slovakia. The most important market for Germany remains, as before, the EU internal market: Well over half of German exports remained in the EU in 2016; France is our most important trade partner. And this close link applies to all countries in the EU, which, after all, conducted nearly two-thirds of their trade in goods within the borders of Europe in 2016.[1]

It is simply wrong when the prophets of a new nationalism preach that Germany would benefit economically if there were no euro. The euro has design errors—that much is undisputed. Its designers failed to buttress it with a political structure. But repairs are underway (key words: banking union, fiscal union). This is no easy task and will take time, but the euro is and will remain indispensable for Germany's economic and political future.

The EU may actually have needed the shock of Brexit. Now it has to show that it listens to its citizens' worries and expectations, and can resolve them. Now it has to take the core concerns of its citizens seriously—for instance, crime prevention, protection from terrorism, and border protection. These issues must be given a plausible and effective response.

However, it must always be added that the basic political decisions in Brussels are made not by the EU Commission, but by the member states. In the end, decisions come from the European Council, where the representatives of the states are assembled. That is why it is wrong to keep claiming that the deficits of European action are always the fault of "Brussels bureaucrats."

During the 1980s I accompanied then German Foreign Minister Hans-Dietrich Genscher, and also Chancellor Kohl, to many major European summits and meetings. After the sessions, back then the national representatives—the chancellors, prime ministers, or foreign ministers—would go to the microphones and announce to their national media, "Today I succeeded, in cooperation with my colleagues from our neighboring countries, in taking the EU a big step forward in the interest of all of us!"

Today the drill is often quite the opposite. After meetings, participants will stand before their national press and say, "Today I once again succeeded, in the interests of our country, in thwarting the EU Commission or preventing adoption of a program!" For instance, after the most recent EU summit in Brussels, the Visegrád states proudly announced that they had defeated the European distribution of asylum seekers based on national quotas.

Former Belgian Foreign Minister Paul-Henri Spaak, one of the founding fathers of the European Community, once made a point worth repeating today:

"In Europe there are only two kinds of states: Small states, and small states that have not yet understood that they are small."

THE WORLD IS GROWING—EUROPE IS SHRINKING

Individual nation-states are nowhere near capable of mastering the challenges coming our way in the age of globalization. From the geopolitical and demographic perspective, a disunited Europe will become ever smaller and less important in the world. Europe's states are too small to hold their own in the world of tomorrow.

We have had relative prosperity in Europe for over seventy years now, and I fear that we have become too accustomed to this comfort. There is no natural law that says our standard of living will remain as high as it is.

From the global perspective, the EU fares well at first glance: In

2018, the global GDP was around US$85 trillion. The EU, with its twenty-eight member states, and the United States each accounted for about one-quarter and China for around 15 percent. By comparison, in the year 1970 the countries of today's EU had a nearly 38 percent share of global GDP, and China just 0.8 percent.

So, Europe's relative share of the global economy is declining because other countries are now achieving and producing more—particularly since China returned to the world stage. Through the "One Belt, One Road" initiative and many other activities, China has become incredibly dynamic and is well on its way to overtaking the United States in terms of economic power. China is already one of the most innovative countries in the world today.

Demographic trends are not encouraging. Today the EU represents a population of 500 million people: more than the United States by half, three times more than Russia, and still nearly half as many as China.

And yet according to the United Nations, Europe is the only region in the world forecasted to experience a drop in population between 2010 and 2060, a reduction of minus 4.9 percent.[2] Europe is also aging. The share of persons aged sixty-five years or older has increased from around 8 percent in 1950 to 16 percent today and will climb to nearly 27 percent by 2050. More than every fourth European will be sixty-five or older! That will present tremendous challenges for social policy, pension policy, and health care systems.

All of this means over time, Europe will have ever more difficulty asserting its interests against the rest of the world.

And what's more, be it climate change, human rights, or free trade—in an increasingly authoritarian and illiberal world, Europe will have to fight even harder for its interests and for a value system from which it has strongly benefited up to now. To have a voice at all, the EU must take on more responsibility for global and security issues in order to actively shape its role in the international system.

Two strategic consequences for Europe result from this development: first, the need for even more Europe, even more integration; and second—and this is a painful insight for some European states—the necessity to organize immigration. There is a great deal to be done to encourage and structure targeted immigration. It is urgent that we consider whom we want to attract and develop programs that result in bringing us "the best and the brightest."

The awareness of a need for joint action on immigration has yet to manifest on the EU's agenda. So far, the focus has been on erecting barriers. Of course, it is hardly surprising that the Iberian Peninsula is not ready to think about immigration programs while half of the young people in Spain are unemployed. The financial and social crisis must be solved first. But in the long term, these two issues cannot be separated.

The prospects for an EU that shapes and creates, rather than spending all its time dealing with the management of internal crises, are better than the current climate of widespread pessimism would suggest. In many European member states, right-wing populists have been denied a decisive victory, such as the Front National in France or the Alternative for Germany (AfD). The wave of populism and nationalism that carried Great Britain out of the EU and Donald Trump into the White House in 2016 is starting to lose force again in continental Europe. For instance, a Eurobarometer poll conducted in spring 2019 showed levels of support for the EU that had previously only been reached right after the fall of the Berlin Wall. In the same survey, 68 percent responded that they strongly believe their countries have benefited from EU membership.

The European economy is also booming again. In 2017 the eurozone was able to record economic growth of 2.4 percent; in the United States, it was 2.2 percent. Since 2013, over 12 million new jobs have been created in the EU.

STRENGTHENING EUROPE'S FOREIGN
AND SECURITY POLICY

Economy and finances have always been topics close to Europeans' hearts. The subject of security, in contrast, has long been neglected. After the Cold War, talk was of the "peace dividend." Defense budgets were slashed. During the Libya intervention in 2011, we had to watch as French and British airplanes ran out of ammunition after just a few days; they had to borrow some from the Americans. Today the German Bundeswehr is in a lamentable state.

Thus we need to make significant progress on foreign and security policy issues and on defense, and do so as fast as possible. EU Commission President Jean-Claude Juncker demanded at the 2018 Munich Security Conference that Europe must become *weltpolitik-fähig*. His insight that Europe has to become a capable player on the world stage, and that we have to strengthen European foreign and security policy to do this, is gaining momentum.

According to a spring 2016 poll by Pew Research Center, 74 percent of the citizens in the ten EU member states polled (including Great Britain) approved of Europe playing a more active role in the world. A special Eurobarometer survey conducted in 2017 showed that 75 percent of EU citizens also support a common security and defense policy.

Despite all the skepticism about EU bureaucracy, apparently Europeans do sense that their own countries are too small to credibly represent their foreign and security policy interests in the world. In past eras, even smaller European states like Portugal and the Netherlands were world powers. Today there are no more European world powers—even the British and the French are now second tier on the global scale, despite their seats on the UN Security Council and their nuclear weapons. This is why foreign and security policy can and must become one of those areas in which the EU has something to offer. Expanding our common foreign and security policy harbors great potential to make Europe fit for the future. After all, the EU is far more than a bloated bureaucratic apparatus and a flood of laws: It ensures peace in Europe and, as an international agenda setter, it can most effectively represent the interests of 500 million Europeans on the global stage.

This is why we have to redouble our efforts in the areas of foreign, development, and defense policy. The cohesion of the EU and its internal and external security cannot be obtained at zero cost. Future generations will not be able to buy anything with a balanced budget if it means that the most important foundation of our prosperity, a peaceful and thriving Europe, has eroded.

IMAGINE: THE EU CALLS AND EVERYONE COMES

Just imagine if the president of the European Commission or the president of the European Council were to say loud and clear, "We are going to try to end the war in Syria—and we invite the powers involved to come together for a peace conference in order to find a solution." Imagine if they all came.

Most observers would find this scenario quite unlikely. But only with more diplomatic courage and initiative can the aspiration to become more capable of geopolitical action actually be realized. Europe has failed to take on the humanitarian catastrophe in Syria for over seven years. The picture of the Ukraine conflict is not much better. In the latter case, Germany and France have undertaken multiple diplomatic attempts to contribute to a solution. But one may well ask, why is the EU not at the negotiating table?

If Europe does not learn to pursue foreign policy with one voice, it will continue to be sidelined diplomatically. In trade policy, we have long seen how the EU can speak with one voice and negotiate successfully. The EU sanctions on Russia because of the Ukraine crisis also demonstrate the power of collective action. But Europe is still struggling to use classical foreign and security policy instruments in a unified and consistent way.

Since 2009 the basis for further development of a common European foreign policy has been the Treaty of Lisbon. This document created, among others, the offices of the EU Council president and the high representative for foreign affairs and security policy, who speak and act for the entire EU.

During the negotiations with Iran, for instance, the three largest EU member states were at the table themselves, but the negotiations were managed under the banner of the EU, that is, by High Representative Catherine Ashton, followed by her successor, Federica Mogherini. This allowed all EU member states, including the many smaller ones, to feel that they were represented at the table. Nevertheless, the EU institutions are often assigned supporting roles when foreign policy crises or strategic challenges arise, including, among others, in the efforts to end the wars in Ukraine and Syria.

Of course, one can point to the Greek government debt crisis and the European debt crisis to argue that, in the end, the individual states set the tone for EU policy. And ultimately, the argument continues, these states represent and fight for very different national interests. This may be true for some areas of policy—frequently for budget, economic, and financial policy, for instance—but in foreign and security policy, there are generally not that many major differences.

In principle, a formula that can be implemented in practice should not be too hard to find, as former Polish Foreign Minister Radek Sikorski noted: First the member states must assess whether a certain foreign policy issue should better be treated separately or by the EU. In the large majority of cases in which the decision is cooperative action, the member states must then give the EU institutions the latitude to act and grant them every possible support.

With its financial resources, personnel, and creative capacities, Germany can play a leading role in paving the way for European unity. In exchange, it would be helpful if Germany would also support European security and defense efforts with the needed resources.

SUFFICIENT BACKING FOR THE MILITARY

Europe's problematic absence in Syria has already been discussed. More active participation in crisis management is not only a moral imperative, but also, and primarily, an imperative of realpolitik: After all, besides Syria's immediate neighbors, it is Europe that has had to handle the stream of refugees fleeing from the war.

In other areas, too, EU members pursue a foreign and security policy that does more to weaken Europe's global position than to strengthen it. A good bilateral relationship with China instead of a unified EU China policy may seem advantageous to one EU state or the other in the short and medium terms, but in the long run it is counterproductive. For there is nothing Beijing—or Moscow— would rather do than continue to skillfully play EU partners against each other.

Credibility in foreign policy and diplomacy must be backed up by an adequate military. Frederick the Great is supposed to have said, "Diplomacy without arms is like an orchestra without instruments." Unfortunately, this remains true today. As Sigmar Gabriel put it so aptly at the 2018 Munich Security Conference, we Europeans, who tend to be vegetarians in geopolitics, have to assert ourselves in a world of carnivores. This is why we need European perspectives on defense as well.

In military terms, Europe is in pretty bad shape. Since the end of the Cold War, our arms stockpiles have shrunk dramatically, become outdated, or to make matters worse, are only partly in working condition. In some EU countries, more than a third of the weapons systems, like tanks and combat helicopters, are currently not operational for lack of maintenance. This is due in part to low defense expenditures. We will have to spend considerably more money on defense.

At the 2014 summit in Newport, Wales, in reaction to the Ukraine crisis, NATO members agreed on the establishment of a new crisis intervention force and on an action plan for increasing the alliance's presence on the ground in Eastern Europe. NATO states further agreed to allocate more money to their defense budgets. In the years prior, member states had reduced their defense spending by an average of 20 percent. Russia, in contrast, doubled its military spending in the same period.

The agreement was to aim for at least 2 percent of GDP within a decade, meaning by 2024. By mid-2017 the only countries that had achieved this target were the United States, Great Britain, Estonia, Greece, Romania, and Poland.

"With economic growth of two percent per year, by the year 2024, Germany would have to spend more than 75 billion euros on defense to reach this goal," calculated the *Süddeutsche Zeitung* on February 18, 2017.[3] Not only that, but spending would have to rise by nearly 10 percent annually; this is not very realistic. The 2 percent goal is certainly right, but its implementation is not so simple.

The critical debate about the 2 percent goal in Germany was intensified by Donald Trump, who increased the pressure on NATO members to adhere to the target. This was met with indignation from many in Germany. But in truth, Germany had agreed to this target long before Trump. If we demand accountability, credibility, and trust from the American president, we must demand the same of ourselves. Two percent does seem like quite a lot compared to our current spending level of around 1.2 percent. But, from the historical perspective, 2 percent is pretty low. For many decades, up to the early 2000s, the European NATO members spent an average of more than 2 percent of GDP for defense. Is the world today so much more secure than at the end of the 1990s that we can afford to permanently spend so much less?

This is expressly not about doing Donald Trump a favor or chasing after any percentages. And it is also not about simply buying more weapons.

After all, the easiest way to increase spending would be to raise pay and pensions for soldiers, have barracks repainted, and purchase expensive vehicles for the military bases. But this would not really do anything to increase our combat strength or improve the networking of European forces.

Trump's massive demands play into the hands of those who attempt to score points using the anti-Trump ticket and the scary concept of a "new arms race." In truth, the point is not to blindly spend more money on the military, but to increase our ability to secure the peace through defense and deterrence.

A study by McKinsey & Company, in a joint project with the Munich Security Conference and the Hertie School of Governance in Berlin, suggested improving the networking of European troops, especially with new technologies, to increase their capacity to respond to new challenges. The idea is to provide our forces with modern equipment that will enable them to prevent and to handle crises. Such projects can take many years.

In 2017 I proposed a 3 percent formula, which Federal President Joachim Gauck also supported at the time: If we were to set a target not only for future spending on defense, but one that included humanitarian aid, conflict prevention, and development aid, all told this should add up to 3 percent of GDP.

The 3 percent approach pursues a greater strategic objective by including nonmilitary spending that also contributes to increasing stability and security for us and our strategic environment.

But more money is a minor part of the calculus. The bigger part is cooperation in Europe.

IN THE LONG TERM: A EUROPEAN ARMY

In November 1991, Manfred Wörner, the first German NATO secretary general and German minister of defense before that, gave a remarkable interview to *Der Spiegel* magazine. He said, "In the long run, in my opinion as a European, a political union of Europe is inconceivable without a common foreign and security policy. This also means that there could someday be a common European army."

The follow-up question by *Der Spiegel* was just "Pardon me?" There is no better way to express how unrealistic the idea must have seemed at the time.

Wörner continued, "Why not? I would only have a problem with that if the idea was to build up a European army that is independent and detached from NATO, for the very same purpose that we already have NATO."

At that time the concern about an either-or—either European integration or a close transatlantic alliance—was widespread and not entirely unfounded. Today most American decisionmakers quite rightly emphasize that a strong Europe capable of conducting its own security policy is in America's own interest. There is no longer any serious NATO-EU conflict. This is of enormous benefit. The main remaining U.S. concern is about being shut out of European procurement and support processes such as the newly established EU Defense Fund.

And there are further reasons why the prerequisites for closer coordination on security and defense policy in the EU are much better today: Our armed forces have learned to work together in foreign military operations. Why would we want to change our fundamental mission and restore parochialism as the norm? This would also be a disservice to our soldiers, who have learned on the field how important interoperability, the capability to work together smoothly, is.

"It seems to me that we have already spent far too much time with national navel-gazing, instead of turning our focus to the common European perspective," as former Minister of Defense Ursula von der Leyen said in 2014.

The initial focus of coordination is directed toward common armaments projects—above all, the introduction of modern cost controlling and realistic risk assessment for major European armaments projects. If real change is to be achieved, then the structural conditions of procurement policy must be addressed as well. Budgetary rights, multinational obligations, industrial policy strategy, and military capability planning form a web of factors that must be synchronized in European procurement policy.

Most of today's large-scale armaments projects are already the result of multilateral cooperation and international treaties. It has become a necessity to talk to European partners about who intends to provide which capacities for the combined European forces of the future—and who will renounce which capacities.

Nevertheless, defense procurement is traditionally driven by national industrial policy considerations. Contracts are often granted in order to maintain national industrial capacities or to minimize dependency on foreign technologies and products. Thus there are important domestic and industrial policy reasons to continue developing and acquiring our own technologies and competences. But here, too, we must think European. Then we can concentrate on developing European technologies and maintaining European capacities in the defense and armaments sector.

IN THE SHORT TERM: CREATE SYNERGIES

Defense expenditures have begun to rise again in Europe, but between 2010 and 2014 they dropped by 8 percent. And because each European state made its own cuts in the wake of the financial and economic crisis without any coordination among the partners, the combined loss of European capacities is compounded. The European pillar in the transatlantic alliance is shrinking: In 2007 the military expenditure by the European allies made up 30 percent of spending by NATO members, but in 2013 it was just 25 percent.

Therefore it is high time to start prioritizing defense. But let us not revert to the habits of the nineteenth century, either. With a few exceptions, the states in Europe are small. Is it really so inconceivable that we could all use the same fighter jet, the same frigate, or at least the same ammunition in our rifles?

In all honesty, how many of the EU states will ever find themselves in the position of going to war on their own? The last time a member of the EU conducted a military operation alone was the Falklands War in 1982. That was almost forty years ago. Why should twenty-eight countries, which only operate together anyway, maintain twenty-eight separate small air forces? Does every small European state really need its own general staff college or its own navy, some with more admirals than ships? Why do we need 178 major weapons systems, when the United States makes do with just 30? Wouldn't limited funds be invested much more efficiently if, for instance, Austria were to provide mountain infantry, Portugal naval forces, and the Czech Republic specialists on chemical, biological, radiological, and nuclear (CBRN) defense?

How is it that the EU states have a total of around 1.5 million soldiers, which is essentially the same number as the U.S. armed forces, while the combined fighting power amounts to just a fraction of the American?

In other words, the efficiency of our defense arrangements is catastrophically low. The EU spends its defense euros extremely wastefully. There is incredible latitude for savings. The recipe is to work toward a Europeanization of defense.

The most intelligent way for us to save would be to pool the capacities of the EU states. This starts with procurement. The above-mentioned McKinsey study calculated that common procurement in Europe could save up to 31 percent each year—that is 13 billion euros. Billions, not millions. And this figure does not even include the invaluable benefit that the increased compatibility of equipment would provide.

Obviously, the project of consolidating military capacities and creating a European army in the long term raises more than economic questions. Questions of national sovereignty also play a role: Which capacities can we renounce? Do we trust our partners—and will they trust us?

What does the requirement of parliamentary approval in Germany mean in this context? What happens in terms of security policy after the departure from the EU of the United Kingdom, a member of the P5 on the UN Security Council? Are we going to deal with London like we do with the Norwegian or Swiss capitals, or are there other, perhaps better, ideas? There is a lot of hard work to be done here. The decisionmaking processes will need time—which makes it all the more important to be proactive about putting them on the agenda.

It would be good if more initiatives to continue building a more unified European foreign and security policy came from Berlin, ideally in collaboration with Paris. Such initiatives must break taboos by contemplating the vision of a European army and decisionmaking by majority vote on foreign policy in the EU.

Just imagine if Germany were to introduce into the discussion in Brussels a proposal that future decisions on foreign policy questions would require a qualified majority rather than unanimity.

How often would Germany have been outvoted in the past if such decisions had been made by a qualified majority? Hardly ever. There is only one area imaginable that could actually become tricky for Germany: Israel. An EU majority could conceivably adopt sanctions against Israel that Germany could not support. For this case, an opt-out clause would have to be arranged. On all other issues, Germany would usually be part of a solid majority. On balance, this measure would not be all that risky for Berlin.

A proposal to introduce majority decisions to the EU would certainly not immediately be accepted by all EU member states. Some would say, "No! We refuse to have this part of sovereignty taken away!" In spite of this, such a proposal would, with a single elegant stroke of the pen, permanently put to bed the suspicion that the Germans want to dominate Europe. Instead, the point would be made: Germany places its power and its influence in the service of an effective EU, which is developing into a security union. Germany serves the EU. In short, the risk of such a proposal would be minimal, whereas the chance for benefits to our reputation and substantive progress would be great.

A first step on the road toward majority decisions could be a voluntary veto waiver by the member states: If a vote turns out to be twenty-seven to one, the outnumbered one could waive their right to veto, by abstaining perhaps, and thus enable the EU to take action. Could Germany volunteer and invite others to follow?

Another aspect: European politics have always had a psychological component. That the Southern European countries felt unjustly reprimanded by Germany, particularly during the European debt crisis, is a fact. This raises the question of how Germany can resume its role as the driving force of European integration in a way that would allow small states to feel they are in good hands. One of Helmut Kohl's greatest accomplishments was that his tact and intuition allowed him to convey to small countries like Luxembourg and Portugal that he always took them seriously. Such a policy of "taking everyone with you" can sometimes be strenuous and time-consuming. For Germany, it is a strategic necessity.

Germany's comprehensive commitment to EU foreign and security policy has a great deal to do with significant changes in German military and strategic thinking. When Chancellor Kohl was in power, it was almost inconceivable to send German troops abroad. Everyone believed that German uniforms would remind people of the atrocities that German soldiers had committed in the Second World War.

In the last twenty years, we Germans have learned that this concern was usually unfounded. Today, German soldiers guarantee stability in Kosovo and in Mali. They are warmly welcomed in Lithuania. This was a silent revolution that took place outside the public eye. By now it is possible for Germany to participate in military missions without being criticized as militaristic.

Ten years ago it would have been nearly impossible to imagine the German parliament sending a military contingent to Mali. There was then a widespread belief that the United Kingdom and France were merely defending their postcolonial interests in Africa. Today, Germany has a thousand soldiers participating in the mission in Mali. We have understood: If we do not take part in combating terrorism there, sooner or later terrorism will come to us. So the mission serves European and German interests at the same time—and not just French or British ones.

GERMANY NEEDS A NATIONAL SECURITY COUNCIL

The partners in NATO and the EU must be able to rely on Germany, even in serious conflicts. The German decisionmaking mechanisms in foreign and security policy are not always helpful in this—especially when decisiveness is called for. Time and again, the German federal government advances different opinions in Brussels, depending on which part of the government or which ministry is voicing them. In Brussels, in Washington, and other capitals, such incidents are taken to be typically German. This inability of the Germans to agree on a clear position has gone down in European policy jargon as "the German vote." Through inconsistent or vague behavior, Germany often limits the effectiveness of its foreign and European policy interests. Rather than speaking with one voice, various ministries are pitted against each other. And this is by no means limited to the Federal Chancellery, the Ministry of Defense, and the Foreign Office. Ever more government departments are involved in international decisionmaking processes, including in finance and energy, environmental and development policy, and counterterrorism.

German foreign, security, and defense policy, and German EU policy, need stronger coordination to prevent a German minister from surprising fellow cabinet members—or, just as bad, the Foreign Office finding out from a press release what the chancellor has just announced as policy. Nothing like this would ever happen in Paris. Berlin squanders important opportunities if it does not manage to speak with one voice. German citizens expect this, and so do our partners. The excuse that we always have had coalition governments, which makes harmonizing policy difficult, is not acceptable. After all, what is at stake here is the international pursuit of German interests, not just a little game of coalition poker.

A national security council, based partly on the American model, could help remedy this situation, despite all of the differences between our systems. The United States National Security

Council (NSC) was created by President Harry S. Truman in 1947. The national security advisor runs the NSC, a team of advisors that counsels and assists the president on foreign and security policy. The topics covered by this council today are no longer classical; the staff includes experts on financial policy, climate policy, development assistance, and many other areas. The NSC meets on various levels to prepare decisions that are ultimately binding for the entire administration—coherent decisions. Decisions in Paris and London are made in a similar way.

And there is not even a need to establish a new governmental agency: After all, Germany already has its federal security council (*Bundessicherheitsrat*), in which various ministries meet behind closed doors. However, since the 1980s its discussions have been mostly limited to decisions on arms exports. It could easily be expanded into a comprehensive coordinating body. A federal security council with a broadened responsibility would considerably strengthen the professionalism and coherence within the government, and thus its international clout as well. Germany would then have clear decisions that serve as guidelines for all departments. The head of the foreign policy department of the Federal Chancellery, as national security advisor, could then also be the secretary of the Federal Security Council, perhaps with one deputy from the Foreign Office and a second from the Ministry of Defense. Staff from all of the relevant ministries would work in the Federal Security Council so that specialized departmental knowledge would flow into its discussions. The position papers and draft resolutions prepared there would then be finalized with the chancellor and the ministers, who would "give their blessing." Despite having coalition governments, this would strengthen Germany's ability to speak with one voice, because the departments would be bound to common resolutions by the Federal Security Council and would no longer be able to travel around the world making whatever pronouncements they feel like.

Expert colleagues and I proposed such an upgrade to the Federal Security Council in 1998, after the change of government from Kohl to Schröder—unfortunately, to no avail. Chancellor Schröder warmed to the idea, but Foreign Minister Joschka Fischer did not, because he feared that the bureaucracy would interfere with policy-making. And when the Christian Democratic Union (CDU)/Christian Social Union (CSU) parliamentary group submitted a security strategy for Germany in May 2008, in which the establishment of a national security council was proposed once more, it was rejected by their then coalition partner, the Free Democratic Party (FDP).

As a player acting with initiative and responsibility, Germany must create the conditions necessary to fulfill the growing professional demands on foreign and security policy. Even in 2011, at one of the first climaxes of the euro crisis, Polish Foreign Minister Sikorski, one of my best Polish friends, said he "feared German power less than German inactivity." A Polish foreign minister calling for German leadership to save Europe—a remarkable development.

Step by step, Germany should take on more responsibility, address major global changes, and actively help to shape their resolution. What this requires today, especially in the wake of Trump's election, is concrete political, budgetary, and military decisions. In any case, more than just hopeful political sermons will be needed.

At the same time, German policy in Europe should not be seen as trying to dictate as a central power. On the contrary, it should be to use the weight of Germany's role purposefully and sustainably in order to strengthen the EU's capacity for action on foreign and security policy, and to conclude the incomplete work of the common market and the economic and currency union. An efficient, respected, and crisis-resistant EU should be the goal of forward-looking German foreign policy. Or, in the still valid words of Thomas Mann, not a German Europe, but a European Germany.

NINE

FOREIGN POLICY IN THE TWENTY-FIRST CENTURY

Challenges and Opportunities

GERMANY: NETWORKED AND DEPENDENT LIKE NO OTHER COUNTRY

There is hardly a country in the world that has benefited from the liberal international order as much as Germany. As an export nation, our welfare depends upon orderly world trade flows and the peaceful resolution of disputes between states. We rely on functioning international organizations in which the governments of the world seek common answers to contemporary and future challenges.

In 2014, McKinsey investigated which countries were particularly strongly integrated into the global streams of goods, services, finances, persons, and data. The result was a "Connectedness Index" for 195 countries, which related these total streams to the size of the country. Germany was at the very top of the list. Our country was among the frontrunners in all five categories.[1] In other words, no country is more dependent than Germany on these streams not being interrupted by war, trade barriers, natural catastrophes, or pandemics.

Just imagine closing Germany to any trade with the outside world for longer than just a week. Our export nation would be bankrupt in no time at all. We would not only have to do without Apple iPhones, Greek olive oil, Japanese game consoles, and American sneakers—there would not be any crude oil, either. Crude oil is the most important cargo globally, making up "around one fourth of the cargo on all maritime transports."[2] Crude oil is still the most valuable raw material for the German economy—not only as a fuel for road traffic, but above all for the pharmaceutical and plastics industries. Other raw materials essential for our economy would no longer be able to make the trip from Australia, Colombia, or South Africa to Germany. And vice versa, there would be no more buyers for German cars and machines. German companies have not made their living from German consumers in years. It is no accident that we are a global export champion.

In order for us to live our lives in peace and prosperity, goods and raw materials from all over the world must travel long distances. As we all know, copper and tin do not exactly fall from the sky right at our customs checkpoints. The most important trade flows are channeled through a relatively small number of main traffic routes. The entrances to Europe's ports are just as busy as the Japanese ports, as Shanghai, Singapore, and Hong Kong, and as the east coast of the United States. Ocean straits further concentrate traffic, amassing shipping at the straits of Dover, Gibraltar, Malacca, Lombok, and Hormuz, but also at the Cape of Good Hope on the southern coast of Africa.[3] So we must ensure that all of the goods upon which our prosperity depends reach their destinations safely and intact via these trade routes. But how can we do that?

All it would take to paralyze Wolfsburg or Stuttgart is to block one of the choke points listed above. Pirates—particularly off the Somalian coast and in the Gulf of Aden between Africa and the Arabian Peninsula, where 16,000 ships pass through each year—

are already demonstrating how susceptible these main trade routes are to attacks against our prosperity.[4] In 2019, Iranian activities laid bare these vulnerabilities to the global community in the Strait of Hormuz. Piracy off the African coast already has economic effects in Germany. Because of the current risks, insurance premiums for passage through the Gulf of Aden have risen more than tenfold.[5] Alternative trade channels prolong shipping times and increase fuel consumption. Shipping and logistics companies include the increased costs for global shipping in their pricing models. In the end, consumers pay the price.

So if we want to stay out of world politics, there is a price tag on it one way or another—and the question is how long we can and want to afford it. One thing is clear: The world around us could not care less whether we are busy with our own problems at the moment or whether we would prefer to keep out of the whole mess.

The skepticism of many Germans regarding a more active foreign policy is certainly understandable. Megalomaniacs from Wilhelm II to Adolf Hitler demonstrated the depths to which geopolitical adventurism can sink. Hopefully, our country has been cured of this disease once and for all. The question is, however, has the pendulum swung too far in the other direction—causing us to look away and stay on the sidelines because the problems are complicated, or to rely on someone else taking care of these challenges for us.

But the fact is that today and in the foreseeable future there will not be many actors left willing to take care of things for us. And it is also a fact that many in the world are looking to Berlin, justifiably, with particularly high expectations—because our country is not really as unimportant and powerless as we tend to think.

Especially after the election of Donald Trump, the global press was in agreement: Chancellor Angela Merkel was now a leader of the free world. The chancellor herself made it clear that she found such statements absurd—and, of course, she was right to do so. Even if we wanted to, Germany could not take on the leadership role. We are lacking so much, including the necessary military power and, no less important, a strategic tradition and culture.

Newspaper articles that hail Germany's new importance in the world are certainly flattering, because they are an expression of the hope which many people outside our country associate with Germany. Even though the last parliamentary election and the long months of difficult negotiations to build a government have subdued this enthusiasm somewhat, today we are considered to be a reliable rock in the waves of turmoil, an island of reason in a sea of vanity and irrationality. Yet at the same time such articles are also a wake-up call: We are needed! The traditional guardians of the world order appear to be no longer capable of or willing to accomplish their task. The German federal government has now recognized this and announced it will actively support building a strategic culture, a broader public debate of international security issues.

Naturally, this does not mean that we will be able to solve the world's problems. But if we Germans do not try to make a strong contribution, why should anyone else? Our country is still among the most populous countries on Earth (in 2019 we are seventeenth on this list). And behind the United States, China, and Japan, Germany is the fourth largest economy in the world!

But we like to see ourselves as a large Switzerland, perhaps as a successful trading nation, just not as a political actor on the world stage that resolutely represents European interests—even, in the case of emergency, by threatening or deploying military power. A discrepancy remains between the expectations of our partners and our own self-image: While German power and influence is overestimated abroad, it is underestimated at home.

THERE CAN BE NO WALL AROUND THE
BUCOLIC VILLAGE OF GERMANY

False prophets are attempting to capitalize on Germany's understandable longing for peace and normality. They claim that the best way to evade the complicated and threatening situation in the world would be to close our borders and reserve Germany for the Germans. Others claim it would help if we avoid getting involved anywhere else as a general rule. The root of all evil in the world, after all, is that the West has been intervening everywhere.

This underlying message has become stronger in recent years. Germans bemoan the situation in the world rather than actually doing anything to improve it. The truth is even if we wanted to, we cannot ignore the crises in the world. Either we take action or the crisis will come to us. To believe that Germany is a bucolic village that you can just build a wall around is too naive. Nothing has exposed this fact more forcefully than the coronavirus pandemic.

Of course it is understandable when people in this country question whether we would be overextending ourselves by helping other countries achieve stability and order when there are certainly more than enough problems to be solved at home. How can we commit to combating poverty around the world when the gap between rich and poor is becoming wider in Germany? How can Germany help others—both inside and beyond Europe—to shoulder the economic effects of the coronavirus pandemic when our own economy is taking a massive hit? Why should we spend more money on the military when so many other things do not work? Dilapidated schools, outdated hospitals and defective bridges could certainly use a financial shot in the arm or two.

This skepticism is justified. But more money for security and foreign policy does not necessarily mean less money for social projects and domestic policy; more money for the world does not necessarily mean less money for our home country. This may be the case in the short term, when we have to decide where limited funds are best put to use. But without our country's active involvement in an increasingly chaotic and conflict-ridden world, the foundations of our prosperity will erode in the long term. And then the political and economic margins will shrink away at home. This is why foreign policy is everyone's business. Good foreign policy is foresight and crisis prevention policy.

The degree to which events in other regions of the world have effects on our own country may not be sufficiently clear to some of my fellow German citizens. But one thing is clear: If war were to break out in Asia on the Korean peninsula, for example, the lights would soon go out in Wolfsburg and Ingolstadt, too, and German automakers would be facing huge losses! And unless countries all over the world defeat the coronavirus, Germany remains at constant risk of a rebound—with massive costs to German lives and livelihood.

Foreign policy has consequences for domestic policy, both positive and negative. We can enjoy political and economic security inside our borders only when there is stability and peace outside our borders as well. We must export, or least project, security in order to ensure our own security.

Yet this also means that it has to matter to us how our partners are doing, and especially our neighbors. Germany's interests are intricately interwoven with those of its neighbors. Our interests cannot be defined exclusively. We cannot and must not reject the more active foreign policy our neighbors expect of us. Federal President Gauck indicated this quite clearly in his speech at the 2014 Munich Security Conference.

At the same time, we must muster tact and intuition in this global network of dependencies and partnerships. Germany's geographical position calls for a particularly high level of foreign policy consideration and circumspection. Each of our movements produces a ripple effect across the fabric of European and international relations. We have more neighbors than most countries, and most of them are small.

Germany's central geographic location certainly brings strategic economic advantages, but also ecological and political burdens. As a major transit country, for instance, the Federal Republic must bear a disproportionate share of the costs for Europe's transport infrastructure and is especially reliant on intensive coordination with the rest of Europe. And precisely because we benefit to such a high degree from our common currency, the euro, we have a great responsibility to our partners. Europe is and remains a community of destiny. Things can go well for us in the long term only if they are going well, or at least not badly, for all the others.

NO SIMPLE ANSWERS TO COMPLICATED QUESTIONS

When the conversation turns to foreign policy issues, the ignorance described above is often, unfortunately, joined by a paternalistic megalomania. Just as many soccer fans believe they would be a better coach for the national team, many newspaper readers believe they would be a better foreign minister. Between rounds at the bar, they are then quick to lay out a tough-guy policy, sketch a simple conflict resolution strategy with a few strong words, or even bluster about a military intervention to straighten everyone out in one country or another.

True, it would be better to put a stop to abuses by dictator X or tyrant Y rather than shaking their hands during official visits. Unfortunately, it is not that simple. If foreign policy meant working only with those we like, many challenges could not be approached at all. And if we only deal with real democracies, we would have to ignore most of humanity. Besides, diplomacy is the art of dealing with your adversaries. With your friends, you go out for dinner!

Another popular argument is that the world would be a better place if we Germans would stop exporting arms. It is certainly important to discuss critically whether and where we supply weapons, and why. But a unilateral decision on this issue by Germany would only result in others rushing in to fill the gap and in endangering defense cooperation projects with our partners in Europe. This would be catastrophic, of course, for closer EU integration in the future.

Others assert that the sanctions against Russia should be dropped. The consequences such an action would yield, not only for us, but also for our neighbors and for the principles of our European and international order, are all too readily dismissed.

Yet another group believes that, because of Trump, it is finally time to cut our transatlantic umbilical cord, break off ties with the big brother U.S.A., and finally stand on our own feet. But how can this work when Europe will need many years before it is capable of defending itself? Should we pray that nothing bad happens in the meantime?

There are rarely simple answers in foreign policy. If everything were as simple as it looks over a few beers, the most important problems would have been solved a long time ago. And even complex answers do not always yield good solutions.

Sometimes the least bad answer is the best we can find. As I have already said, foreign policy often takes place in shades of gray, not in black and white.

The complicated interplay of politics, diplomacy, military, and economics means walking the tightrope between setting clear boundaries and showing a willingness to communicate, striking that fine balance between skepticism and trust. All of this cannot be summarized with a few simple slogans. Foreign policy is a never-ending live concert with countless musicians, usually without a conductor or sheet music. The sound will never be completely harmonious. But it does not have to degenerate into deafening noise if everyone succeeds in listening to each other, playing in the same key, with each of the players creatively contributing their own melodies. Not every musician can play first violin, but it is not good if the strongest instrumentalists disappear backstage.

A few weeks before his death, my former boss and long-time

German foreign minister Hans-Dietrich Genscher beseeched me: Take care of the European integration project and of completing our policy of reconciliation with all our neighbors, especially with Russia.

To pursue these objectives, I see the following tasks as most important for German foreign policy:

1. Europe must become more capable of action, more *weltpolitikfähig*. Specifically, this entails majority decisions on foreign policy, a defense union, and reinforcing the protection of Europe's external borders. Germany's key task must be to bring two categories of European states onto the same track: those that know they are small, and those that have not yet fully understood that they are small and still believe they can achieve their objectives by going it alone.

2. Europe costs money, and we must be willing to invest in it. This is particularly true post-coronavirus. Again, Germany benefits disproportionately from European integration. In November 2017, French President Emmanuel Macron formulated his vision for a social Europe: "Une Europe qui protège," a Europe that protects its citizens and companies. Macron called for more investment in education and a stronger social safety net. He understood what many Germans apparently have yet to grasp: The EU is a project for safeguarding the future! What good would a balanced budget do us if the centrifugal forces in the EU win and the EU reverts back into a grouping of hostile nation-states? An EU that is capable of action and protects its citizens is the best investment in the future by far. It is wrong to constantly demand that Europe not become more expensive.

3. Germany must develop a strategic culture. Federal President Gauck already articulated this clearly back in 2014: Germany must take on more responsibility. The special role we have

claimed on the basis of our history, namely pacifist abstinence, will no longer be accepted by our allies. Realism is necessary: Without military instruments of power, diplomacy remains anemic. The point is not to use our weapons, but to possess them so that we cannot be pushed around and threatened by others—ideally, with the result that we do not need to use them. Unfortunately, creating peace entirely without weapons works very rarely in our world today. The pacifist merely delegates the conflict and its solution to others. This is convenient but shows no sense of responsibility and is thus morally questionable.

4. We must cultivate and maintain partnerships and alliances. This counts especially for our partnership with the United States. Anti-American voices in Germany are now proposing to abandon this relationship once and for all. I can only recommend not to jeopardize the transatlantic connection that has proven reliable for decades, but rather to endeavor to continue it even in these extremely dissonant times. The rallying cry must be, "Engage, engage, engage!" America is far more than Donald Trump! And there will be an America after Trump, just as there will be a Russia after Putin, by the way. Foreign policy is smart when it is designed for the long term. This applies also to one of the central policy challenges on the horizon, how to deal with China.

5. We must develop a European and, ultimately, transatlantic China strategy. To date, Europe is badly equipped to respond to the growing challenges from China that loom on the horizon: The European debate on China is outdated, the EU lacks a common approach vis-à-vis Beijing, and Europe's policy is hardly coordinated with that of the United States. As Washington hotly debates the strategic implications of an era of Sino-American competition and rivalry, the most recent European document on China, published in March 2019 by the EU Com-

mission, reads like a U.S. paper from a decade ago. And despite efforts to display a united front toward China—as when Emmanuel Macron invited Angela Merkel and EU Commission President Juncker to his meetings with Chinese leaders in March 2019—there is no agreed EU China strategy. The opposite is true: Beijing is growing its leverage over individual EU member states, hoping that it translates into a de facto veto power over decisions in Brussels. And while there is growing awareness in Europe that Washington and Brussels share common interests on a number of issues, the current transatlantic crisis of trust has certainly not helped both partners work toward a concerted strategy. Against this background, Germany must help push the EU to seriously address the challenge and develop a joint approach toward China. This is a necessary precondition for better transatlantic policy coordination on China—coordination that is direly needed.

6. We must overcome division within Europe. It remains an important German task to find a settlement with our large neighbor in the East, Russia. As Federal President Richard von Weizsäcker demanded nearly thirty years ago, on the Day of German Unity in 1990: After the collapse of the wall through Berlin and Germany, we must ensure that a new dividing line is not drawn through Europe farther to the east. But the door to the Common European Home must not be kept open to Russia out of a position of weakness; Russia's reentry must be coupled with a clear demand for reciprocity. It takes two to tango! And nothing in our relationship with Russia may happen without consulting the states "in between." Too many bad memories and fears still linger in Warsaw and are also present in Kyiv today.

7. Trust is the greatest good in foreign policy. No matter how the rhetoric and mood might escalate in the rest of the world, or even in other European countries, Germany should pursue its

foreign policy with a steady hand and in a spirit of consistency. A quote from Bremen's Mayor Arnold Duckwitz in the nineteenth century serves as a good motto for German foreign policy: "A small state like Bremen should never be seen as an obstacle to the prosperity of the nation at large; on the contrary, it should take such a position that its independence is regarded as good fortune for the whole nation, and its existence as a necessity. Therein lies the safest guarantee of its survival."

In the twenty-first century, power is no longer based only on military resources, on so-called hard power. What is becoming of ever greater importance instead is soft power, a term coined by the American political scientist Joseph S. Nye. For him the EU was the best example of how "functioning as an exemplary model, attractiveness, and conveying its own norms and values"[6] like democracy and human rights count more than weapons and soldiers. This is why the EU enjoys respect and authority around the globe, because it "appears on the world stage according to its self-conception as a 'civilian power'"[7]—and relies more strongly than others on diplomacy and civil conflict management. Of course, the EU would strengthen its capacity to act if, should the worst happen, it were also capable of military action or at least be able to defend itself more credibly.

A NEW CHALLENGE FOR FOREIGN POLICY IN THE TWENTY-FIRST CENTURY

Winning over others to one's own ideas and convictions is a more sustainable way to achieve political objectives than dragging others over to one's side through pressure and sanctions. The EU's enlargement and neighborhood policies therefore belong to Brussels' "soft power" just as much as development or climate policy, or measures to secure and regulate digital infrastructure.

As mentioned above, the challenges of foreign and security policy are no longer merely questions of war and peace.

The coronavirus pandemic disperses any remaining doubt that health crises pose a serious threat to international security. As the virus kills people in all parts of the world, measures to halt its spread cause economies to plunge into recession and threaten to destabilize entire states, and as extremists capitalize on the disruptions caused by the pandemic, the world forcefully witnesses the inextricable link between international security, global stability, and health. And this link is not new: Ever since the plague, the "black death" that decimated Europe's population by a third in the fourteenth century, states have been aware of the catastrophic threat posed by disease and have attempted to protect their inhabitants from deadly epidemics.

Yet, with globalization and urbanization, the risk that diseases spread beyond borders has increased tremendously. "The health of one person is, increasingly, the health of others as well," Chancellor Merkel stated in 2017. Or as UN Under-Secretary-General and Emergency Relief Coordinator Mark Lowcock put it, "No one is safe until everyone is safe." And yet, many states do not have at their disposal the systems stipulated in international health regulations, which would allow them to detect and combat infectious diseases within their own borders. This is particularly true for fragile and conflict-ridden countries of the Global South. Also, it has proven to be utterly difficult to break what Stefan Oschmann and I describe as a vicious cycle of panic and neglect that typically marks the global response to pandemics. To help break this cycle, in 2016, the MSC initiated a Health Security Series, thereby contributing to a continuous debate on the most pressing challenges in the field of global health security and pandemic preparedness among governments, international organizations, NGOs, research institutions, and the private sector.

In fact, today's risks for our collective health—and thus security—are diverse. They also include the mounting failures of antibiotics to treat infections. Global warming likewise comes with consequences for the health of the world's population: The expansion of the mosquito's habitat, for instance, has resulted in severe dengue fever outbreaks spreading from just seven countries to one hundred.

Another major nontraditional security issue that will occupy Europe in the years ahead is the question of how the continent intends to deal with the constantly growing pressure of migration from Africa. Angela Merkel proposed addressing the issue with a Marshall Plan for Africa. Helping the fast-growing African continent to create employment, growth, and stability in the coming century will be a huge task for Europe and the entire international community. This challenge will be magnified by the impact of the coronavirus pandemic, which will have massive ramifications for development and stability in Africa.

Above and beyond this, climate change is a growing threat to international security. A higher incidence of natural catastrophes leads to flows of refugees and conflicts over basic resources like food and water. We can expect increases in extreme meteorological events, drought periods, and land degradation, as well as the rise of sea levels. All of these will exacerbate political fragility and resource conflicts, economic hardships, and mass migrations, and incite ethnic tensions and civil wars.

In 2018, around 70 percent of people around the world expressly classified climate change as a national security threat. For this reason, the breakthrough climate agreement signed in Paris in December 2015 was a major achievement of international diplomacy. Too bad the United States failed to stay on board!

The latest major challenge for foreign and security policy is cybersecurity and artificial intelligence (AI). The greatest damage caused by cyberattacks to date has been due to the theft of government and corporate data, as well as private data. However, reports about an attack on a Ukrainian utility, shutting down a major electricity grid and affecting 700,000 households, show the necessity of steeling ourselves against more aggressive kinds of cyberattacks. The scandal surrounding the use of Facebook data for subtle interference in American elections, as was apparently undertaken by the British firm Cambridge Analytica in 2016, shows the growing importance of technical questions for national sovereignty and security. In September 2015 the United States and China signed a cyber agreement in which the two governments promised not to engage in or knowingly support the cyber-based theft of intellectual property. But agreements like this are directed toward the commercial sector, not toward government data—if they are complied with at all.

States and non-state actors alike are proposing initiatives to regulate lethal autonomous weapons systems (LAWS). Armies around the world already use robots to defuse explosives, and new tasks and possibilities are emerging. Companies are developing armed robots and automatic gun turrets that can identify, pursue, and shoot down targets. The United States already uses drones, remote-controlled by soldiers in the desert of Nevada, to attack targets as far away as Yemen or Pakistan.

Advances in artificial intelligence have particular potential to fundamentally change the global security situation and the conditions contributing to peace and stability. The actual effects of the technological advances are difficult to estimate. However, it is probable that they will permanently change the relationship between human and machine. For instance, how will it influence military strategic planning when the speed at which intelligent machines work soon overtakes the human capacity to understand these processes? Moreover, we cannot rule out the possibility that AI will turn the previous logic of military superiority completely on its head. Power in the twenty-first century, as China and Russia already believe, will be a question of technological leadership. That is why they are investing huge sums in their AI capabilities in the hope of thereby overtaking the United States as the strongest military power. And, finally, if machines are soon able to act on the battlefield without any human control or authorization, this poses profound ethical dilemmas. For instance, what does this possibility mean for international humanitarian law? Just as physicists warned about nuclear weapons in the 1940s, today's experts in the field of artificial intelligence are urging political decisionmakers to take measures to prevent an arms race in this area. The United Nations has begun dealing with this topic in the framework of the Convention on Certain Conventional Weapons (CCCW).

These processes of global change are directly felt by the individual. They have immediate consequences for personal freedom and security. That is why it is so important that we take the current developments and future hazards seriously and—instead of looking away—actively address them together. This is the only way we can steel ourselves for what may come.

There have certainly been times when foreign policy had simpler tasks with which to deal. But there have also been periods that were much worse. In spite of the many diverse challenges, I look optimistically into the future. In my long career, I have learned that persistent work can go a long way in making things take a turn for the better.

I am convinced that efforts toward peace and security pay off; I believe in a more peaceful global future. But we will not reach that future if we believe we can wait out, or even ignore, the huge challenges currently confronting us.

We must resolutely confront the loss of trust in so many places in the world. And we must do so confident in ourselves that we can solve problems if only we tackle them with enough determination and diligence. As the poet Friedrich Hölderlin, who grew up in my hometown of Nürtingen, put it so beautifully, "Where there is danger some / Salvation grows there too."[8]

NOTES

Chapter 1

1. Tobias Bunde and others, *Munich Security Report 2019: Who Will Pick Up the Pieces?* Munich Security Conference 2019, https://bit.ly/2E7AMee, p. 6.

2. Bunde, *Munich Security Report 2019*, p. 8.

3. Bunde, *Munich Security Report 2019*, p. 9.

4. Hans M. Kristensen and Robert S. Norris, *Status of World Nuclear Forces,* Federation of American Scientists, https://fas.org/issues/nuclear-wea pons/status-world-nuclear-forces/; see also SIPRI, *Modernization of Nuclear Weapons Continues; Number of Peacekeepers Declines: New SIPRI Yearbook Out Now,* June 18, 2018, www.sipri.org/media/press-release/2018/moderni zation-nuclear-weapons-continues-number-peacekeepers-declines-new -sipri-yearbook-out-now.

5. Ibid.

6. Bunde, *Munich Security Report 2019*, p. 16.

7. Bunde, *Munich Security Report 2019*, p. 16; Paul Mozur, "Inside China's Dystopian Dreams: A.I., Shame and Lots of Cameras," *New York Times*, July 8, 2018, https://nyti.ms/2NAbGaP.

8. Bunde, *Munich Security Report 2019*, p. 13.

9. Francois Heisbourg and Maximilian Terhalle, "6 Post-Cold War Taboos Europe Must Now Face," *Politico*, December 28, 2018, www.politico.eu/arti cle/6-post-cold-war-taboos-europe-must-now-face-merkel-macron-trump -nato-eurozone-reform/.

10. Richard Wike and others, "America's International Image Continues to Suffer," Pew Research Center, October 1, 2018, www.pewglobal.org/2018 /10/01/americas-international-image-continues-to-suffer/.

Chapter 2

1. Regierungserklärung des Bundeskanzlers Gerhard Schröder zu den Anschlägen in den Vereinigten Staaten von Amerika vom 12.09.2001, ["Chancellor Gerhard Schröder's Government Statement on the Attacks in the United States from September 12, 2001,"] www.documentarchiv.de/ brd/2001/rede_schroeder_terror-usa.html.

2. "What Is the Theme of 'Embassy' by W.H. Auden?," www.gradesaver. com/wall-street/q-and-a/what-is-the-theme-of-embassy-by-wh-auden -286748.

Chapter 3

1. Ben Blanchard and Chris Buckley, "The American Definition of Torture," *Stern*, December 7, 2005, www.stern.de/politik/ausland/hintergrund -die-amerikanische-definition-von-folter-3496414.html.

2. Barack Obama, "Remarks by the President on a New Beginning," The White House, June 4, 2009, https://obamawhitehouse.archives.gov/the-press -office/remarks-president-cairo-university-6-04-09.

3. Wolfgang Ischinger, "How Europe Should Deal with the New Conditions in Washington—and How Not," *Süddeutsche Zeitung*, February 14, 2017, www.sueddeutsche.de/politik/aussenansicht-einbinden-einfluss-neh men-1.3378986.

Chapter 4

1. These lines are a slightly adapted version of the lines found in Wolfgang Ischinger, "30 Years after the Wall's Fall, Europe's New Divisions," *Politico*, November 9, 2019, www.politico.eu/article/german-reunification-peace -in-europe-berlin-wall-anniversary/.

2. Vladimir Putin, "Speech and the Following Discussion at the Munich

Conference on Security Policy," February 10, 2007, http://en.kremlin.ru/events/president/transcripts/24034.

3. Hans M. Kristensen and Robert S. Norris, *Status of World Nuclear Forces*, Federation of American Scientists, https://fas.org/issues/nuclear-weapons/status-world-nuclear-forces/.

Chapter 5

1. Nobel laureate Tawakkul Karman cited in Michael Thumann, "Ich bin bereit zu sterben," *Die Zeit*, October 13, 2011, https://www.zeit.de/2011/42/P-Tawakkul-Karman.

2. Jana Hauschild, "Personality of GDR Citizens: One Country, Two Souls," *Der Spiegel*, June 9, 2016, www.spiegel.de/wissenschaft/mensch/ddr-buerger-persoenlichkeit-ein-land-zwei-seelen-a-1096449.html.

3. André Glucksmann, "We Have to Protect," *Die Welt*, March 29, 2011, www.welt.de/print/die_welt/debatte/article12994941/Wir-muessen-schuetzen.html.

4. Joachim Gauck, "Wir müssen sehen lernen, was ist," acceptance speech for the Ludwig-Börne-Preis 2011, February 21, 2012, in Gauck, "Nicht den Ängsten folgen, den Mut wählen," *Siedler Verlag,* 2013.

5. "Münchner Sicherheitskonferenz. Gaucks Eröffnungsrede im Wortlaut," *Die Zeit*, January 31, 2014, www.zeit.de/politik/ausland/2014-01/gauck-muenchner-sicherheitskonferenz-eroeffnungsrede.

6. Gauck, acceptance speech for the Ludwig-Börne-Preis.

7. Glucksmann, "We Have to Protect."

8. Anne-Marie Slaughter, "Hilfe für die Wehrlosen. Ein Plädoyer für den Libya-Krieg—und gegen seine Ausweitung," *Die Zeit*, April 7, 2011, https://www.zeit.de/2011/15/Libyen.

Chapter 6

1. Manfred Rowold, "Dayton—Synonymous with Peace or War," *Die Welt*, November 3, 1995, www.welt.de/print-welt/article663530/Dayton-Synonym-fuer-Frieden-oder-Krieg.html.

2. Printed in Manfred Rowold, "Dayton—Synonymous with Peace or War," *Die Welt*, November 3, 1995, —picture alliance/ASSOCIATED PRESS, Joe Marquette.

3. Rowold, "Dayton—Synonymous with Peace or War."

4. Ibid.

5. Federal Foreign Office (Auswärtiges Amt), "Deutsche Außenpolitik 1995. Auf dem Weg zu einer Friedensregelung für Bosnien und Herzegowina - 53 Telegramme aus Dayton. Eine Dokumentation," Bonn, 1998.

6. *Der Spiegel*, "Greift den Strohhalm. Die deutsche Rolle bei den Friedensgesprächen in Dayton," November 27, 1995, www.spiegel.de/spiegel/print/d-9236636.html.

7. Brian Rathbun, "The Rarity of Realpolitik: What Bismarck's Rationality Reveals about International Politics," *International Security*, vol. 43, no. 1, Summer 2018, p. 33, www.mitpressjournals.org/doi/pdf/10.1162/isec_a_00323.

8. Ibid.

9. The paragraphs from "Never before . . ." to ". . . more costly than action" come from the following guest commentary: Wolfgang Ischinger, "Europe Has Failed with Syria," Munich Security Conference, German version published in Handelsblatt, October 12, 2016, https://securityconference.org/en/news/full/europe-has-failed-with-syria/.

Chapter 7

1. Donald Trump, "Statement by President Trump on Syria," The White House, April 13, 2018, www.whitehouse.gov/briefings-statements/statement-president-trump-syria/.

2. For the full German article summarized here, see Claus Kreß, "Wird die humanitäre Intervention strafbar?" *Frankfurter Allgemeine Zeitung*, November 9, 2017, https://kress.jura.uni-koeln.de/sites/iipsl/Home/FAZ131117.pdf.

3. List of vetos in the UN Security Council since 1946: www.un.org/depts/dhl/resguide/scact_veto_table_en.htm.

4. Georg Kreis, "Umstrittenes Privileg der Mächtigen," NZZ, October 23, 2013, www.nzz.ch/umstrittenes-privileg-der-maechtigen-1.18171922.

5. "The US and Allies Turn Off the Oil Tap in North Korea," *Die Welt*, November 15, 2002, www.welt.de/print-welt/article421668/USA-und-Verbuendete-drehen-North Korea-den-Oelhahn-zu.html.

6. Stephan Ueberbach, "Braucht die Welt G20-Gipfel? Contra. Das ist Kolonialismus 2.0," SWR Aktuell, July 7, 2017.

7. Peter Heilbrunner, "Braucht die Welt G20-Gipfel? Pro. Das Sprechen an sich ist ein Wert," SWR Aktuell, July 7, 2017.

Chapter 8

1. Eurostat, "Internationaler Warenverkehr im Jahr 2016," http://ec.eur opa.eu/eurostat/documents/2995521/7958470/6-29032017-AP-DE.pdf/df5 d18a8-7539-4ca3-88a5-c98a0da22382.

2. Eurostat/UN Department of Economic and Social Affairs (UN/DESA), "Population Status and Development," Federal Agency for Civic Education, October 18, 2018, www.bpb.de/nachschlagen/zahlen-und-fakten/europa/70 497/bevoelkerungsstand-und-entwicklung.

3. "Erreicht Deutschland das Zwei-Prozent-Ziel der Nato?" SZ.de, February 18, 2017, www.sueddeutsche.de/politik/international-erreicht-deutschland-das-zwei-prozent-ziel-der-nato-dpa.urn-newsml-dpa-com -20090101-170218-99-341518.

Chapter 9

1. James Manyika and others, *Global Flows in a Digital Age*, McKinsey Global Institute, April 2014, www.mckinsey.com/business-functions/strat egy-and-corporate-finance/our-insights/global-flows-in-a-digital-age.

2. World Ocean Review, "A Dynamic Market—International Shipping," 2010, https://worldoceanreview.com/wor-1/transport/der-weltseeverkehr/.

3. Ibid.

4. World Ocean Review, "Piracy and Terrorism in Global Shipping," 2010, https://worldoceanreview.com/wor-1/transport/piraterie-und-terrorismus/.

5. Ibid.

6. M. Große Hüttmann, "Soft Power," Federal Agency for Civic Education, www.bpb.de/nachschlagen/lexika/das-europalexikon/177268/soft-power.

7. Ibid.

8. Friedrich Hölderlin, "Patmos, 1803" in *Hölderlin, „Sämtliche Werke,"* *Kleine Stuttgarter Ausgabe,* edited by Friedrich Beißner, Vol. II, *Stuttgart 1953.* German version: „Wo aber Gefahr ist, wächst das Rettende auch."

NAME INDEX

Names starting with "al-" are alphabetized by remaining portion of the name.

Abdullah (Saudi Arabia), 120
Aeschylus, 19
Annan, Kofi, 162
Ashton, Catherine, 92, 122, 215
al-Assad, Bashar, 68–69, 115, 121–24, 157–62, 167
al-Assad, Hafiz, 120–21
Auden, W. H., 49–50

Ban Ki-Moon, 122
Ben Ali, Zine El Abidine, 118, 124
Bildt, Carl, 146
bin Laden, Osama, 160
Bismarck, Otto von, 23, 151
Blot, Jacques, 146

Bouazizi, Mohamed, 116
Bouteflika, Abdelaziz, 118–19
Brahimi, Lakhdar, 162
Brandt, Willy, 40, 66, 102
Bremmer, Ian, 11
Browne, Des, 111
Burkhalter, Didier, 92, 103
Bush, George H. W., 2, 14, 57–58, 80
Bush, George W., 2, 46–49, 54, 60, 64–65, 87, 159–60, 184

Carter, Jimmy, 1–2
Catherine the Great (Russia), 79
Ceaușescu, Nicholae, 2
Cheney, Dick, 48, 60

Chirac, Jacques, 2, 86
Christopher, Warren, 145, 146, 148, 150
Clinton, Bill, 58, 80, 86, 146
Clinton, Hillary, 22, 122, 133, 163

Daalder, Ivo, 191
Däubler-Gmelin, Herta, 48
de Gasperi, Alcide, 198
de Gaulle, Charles, 198, 201
de Mistura, Staffan, 3
Deschitsa, Andrey, 92
Diana (Princess of Wales), 189
Duckwitz, Arnold, 238

Eisenhower, Dwight D., 107
Elizabeth II (England), 31–32, 34–37

Falke-Ischinger, Jutta, 1, 35, 58, 63
Figgis, Anthony, 35
Fischer, Joschka, 59, 130, 173, 226
Fischer, Oskar, 41
Frederick the Great (Prussia), 216

Gabriel, Sigmar, 22, 204, 216
Gates, Robert, 53
Gauck, Joachim, 128, 131, 132, 218, 232, 235
Genscher, Hans-Dietrich, 16, 37–39, 41, 210, 235
Gibbs, Robert, 66
Glucksmann, André, 128, 133
Gorbachev, Mikhail, 2, 13, 57, 66, 79–81
Grenell, Richard, 33
Gromyko, Andrei, 2
Guterres, António, 185, 191

Haass, Richard, 74
Hallstein, Walter, 197
Hitler, Adolf, 17, 23, 48, 229
Holbrooke, Richard, 63, 145, 146, 149, 150, 165
Hölderlin, Friedrich, 242
Hollande, François, 97
Honecker, Erich, 40

Ivanov, Igor S., 2, 111, 146
Izetbegović, Alija, 17, 145, 146, 151

Jefferson, Thomas, 54
Joulwan, George, 148
al-Jubeir, Adel, 2
Juncker, Jean-Claude, 191, 197, 213, 237

Karadžić, Radovan, 146
Karman, Tawakkol, 124
Kern, Christian, 204
Kerry, John, 92, 97, 165
Khomeini, Ruholla (Ayatollah), 39
Kim Jong-un, 131, 183, 185
Kimmitt, Bob, 45
Kissinger, Henry, 63, 99, 165
Kleist, Ewald von, 191
Kohl, Helmut, 2, 37–39, 84, 86, 151, 207, 210, 223
Koschnick, Hans, 150
Krause, Ina, 44, 45
Kreß, Claus, 168–69
Kuchma, Leonid, 88

Lake, Tony, 148
Lambsdorff, Otto Graf, 37
Lavrov, Sergey, 92
Lowcock, Mark, 239

Macron, Emmanuel, 33, 207, 235, 237
Mamedov, Georgiy, 101
Mangold, Klaus, 83
Mann, Thomas, 226
Marschall, Christoph von, 28
Medvedev, Dmitry, 88, 109, 122
Merkel, Angela, 21, 23, 28, 32, 33, 45–46, 51–52, 62, 68, 70, 74, 75, 87, 93, 96, 155, 159–60, 179, 229, 237, 239, 240
Middleton, Kate (Duchess of Cambridge), 31–32
Milošević, Slobodan, 2, 17, 138–39, 144–46, 148, 153, 158, 173–74
Mitterrand, François, 2, 207
Mladić, Ratko, 146, 154
Mogherini, Federica, 215
Monnet, Jean, 198
Monroe, James, 55
Moon Jae-in, 185
Mronz, Michael, 36, 37
Mubarak, Hosni, 69, 117–18
Müller, Sven, 42

Napoleon Bonaparte, 124
Netanyahu, Benjamin, 191
Neville-Jones, Pauline, 146
Nunn, Sam, 111
Nye, Joseph S., 238

Obama, Barack, 7, 25–26, 65–71, 109, 123, 143–44, 161, 208
Olaf V (Norway), 38
O'Reilly, Bill, 60–61
Oschmann, Stefan, 239
Owen, David, 142

Pence, Mike, 191
Peres, Shimon, 66
Perle, Richard, 125
Phillips, Zara, 36, 37
Pillay, Navanethem, 122
Pinker, Steven, 14
Poroshenko, Petro, 2, 93, 97
Powell, Colin, 63
Prinz, Detlef, 61
Putin, Vladimir, 2, 7, 20, 21, 28, 72, 80–83, 86, 87, 90, 93, 95–96, 100, 108, 111–12, 131–32, 187

Qaddafi, Muammar, 118–20, 122–23, 129–31, 134, 185

Rasmussen, Anders Fogh, 87
Reagan, Ronald, 2, 39, 57
Rice, Condoleeza, 48, 126, 178–79
Roosevelt, Franklin D., 55–56
Rumsfeld, Donald, 59

Saddam Hussein, 47, 49, 61, 126, 127
Sarkozy, Nicolas, 87, 163
Sarotte, Mary Elise, 80
Schmidt, Harald, 62
Schmidt, Helmut, 37
Schröder, Gerhard, 46–49, 58, 60, 62, 83, 226
Schuman, Robert, 198
Shevardnadze, Eduard, 41
Sikorski, Radek, 215, 226
Slaughter, Anne-Marie, 133
Spaak, Paul-Henri, 210
Steiner, Michael, 149
Steinmeier, Frank-Walter, 3
Stoltenberg, Jens, 168, 191
Surkov, Vladislav, 112

Talbott, Strobe, 74

Thatcher, Margaret, 2, 201

Thucydides, 18–19

Thumann, Michael, 28

Tito, Josip Broz, 138

Truman, Harry S., 225

Trump, Donald, 1–3, 10, 11, 19, 21, 25, 33, 52, 53, 64, 71–73, 108, 111–12, 131, 152, 167, 183, 185, 200–01, 212, 217–18, 226, 229, 234, 236

Trump, Melania, 1

Tuđman, Franjo, 17, 145, 146

Twain, Mark, 198

Tymoshenko, Yulia, 88

Ulrich, Bernd, 27

Ungers, Oswald Mathias, 62, 63

Vance, Cyrus, 142

von der Leyen, Ursula, 197, 219

Wallert family, 129–31

Washington, George, 54

Weizsäcker, Richard von, 80, 237

Westerwelle, Guido, 36

Wilhelm II (Germany), 229

William (Duke of Cambridge), 31–32

Williams, Jody, 189

Wilson, Woodrow, 55

Wolfowitz, Paul, 59, 125

Wörner, Manfred, 218–19

Xi Jinping, 6, 10, 20, 185, 205

Yanukovych, Viktor, 88, 89, 93

Yeltsin, Boris, 81, 84, 88

Zarif, Mohammad Javad, 2

Zoellick, Robert, 12

SUBJECT INDEX

Aachen, Treaty of (2019), 208

Abu-Ghraib prison, 65

Abu Sayyaf terror organization, 129–30

Accreditation of ambassadors, 34

Afghanistan: Taliban in, 23, 47; terrorist attacks in, 5; U.S. military operations in, 65

Africa: Ebola outbreak in, 192; lack of representation on Security Council, 178; migration from, 240; ongoing conflicts in, 4; piracy in, 228–29; terrorism threats in, 223. *See also specific countries*

Agenda 21 (UN), 13

AI (artificial intelligence), 33, 192, 240–42

Albanian insurgency in Macedonia (2001), 139

Algeria, Arab Spring in, 116, 118–19

al Qaida, 5, 57

Ambassadors: accreditation of, 34; criticisms of host country by, 34; hospitality of, 62–63; installation process for, 33–37; interpersonal interactions of, 45–46; press appearances by, 61. *See also* Diplomacy

America First agenda, 19, 72–73

American exceptionalism, 54

Amsterdam, Treaty of (1999), 202

Annexation of Crimea (2014): dangers posed by, 2, 11, 21; events leading up to, 88–90; international response to, 78, 79, 91, 98;

Annexation of Crimea (2014) (*cont.*) Russian justifications for, 104, 180; as violation of international law, 91, 95, 184–85

Arab League, 119–20, 122, 133, 135

Arab Spring, 26, 69, 115–22, 124

Arms races, 6, 57, 74, 218, 242. *See also* Weapons

Article 5 (NATO), 3, 25

Artificial intelligence (AI), 33, 192, 240–42

Authoritarian states: and capitalism, 9–10; civil society in, 190; growth of, 5, 23, 211; response to Arab Spring by, 117–19; U.S. cooperation with, 57

Autocratic states, 9, 25, 26, 72, 123

Axis of evil, 64, 184

Ba'ath Party, 120–22

Balkan wars (1991–2001), 137–55; Albanian insurgency in Macedonia (2001), 139; casualties resulting from, 139; consequences of, 154–55; contact group for, 148–52, 165, 188; Croatian War of Independence (1991–1995), 139–40; diplomatic negotiations during, 70; genocide during, 132, 140–42, 154; Kosovo War (1999), 58, 135, 139, 153, 169, 173–74; lessons learned from, 137–38; military force utilized in, 138, 143–44; refugee populations from, 139, 140; Slovenian War of Independence (1991), 139–40; war crimes during, 140, 146, 154. *See also* Bosnian War

Baltic states: EU membership for, 82; independence of, 106; NATO membership for, 86; Russia as viewed by, 78, 106, 204

Belt and Road Initiative (BRI), 205, 211

Berlin Bar, 62–63

Berlin Process, 155

Berlin Wall, fall of (1991), 14, 79, 80, 83, 111, 212

Bertelsmann Stiftung Transformation Index, 9

Birther movement, 68

Black death, 239

Black Sea Fleet Accords (1999), 88, 89, 95

Boko Haram, 5

Bosnian War (1992–1995), 139–53; casualties resulting from, 139; and Dayton Accords, 149, 152–53, 158, 188; genocide during, 132, 140–42; international response to, 58, 141–44; military force utilized in, 144; peace negotiations during, 17, 111, 145–52

Brexit, 22, 24, 197–201, 209

BRI (Belt and Road Initiative), 205, 211

Brinkmanship, 8

Budapest Memorandum (1994), 95, 184–85

Bundeswehr, 38, 52, 98, 213

Cambridge Analytica, 241

CCCW (Convention on Certain Conventional Weapons), 242

Central and Eastern European (CEE) states: cooperation with

China, 205; EU membership
for, 80, 82; NATO expansion to,
13–14, 80, 82, 84–86; Russia as
viewed by, 78, 101; U.S. anti-missile shield for, 109. *See also*
specific countries

Charter of Paris for a New Europe
(1990), 16, 82, 84, 91, 94–95, 153

Charter of the United Nations
(1945), 95, 170, 180, 181

Chemical weapons: comprehensive
ban on, 183; as justification for
Iraq War, 126; in Syrian civil
war, 4, 68–69, 135, 161, 167

Child mortality rates, 15

China: authoritarianism in, 9–10;
Belt and Road Initiative, 205,
211; contract for natural gas
from Russia, 79; cyber agreement with U.S., 241; EU strategy
toward, 236–37; human rights
violations in, 20; in Iran nuclear
deal, 69; in liberal world order,
12, 205; manipulation of public
opinion by, 20; and nonintervention principle, 132; nuclear
weapons in, 6; poverty reduction in, 9, 15; Security Council
vetoes by, 163, 172–73; as share
of global GDP, 211; in South
China Sea disputes, 5, 96, 205;
Tiananmen Square protests in
(1989), 117

CIS (Commonwealth of Independent States), 81

Civil society: activism in, 75–76,
93; democratic, 10, 120, 189;
global influence of, 17, 186,

188–89; at Munich Security
Conference, 192–93; NGOs in,
99, 121, 188–90, 239; promotion
of, 98–99

Civil wars: and climate change, 240;
internationalized, 4; in Iraq, 127;
in Libya, 120, 134; rebuilding
process following, 5; in Somalia,
5; in Yemen, 2, 4, 23. *See also*
Syrian civil war

Climate change, 11, 73, 192, 200,
211, 240

Cold War: arms race during, 57;
beginnings of, 56; containment
policy during, 57; end of, 8,
13–16, 82, 109; mutual deterrence strategy during, 52; NATO
solidarity during, 98; shared
memories of, 64; United Nations
during, 11, 170. *See also* Nuclear
weapons

Common European Home, 13, 80,
237

Commonwealth of Independent
States (CIS), 81

Conference on Security and Co-operation in Europe (CSCE), 13, 16,
82, 102, 153. *See also* Organization for Security and Co-operation in Europe

Connectedness Index, 227

Consensus principle for foreign
policy, 203

Contact groups, 148–52, 163–66,
188

Containment policy, 57

Convention on Certain Conventional Weapons (CCCW), 242

Coronavirus (COVID-19) pandemic (2020): economic effects of, 206, 231; global response to, 74, 232, 240; as international security threat, 3, 239

Crimea: Black Sea Fleet naval base in, 81, 88; referendum on status of, 90, 91. *See also* Annexation of Crimea

Crimes against humanity, 131–33, 154, 171

Crisis diplomacy, 72, 97

Croatian War of Independence (1991–1995), 139–40

CSCE. *See* Conference on Security and Co-operation in Europe

Cuban Missile Crisis (1962), 57

Cuban Revolution (1959), 124

Cyberattacks, 24, 112, 190, 240–41

Damascus Spring, 121

Dayton Accords (1995), 149, 152–53, 158, 188

Debt crisis in EU, 208, 215, 223

Democracy: and American exceptionalism, 54; attacks on, 9–10, 105, 112; Charter of Paris on, 16, 153; consolidation in Europe, 80; illiberal, 10; international advancement of, 12; transition to, 124–27

Dengue fever, 240

Deterrence strategies, 52

Diplomacy, 31–50; art of, 69, 233; by British royal family, 31–32; complicated nature of, 33–34, 49–50, 152; credibility in, 216; crisis, 72, 97; and East German refugees, 40–44; expansion of options in, 159; interpersonal interactions in, 33, 45–46; life-changing impact of, 40–45; military instruments of power for, 236; misunderstandings in, 45–47, 49; moral risks in, 131; Normandy negotiation format, 70, 107; political gestures in, 37–40; public, 62; shuttle, 149; summit, 108; trust as critical factor in, 37, 45–49. *See also* Ambassadors

Donbass region, conflict in, 91–94, 105

Drone technology, 24, 241

Eastern Europe. *See* Central and Eastern European states

East Germany: democratic transition in, 125; peaceful revolution in, 116; refugees from, 16, 40–44; roundtable talks in, 92

Ebola virus, 192

Economic power, 12, 53, 197, 211

EDC (European Defence Community), 201

EFTA (European Free Trade Association), 198

Egypt: Arab Spring in, 69, 117–18; as heart of Arab world, 66; Tahrir Square protests in, 118

ELN (European Leadership Network), 7–8

Élysée Treaty (1963), 207

Ethnic cleansing. *See* Genocide

EU. *See* European Union

Euro crisis, 65, 205, 208, 226

Euromaidan movement, 89, 93

European Citizens' Initiative, 203

European Community. *See* European Union

European Defence Community (EDC), 201

European Free Trade Association (EFTA), 198

European Leadership Network (ELN), 7–8

European Union (EU): and Balkan wars, 148; challenges facing, 24, 195, 196; debt crisis in, 208, 215, 223; democratic attacks in, 10; demographic trends in, 211; establishment of, 13; expansion of, 13–14, 80, 155, 202, 238; financial and economic stability for, 206, 212; foreign policy for, 203–05, 213–16, 218, 222, 236–37; immigration policy for, 212; institutional reform of, 201–03; internal cohesion of, 156, 199, 214; joint projects within, 205–06; necessity of, 199–201; as peacemaker, 24, 199; precursors to, 137; refugee crisis in, 140, 156, 205, 216; sanctions imposed by, 78, 91, 122, 159, 214; as scapegoat for member nations, 197–98, 209; security and defense policy for, 206–07, 213–22; as share of global GDP, 211; and Syrian civil war, 122, 156–57, 161–66; tariffs on imports from, 10, 64, 76, 200–201; U.S. relationship with,

14, 52–54, 58, 74–76, 236; voting procedures within, 202, 222–23, 235. *See also specific countries*

Expansionist foreign policy, 112

Extended nuclear deterrence, 52

Falklands War (1982), 221

Federal Republic of Germany. *See* West Germany

Fog of war, 17–18

Foreign policy: challenges in, 238–42; consensus principle for, 203; credibility in, 216; dilemmas in, 112–13, 128–29, 233–34; domestic policy impacted by, 232; elements for success, 77–78; expansionist, 112; interventionist, 54–56, 58; isolationist, 54–55; long-term design of, 236; predictive power in, 22; of preemptive security, 64; revisionist, 94–97; security-related, 206–07, 213–26, 231–32; skepticism related to, 229, 231–32; spectrum of options in, 27, 129, 143; strategic patience in, 18; trust in, 237–38; unreliability of, 25, 72. *See also* Diplomacy

France: and Balkan wars, 148; on common European defense, 28; on East German refugee crisis, 41; German-Franco relationship, 207–09; in Iran nuclear deal, 69, 74; Iraq War opposed by, 48, 127; Libya intervention by, 119, 213; in Normandy negotiation format, 70, 107; Security Council

France (*cont.*)
vetoes by, 172; and Syrian civil war, 167–68
Franco-German duo *(couple franco-allemand)*, 207
Freedom House, 9
Free trade, 3, 10, 14, 100, 198, 211
French Revolution, 124
Friendship Treaty (1997), 95

G7 summits, 11, 74, 79, 186
G8 summits, 72, 79, 90, 99, 186–88
G20 summits, 11, 96, 111, 186–88
General Assembly (UN), 132, 178, 182
Genocide: in Balkan wars, 132, 140–42, 154; in Libya, 119; and nonintervention principle, 131; and Responsibility to Protect, 132–34, 169; in Rwanda, 132; UN prosecution of, 154, 171–72
Georgia, Russian intervention in (2008), 78, 87, 105, 180–81
German Democratic Republic (GDR). *See* East Germany
German-Polish Border Treaty (1990), 176
Germany: ambassador installation process in, 34; and Balkan wars, 141, 148–49; Bundeswehr in, 38, 52, 98, 213; crisis of confidence between U.S. and, 47–49; democratic transition in, 125–27; diplomatic relations with Iran, 39; foreign policy for, 195–96, 222–26, 229–32, 235–38; foundations of German-Amer-

ican relationship, 63–64; Franco-German relationship, 207–09; global connectedness of, 227–28, 232–33; historical guilt of, 131–32; international responsibilities of, 27–29, 223, 229–32, 235–36; in Iran nuclear deal, 69, 74; Iraq War opposed by, 48, 60–61, 64, 127; in liberal world order, 227; NATO defense expenditures from, 53, 217; and nonintervention principle, 128, 131–32; in Normandy negotiation format, 70, 107; post-World War II recovery in, 16; response to 9/11 attacks, 17, 46, 60; reunification of, 2, 14, 40, 53, 64, 79–80, 198; Russia's relationship with, 79–81, 83; on Security Council, 170, 177–79; security policy for, 222–26, 231–32; and Syrian civil war, 123–24, 157, 161, 168; terrorist threats in, 5–6; visit by British royal family, 31–32; in Wallert family rescue, 129–31. *See also* East Germany; West Germany
Gestures, political, 37–40
Global commons, 69
Global governance, 12, 13, 19
Global warming. *See* Climate change
Global war on terror, 64–65
Global Zero campaign, 182, 183
Gray zones in international law, 168–69, 174
"G-Zero world" phenomenon, 11

Hard power, 77, 238

Health crises: black death, 239; and climate change, 240; community response to, 56; dengue fever, 240; Ebola virus, 192; as international security threats, 239; mortality rate reductions in, 15. *See also* Coronavirus pandemic

Helsinki Final Act of 1975, 82, 94, 95, 102

Hezbollah, 161

Human rights: and American exceptionalism, 54; in autocratic states, 9; Charter of Paris on, 16, 153; Helsinki Final Act on, 102; international progress on, 12, 14, 169; and interrogation techniques, 65; violations of, 20, 65, 120, 131, 133

Illiberal democracy, 10

Immigration policy, 212

Intermediate-Range Nuclear Forces (INF) Treaty (1987), 7, 109, 182

International Campaign to Ban Landmines (ICBL), 189

International Criminal Court, 169, 171–72

Internationalized civil wars, 4

International trade. *See* Trade

Interrogation techniques, 65

Interventionist foreign policy, 54–56, 58

Iran: in axis of evil, 64; diplomatic relations with Germany, 39; nuclear deal with, 11, 25, 33, 69, 73–74, 152, 165; revolution in (1979), 124; in Yemeni civil war, 4

Iraq: in axis of evil, 64; civil war in, 127; invasion of Kuwait by, 58; terrorist attacks in, 5

Iraq War (2003–2011): casualties resulting from, 54, 127; dangers posed by, 2; human rights abuses during, 65; justifications for, 126, 176; opposition to, 48, 60–61, 64, 127; and preemptive security policy, 64

Islamic State (IS): emergence of, 127, 156, 160; predictive power regarding, 22; terrorist attacks by, 5

Isolationist foreign policy, 54–55

Israeli-Palestinian conflict, 5, 66

Just war, 128

Korea. *See* North Korea; South Korea

Korean Energy Development Organization (KEDO), 184

Kosovo War (1999), 58, 135, 139, 153, 169, 173–74

Kurds, 5, 126, 160

Kuwait: Arab Spring in, 116; Iraqi invasion of (1990), 58

Land mines, global ban on, 188–89

"Leading from behind" strategy, 70–71

League of Nations, 55

Lethal autonomous weapons systems (LAWS), 241

Liberal world order, 2–3, 12, 19, 73–75, 205, 227

Libya: Arab Spring in, 116, 118–20; civil war in, 120, 134; collapse of state apparatus in, 4, 119; interventions in, 70–71, 119–20, 128, 133–35, 213; Lockerbie bombing by (1988), 130; no-fly zone over, 27, 119, 120, 133; regime change in, 123

Life expectancy, 15

Lisbon, Treaty of (2009), 68, 202–03, 215

Literacy rates, 15

Lockerbie bombing (1988), 130

Maastricht Treaty (1992), 201

Macedonia, Albanian insurgency in (2001), 139

Malaysia Airlines crash (2014), 94

McKinsey & Company, 218, 221, 227

Membership Action Plan (MAP), 87

Middle East: Arab Spring in, 26, 69, 115–22, 124; Israeli-Palestinian conflict in, 5, 66; nuclear threats in, 7; peace process in, 65–67; predictive power regarding, 22. *See also specific countries*

Military spending, 3, 52, 84, 108, 217–21

Mine Ban Treaty (1997), 189

Minsk I Agreement (2014), 70, 94, 97

Minsk II Agreement (2015), 97, 99–100

Monroe Doctrine (1823), 55

Munich Security Conference (MSC): agenda setting for, 21, 192; civil society actors at, 192–93; on global power shifts, 19; Health Security Series, 239; history and evolution of, 190–93; leadership of, 2, 17; and New START initiative, 110; participants of, 83, 124, 191–93, 213, 232; on territorial integrity, 96; "To the Brink–and Back?" program, 2

Mutual deterrence strategy, 52

Nationalism, 10, 56, 156, 195–98, 209, 212

National Security Council, U.S. (NSC), 224–25

Nation-states, 23, 200, 210, 235

NATO (North Atlantic Treaty Organization): on annexation of Crimea, 98; Article 5 of, 3, 25; Balkan wars intervention by, 142, 144; during Cold War, 98; crisis intervention force, 216–17; escalation threats involving, 6–8; expansion of, 13, 80, 82, 84–87, 104, 108; extended nuclear deterrence through, 52; internal cohesion of, 72; Membership Action Plan from, 87; Putin on, 83; response to 9/11 attacks, 59; share of defense expenditures for, 53, 71, 217; and Syrian civil war, 168; Trump on, 25, 53, 71–73, 217

NATO-Russia Founding Act of 1997, 85, 86, 95, 105

Neoconservative intellectuals (neocons), 125–26

New START (New Strategic Arms
Reduction Treaty, 2010), 7,
109–10, 182

Nice, Treaty of (2003), 202

9/11 terrorist attacks (2001), 2, 17,
46, 58–60, 64

Nongovernmental organizations
(NGOs), 99, 121, 188–90, 239

Nonintervention principle, 55, 102,
128, 131–32, 175

Non-Proliferation of Nuclear Weapons Treaty (NPT) (1968), 182–84

Normandy negotiation format, 70,
107

North Korea: in axis of evil, 64, 184;
nuclear weapons in, 7, 183–85;
sanctions against, 183, 185;
South Korean relations with, 5,
184, 185

NPT (Non-Proliferation of Nuclear
Weapons Treaty) (1968), 182–84

NSC (National Security Council,
U.S.), 224–25

Nuclear weapons: arms control
treaties, 7, 109–10, 182–84;
during Cold War, 52, 57; and
deterrence strategies, 52; disarmament efforts, 13, 57, 67, 95,
183–84; disputes regarding, 5;
escalation threats involving,
6–8, 57; global stockpile of, 108;
Global Zero campaign on, 182,
183; terrorist acquisition of,
112

Organization for Security and
Co-operation in Europe (OSCE),
13, 89, 92–94, 100–03, 152. *See
also* Conference on Security and
Co-operation in Europe

Ostpolitik, 40, 66, 102

Ottawa Treaty (1997), 189

Pacifism, 28, 128, 173, 236

Pandemic. *See* Coronavirus
pandemic

Paris Agreement (2015), 11, 73, 240

Peace: consolidation in Europe, 80;
difficulties in achievement of,
18–24; as diplomatic goal, 45;
in Middle East, 65–67; military
force as element of, 17, 54, 138,
143–44, 236; in new world order,
58; sustainability as generational
task, 155; UN operations for, 107,
141, 171, 172; Vance-Owen peace
plan, 142, 143

Peace dividend, 13, 213

Pearl Harbor attack (1941), 55, 59

Pew Research Center, 25, 213

Piracy, 228–29

Political gestures, 37–40

Populism, 23, 156, 196, 198, 212

Potsdam Agreement (1945), 175

Poverty, 9, 14–15, 231

Power: in authoritarian states,
117; balance of, 177; of collective action, 214; corporate, 190;
economic, 12, 53, 197, 211; global
shifts in, 18–19; hard, 77, 238;
nation-state's monopoly of, 23,
24; political, 160; predictive,

Power (*cont.*)
21–22; of self-fulfilling prophe-
cies, 45; smart, 77; soft, 71, 77, 78,
238; veto, 94, 107, 135, 163, 170,
172–77
Predictive power, 21–22
Preemptive security policy, 64
Prohibition of Nuclear Weapons,
Treaty on the (2017), 182
Protectionism, 73, 75
Proximity talks, 149
Proxy wars, 157
Public diplomacy, 62
Public opinion, manipulation of, 20
Putin Doctrine, 95–96

Qualified majority voting, 202,
222

Realpolitik, 26, 76, 129, 216
Red Cross benefit ball (2005), 1
Refugees: from Balkan wars, 139,
140; and climate change, 240;
East German, 16, 40–44; EU
crisis of, 140, 156, 205, 216;
global prevalence of, 3; quotas
for, 24, 210; from Syrian civil
war, 4, 156, 216; UN efforts
involving, 172
Regime change, 123–24, 126, 129,
134
Responsibility to Protect (R2P),
132–35, 169
Revisionist foreign policy, 94–97
Russia: authoritarianism in, 10; and
Balkan wars, 141–42, 148; and
Common European Home, 13,
80, 237; contracts for natural gas
from, 79, 88; in Donbass conflict, 91–94, 105; ejection from
G8 summits, 79, 187; escalation threats involving, 6–8; in
European security architecture,
97–99, 112; expansionist foreign
policy of, 112; fear of, 78, 101,
106; Friendship Treaty with
Ukraine (1997), 95; Georgia intervention by (2008), 78, 87, 105,
180–81; Germany's relationship
with, 79–81, 83; in Iran nuclear
deal, 69; Malaysia Airlines crash
caused by, 94; manipulation of
public opinion by, 20; on NATO
expansion, 82, 84–87, 104, 108;
and nonintervention principle,
132; in Normandy negotiation
format, 70, 107; nuclear weapons
in, 6, 7, 108–10; as pseudo-giant,
77–79; revisionist foreign policy
of, 94–97; sanctions against,
72, 78, 82, 91, 99–100, 214, 234;
Security Council vetoes by, 94,
163, 172, 173; and Syrian civil
war, 123, 161, 168; violation of
international principles, 95. *See
also* Annexation of Crimea;
Soviet Union
Russian Revolution (1917), 124
Rwanda: criminal tribunal for, 171;
genocide in, 132; rebuilding
following civil war in, 5

SALT (Strategic Arms Limitation
Treaty, 1972), 182

Sanctions: on North Korea, 183, 185; purpose of, 99, 159; on Russia, 72, 78, 82, 91, 99–100, 214, 234; on Serbia, 146; on Syria, 122, 159, 160; targeted (smart), 160

Saudi Arabia: nuclear weapons in, 7; relationship with Libya, 120; and Syrian civil war, 123, 161; in Yemeni civil war, 4

Schengen Area, 205, 206, 209

Security Council (UN): criticisms of, 172–79; Dayton Accords accepted by, 188; Iraq War discussions in, 48; membership structure, 170, 177; on no-fly zone over Libya, 27, 119; reform proposals for, 177–79; on Responsibility to Protect, 133; Russian succession to Soviet seat on, 81; sanctions imposed by, 160, 183, 185; successes of, 171; on Syrian civil war, 122, 163; veto power in, 94, 107, 135, 163, 170, 172–77

Self-determination of states, 82, 138–39, 169, 175

Self-fulfilling prophecies, 8, 45

September 11 attacks. See 9/11 terrorist attacks

Shuttle diplomacy, 149

Slovenian War of Independence (1991), 139–40

Smart power, 77

Smart (targeted) sanctions, 160

Social media, 20, 192

Soft power, 71, 77, 78, 238

South China Sea, territorial disputes in, 5, 96, 205

South Korea: North Korean relations with, 5, 184, 185; U.S. alliance with, 57, 184

Soviet Union: collapse of, 2, 3, 14, 73, 81, 106; containment policy against, 57; in modernization of North Korean energy sector, 183–84; nuclear weapons in, 57, 109. See also Cold War; Russia

Srebrenica massacre (1995), 140–41, 154

Strategic Arms Limitation Treaty (SALT, 1972), 182

Summit diplomacy, 108

Syrian civil war: and Arab Spring, 115, 121–22; casualties resulting from, 3–4, 68, 159; chemical weapon use in, 4, 68–69, 135, 161, 167; combatants in, 23; contact group for, 163–66; dangers posed by, 2, 157–58; events leading up to, 115, 120–22; as geostrategic conflict, 160; international response to, 122–24, 156–64, 167–68, 214; refugee populations from, 4, 156, 216

Tahrir Square protests (2011), 118

Taliban: conflicts involving, 4, 23; sanctions against, 160; terrorist attacks by, 5; training for, 57; U.S. actions against, 47

Targeted (smart) sanctions, 160

Tariffs, 10, 64, 76, 200–01

Technology: artificial intelligence, 33, 192, 240–42; cyberattacks, 24, 112, 190, 240–41; drones, 24, 241; in manipulation of public opinion, 20; social media, 20, 192; as soft power, 71

Territorial integrity, 95–96, 175, 184–85

Terrorism: global war on terror, 64–65; growing threats of, 5–6, 156, 223; 9/11 attacks (2001), 2, 17, 46, 58–60, 64; and nuclear weapons, 112; state sponsorship of, 64; and technological advances, 190. *See also specific terrorist groups*

Thirty Years' War (1618–1648), 137

Thucydides's trap, 18–19

Tiananmen Square protests (1989), 117

Torture, 65

TPP (Trans-Pacific Partnership), 73

Trade: collective action of EU on, 214; free trade, 3, 10, 14, 100, 198, 211; global nature of, 228; piracy impacting, 228–29; and tariffs, 10, 64, 76, 200–01; and World Trade Organization, 10, 12

Trade wars, 10, 186

Transformation Index, 9

Trans-Pacific Partnership (TPP), 73

Treaties. *See specific names of treaties*

Trudering speech (2017), 51–52, 70, 75

Trust: building and restoring, 107, 206; in contract negotiations, 33;

in diplomatic relationships, 37, 45–49; in foreign policy, 237–38; in government, 19–21, 65; in international order, 74; loss of, 19–21, 242; in resolution of conflict, 18, 105

Tunisia, Arab Spring in, 115–17, 124

Turkey: authoritarianism in, 5; in EU membership negotiations, 87, 156; Kurdish conflict with, 5; and Syrian civil war, 122, 123

Ukraine: and Black Sea Fleet Accords, 88, 89, 95; civil society in, 93, 98–99; cyberattacks in, 240–41; Donbass conflict in, 91–94, 105; Euromaidan movement in, 89, 93; Friendship Treaty with Russia (1997), 95; and Minsk Agreements, 70, 94, 97, 99–100; NATO partnership with, 85, 87; in Normandy negotiation format, 70, 107; nuclear weapons relinquished by, 13, 95, 184; oil and gas resources in, 90–91; territorial integrity of, 184–85. *See also* Annexation of Crimea

UN. *See* United Nations

UNESCO (United Nations Educational, Scientific and Cultural Organization), 73

UNHCR (United Nations High Commissioner for Refugees), 172

UNICEF (United Nations Children's Fund), 172

United Kingdom: ambassador installation process in, 34–37; and

Balkan wars, 148; and Brexit, 22, 24, 197–201, 209; diplomacy as utilized by, 31–32; on East German refugee crisis, 41; in Iran nuclear deal, 69, 74; Libya intervention by, 119, 213; Security Council vetoes by, 172; and Syrian civil war, 167–68

United Nations (UN), 169–83; challenges facing, 11; Charter of, 95, 170, 180, 181; during Cold War, 11, 170; Conference on Environment and Development, 12–13; Convention on Certain Conventional Weapons, 242; criminal tribunals established by, 146, 154, 171–72; criticisms of, 172–83, 186; General Assembly, 132, 178, 182; G20 summits compared to, 187; history of, 169–70; monopoly on use of force, 179–81; peacekeeping operations of, 107, 141, 171, 172, 181; World Food Programme, 172; world order of, 23–24. *See also* Security Council

United Nations Children's Fund (UNICEF), 172

United Nations Educational, Scientific and Cultural Organization (UNESCO), 73

United Nations High Commissioner for Refugees (UNHCR), 172

United States: and American exceptionalism, 54; and Balkan wars, 142, 144, 148–50; containment policy of, 57; crisis of confidence between Germany and, 47–49; cyber agreement with China, 241; on East German refugee crisis, 41; election interference in, 20, 108, 241; EU relationship with, 14, 52–54, 58, 74–76, 236; foreign policy strategies of, 54–58; foundations of German-American relationship, 63–64; interventionist policies of, 54–56, 58; in Iran nuclear deal, 11, 25, 33, 69, 73–74, 152; isolationist policies of, 54–55; "leading from behind" strategy of, 70–71; liberal democracy under attack in, 10; Libya intervention by, 70, 71, 119, 133; National Security Council of, 224–25; NATO defense expenditures from, 53; and 9/11 terrorist attacks (2001), 2, 17, 46, 58–60, 64; nuclear weapons in, 6, 7, 57, 108–10; in Pacific region, 25–26; and Pearl Harbor attack (1941), 55, 59; preemptive security policy of, 64; retreat from role as global protector, 19, 68–71, 74; sanctions imposed by, 72, 91, 99, 122, 159, 185; Security Council vetoes by, 172, 173; as share of global GDP, 211; and Syrian civil war, 122, 167–68; unipolar moment for, 18, 57, 83, 125–26; withdrawal from international agreements and organizations, 11, 33, 73, 152, 240. *See also* Cold War

Vance-Owen peace plan (1993), 142, 143

Visegrád states, 198, 210

War: fog of, 17–18; global war on terror, 64–65; just war, 128; in preservation of peace, 143–44; proxy wars, 157; trade wars, 10, 186. *See also* Civil wars; *specific names of wars*

War crimes, 131–33, 140, 146, 154, 171

Warsaw, Treaty of (1970), 175

Warsaw Pact, 82, 84, 102

Weapons: and arms races, 6, 57, 74, 218, 242; Convention on Certain Conventional Weapons, 242; cyberattacks as, 24, 112, 190, 240–41; as diplomatic tool, 236; and drone technology, 24, 241; land mines, 188–89; lethal autonomous weapons systems, 241; procurement of, 219–21, 233–34; terrorist acquisition of, 171. *See also* Chemical weapons; Nuclear weapons

Wehrkunde. *See* Munich Security Conference

Weltpolitikfähig, 213, 235

West Germany: East German refugees taken in by, 16, 40–44; NATO support during Cold War, 98; peaceful demonstrations in, 116; policy objectives of, 14

Westphalia, Treaty of (1648), 132, 137

World Health Organization, 15

World Trade Organization, 10, 12

World War I, 23, 55, 119, 138

World War II: commitment to rebuilding after, 155; internationalist view following, 56, 73; as nation-state conflict, 23; Pearl Harbor attack during, 55, 59; territorial changes following, 175

Yemen: Arab Spring in, 124; civil war in, 2, 4, 23

Yugoslavia: criminal tribunal for, 140, 154, 171; ethnic and religious diversity in, 138; independence movements within, 139–40. *See also* Balkan wars